7. 34

AMERICAN
WOMEN POETS

AMERICAN WOMEN POETS
Pioneers of Modern Poetry

JEAN GOULD

Dodd, Mead & Company, New York

In memory of
three modern poets
taken from us too soon:
Jean Garrigue (1912–1970)
Elizabeth Bishop (1911–1979)
and
Muriel Rukeyser (1913–1980)

1 2 3 4 5 6 7 8 9 10

Library of Congress Cataloging in Publication Data

Gould, Jean, 1909–
   American women poets.

   Includes index and bibliography.
      1.   Women poets—United States—Biography.
   2.   American poetry—Women authors—History and criticism.
   I.   Title.
PS151.G6   811'.009'9287   79-25670
ISBN 0-396-07828-1

CONTENTS

ACKNOWLEDGMENTS

RESEARCH on this collection of biographical sketches was begun in 1975, shortly after my full-length portrait of Amy Lowell was published. In those five years the number of notable American poets who are women has grown to such proportions that it was decided to publish the work in two parts. Since most of the women who were pioneers in the evolution of modern poetry begun in 1900 are now gone, I have had to rely principally on past records for material on the lives of those included in this first volume.

However, I am indebted to a number of contemporary poets who will appear in Volume II for reminiscences and anecdotes about Sara Teasdale, Marianne Moore, Louise Bogan, and other early figures. Muriel Rukeyser, whose untimely death occurred as these acknowledgments were being written, May Swenson, Jane Mayhall, Jean Burden, and Isabella Gardner, in the course of discussing their own careers, recalled various incidents and characteristics of their fellow poets who were older and well established when they began publishing. They gave me a closeup view of Marianne Moore and Elizabeth Bishop, whom I had met but not really known. The latter's sudden death in October 1979 put an end to our interviews.

Lesley Frost Ballantine contributed recollections of the rare friendship between Frost and Miss Moore, a kind of sparring camaraderie between these two disparate poets. Arthur Gregor, who knew Moore well in her last years, spoke of her in his recollections of Jean Garrigue, telling me of the time Jean and he took Marianne to dinner in celebration of her eightieth birthday. And Michel Farano, close friend of the Untermeyers until their deaths, knew both Sara Teasdale and Amy Lowell, and generously shared his reminiscences of those two distinctive poets. Babette Deutsch was most helpful in supplying notes of her own career.

I am particularly grateful to Connie (Mrs. Ralph) Easton, of Charlottesville, Virginia, niece of Elinor Wylie, who gave me much information concerning the family background of her famous aunt, and furnished her own memories of a visit to Wylie's apartment near the end of the poet's life. I am indebted to James Kraft, dean of the Adult Education Division of the New School for Social Research and editor of *The Letters of Witter Bynner,* for assistance in gaining permission from the Witter Bynner Foundation for Poetry to quote excerpts from hitherto unpublished letters that Bynner wrote to Edna Millay and to Arthur Ficke. The former was in connection with the "triangle" relationship of the three poets, and the latter expressed Bynner's confidential opinion of the poems in Millay's volume, *The Buck in the Snow.*

The daughter of early Imagist poet H.D., Perdita (Mrs. John) Schaffner, kindly gave me a description of her life as a child and growing up with her poet-mother and their close friend "Bryher" (Winifred Ellerman) during the twenties and thirties. Adelaide Schulkind (Mrs. Walter) Frank, one of the founders and executive secretary of The League for Mutual Aid, corroborated and added to Muriel Rukeyser's own recollections of her early struggles and the financial assistance afforded her by the League. Mrs. Frank also gave personal help to Rukeyser and others, including black poet Pauli Murray.

To writer, critic, and editor Paul Kresh, and to painter Penrod Scofield, go my thanks for information concerning the recorded readings made by several of the poets discussed here, and of Muriel Rukeyser's last projects. Mr. Kresh, as editor of the Spoken Arts series, *Treasury of 100 Modern American Poets Reading Their Poems,* gave me an account of tracking down and working with a hundred poets, a number of whom are included in this study. Also editor of the recently released Spoken Arts series, *Twenty-five Jewish Poets Reading Their Poems,* Kresh told me of Muriel Rukeyser's participation despite her illness, to the extent that she was the only one of the twenty-five who has a whole side of a disc devoted to her poetry. Penrod Scofield, who had illustrated four of her "Akiba" poems when they appeared in the *American Judaism Reader* (1967, edited by Paul Kresh), a collection of the best poems, essays, and short stories that the magazine had published, was consulting with Rukeyser on a prose-poem text she had agreed to write for a book comprising Scofield's drawings and watercolors of New York's "bag-ladies," a project left unrealized by her death.

Louis Rachow, librarian of the Walter Hampden Memorial Library and Theatre Collection at the Players Club, was most cooperative in granting permission to reprint the photograph of Edna St. Vincent Millay, and in furnishing the reproduction included here.* The same sort of assistance was given by Deborah Kelley and the staff of the photograph division at the Houghton Library of Harvard University in regard to the photograph of Amy Lowell.* I am also indebted to the staff of the Anderson Library of the University of Virginia for access to their recent acquisition, the love letters of Elinor Wylie to William Rose Benet, covering the three-year period just before their marriage in 1923.

* The photographs of both Edna Millay and Amy Lowell were included in my full-length biographies of these two poets.

To all of the above and those who assisted in the editing and proofreading of the manuscript, I am most grateful. Finally, I wish to express my gratitude to Director William Smart and the excellent staff at the Virginia Center for the Creative Arts at Sweet Briar for granting me residence periods during 1978 and 1979, when the major portion of the manuscript was written, and to the MacDowell Colony, where writing was begun in 1977.

FOREWORD

UNTIL the twentieth century, women, although recognized to a greater degree in poetry than in the other creative arts, were still relegated to second place in this field of literature. Histories of poetry in America give ample proof that there was no dearth of poets among women, but the work of only a few has survived. In 1858 a big volume entitled *American Female Poets* contained nearly a thousand pages of poetry written by nineteenth-century women, most of them writing lines of strict Victorian verse on prescribed subjects, often expressing maudlin emotion in iambic pentameter. And most of them are now forgotten.

Recent histories, such as *The Poet in America, 1650 to the Present* by Albert Gelpi (1973) and *A Short History of American Poetry* by Donald Barlow Stauffer (1974), go back to the seventeenth century with Anne Bradstreet (1612–1672) and Phyliss Wheatley (1753–1784), but mention practically no more poets of their sex until modern times. Stauffer's first chapter, "The Beginnings to 1765," discusses ten poets, and Anne Bradstreet is the only woman among them. Following her no other woman is given any consideration, even by name, until Emily Dickinson at the close of the nineteenth century. Other late nineteenth/ early twentieth-century names among women poets besides Dickinson are Lizette Woodward Reese and Emma Lazarus, the latter principally known for the portion of one of her sonnets that is inscribed on the Statue of Liberty. Male poets fill the chapters dealing with the generations of poets in between.

While Emily Dickinson's monumental genius, unveiled in 1890, broke with tradition and paved the way for modern verse, her younger sister poets still had rough going. When Edna St. Vincent Millay's poem "Renascence" was first published in 1912, such knowledgeable poets as Witter Bynner and Arthur Davison Ficke refused to believe the biographical note stating her sex and age. They felt that "no sweet young thing of twenty could have written a poem with the depth and vision of 'Renascence.' " They asserted, "It takes a brawny male of forty-five to do that." She retorted in a letter to them that she "simply would *not* be a male!"

Although Edna Millay, Amy Lowell, and Marianne Moore did much in different ways to bring women to the fore in the world of poetry during the first quarter of the century, placing them on an equal footing professionally with the opposite sex, their achievements made little immediate impression on their male counterparts. William Rose Benét wrote as late as 1933, in an opinion he no doubt meant to be complimentary, "Anna Hempstead Branch's *Nimrod* and Lola Ridge's *Firehead* are fit to stand with any of the longer poems written by men in America." This unconscious but monstrous piece of male chauvinism apparently passed unnoticed at the time. Though he modified it by adding that "she [Miss Ridge] . . . is one of the chosen few, whether men or women, to whom the epithet 'genius' does not seem inapplicable," his statement is nonetheless indicative of the way women were regarded in poetry until the mid-twentieth-century or even later.

It remained for the poets among women of the era following World War II and the Korean conflict to demand equal consideration and recognition in poetry as in all other areas of human endeavor. With the coincidence of the women's liberation movement and the fight for civil rights generally, a new element has been added with the emergence of black women eager to join forces with other women in the fight for recognition as poets, regardless of sex.

It is the purpose of the biographical studies that follow to show not only the important role played by outstanding women in the evolution of modern poetry, but also to give a sense of the struggle waged by these women for equality of treatment in the arts.

1

The "Little Tippler":
EMILY DICKINSON,
Herald of a New Era in Poetry

UNRECOGNIZED until four years after her death in 1886, Emily Dickinson was the foremost of her sex among those who brought about the revolution that eventually resulted in modern American poetry. Though she died fourteen years before the twentieth century began, Emily Dickinson's unconscious innovations—her spare, unevenly accented lines, random rhymes, and amazing images—marked the beginning of the feminine influence in modern American poetry. "Feminine" here is not intended to indicate soft or delicate content, but merely to designate gender. The fact is that Emily Dickinson, a member of the then so-called "weaker sex," made some of the strongest, most profound statements in the annals of American poetry. Fifty years before her first volume was published posthumously in 1890, Walt Whitman was shouting the same ideas in essence, but he was a speechmaker, with his free-flowing, overflowing lines of prose poetry. Emily was a lyrist. She led the way toward Imagism before its appearance in the United States.

The question has been asked in recent years; Why separate writers of poetry by sex? As Babette Deutsch drily remarked to her class at Columbia University, "There is no such creature as a poetess: You're either a poet, or you're not." Before her, Amy Lowell, Edna Millay, and other prominent figures fought to banish the term from literary nomenclature, and with some success, although it still crops up occasionally.

Emily's staunchest advisers and mentors, Colonel Thomas W. Higginson and Dr. Josiah T. Holland, both experienced writers who admired her gift for poetic expression, felt that her poems were, in Holland's words, "not suitable for publication." Higginson's attitude is all the more curious, since he realized at once that hers was a "wholly new and original poetic genius." Even so he advised her to keep her poems under cover, and he referred to her as "my partially cracked poetess at Amherst," an indication that he was far from understanding her.

"The truth was," George Whicher wrote in his discerning biography *This Was a Poet*, published in 1938, "that a woman poet was a woman poet to Higginson, and even Emily Dickinson was nothing more. . . . Feminine genius was all of a piece to him, whether manifested by a Lucy Stone, an Anne Whitney, an Emily Dickinson, or a Queen Victoria. He approved it in the lump in a warm blur of chivalrous devotion, giving his allegiance to Woman in the abstract as he had previously given it to the Negro Slave. This temper of mind did not make for critical discrimination." Higginson had bracketed Emily with his sister Louisa in lecturing before the Woman's Club on "Two Unknown Poetesses," a title that speaks volumes for his inability to judge the true value of Emily's work or its distinctiveness in relation to that of her contemporaries. When her first volume created a sensation in the literary world, he was as much surprised as delighted.

Even Samuel Bowles, editor of the *Springfield Republican*, a friend of the Dickinson family, and most recently cited as one of Emily's love objects—the man who published two of the few poems to appear in print during her lifetime and who would have printed more if she had given permission—hardly seemed to appreciate fully her artistry and command of the poet's craft. In referring to the second poem he published, containing her precise picture of a snake beginning with the line, "A narrow Fellow in the Grass/Occasionally rides," Bowles showed a singularly mundane reaction. His comment, stemming from the third stanza, which opens, "He likes a Boggy Acre/A Floor too cool for Corn," was typical of the country editor whose knowledge of agriculture was as great, if not greater than his love of literature. "How did that girl ever know that a boggy field wasn't good for corn?" he wondered, but he offered no more for the record by way of the admiration he must have felt, since he frequently pressed her for more poems. Yet when she refused with finality, he did not persist.

Only her friend Helen Hunt Jackson kept urging her to publish. Mrs. Jackson had made a career for herself as a writer after suffering the deep loss of her first husband, Major Edward Hunt, in a shipyard accident during the early days of the Civil War, followed by the untimely death of their ten-year-old son. Helen felt it imperative that Emily's poetry be revealed to the public. "You are a great poet," she wrote to her childhood playmate after reading the lines published in the *Springfield Republican* plus a few more she begged the poet to let her see, "and it is a wrong to the day you live in that you will not sing aloud. When you are what men call dead, you will be sorry you were so stingy."

This is the strongest, most forthright and perceptive statement concerning the Dickinson genius ever made directly to the poet herself; and significantly, pertinent to the present study, it came from a woman. None of Emily's male mentors or advisers had the vision to see her as a great poet, no matter how much they might admire her talent or find in her a dazzling brilliance. Unfortunately, however, when Helen finally persuaded Emily to submit some poems for an anthology she was compiling. and, in ironic coincidence, chose the one dealing with success itself, she saw fit to emend two lines, thereby altering the accent and the impact of the poem that begins, "Success is counted sweetest/By those who ne'er succeed." The important close, referring to the "definition . . . of Victory," cites a felled soldier, . . . "defeated—dying—/On whose forbidden ear/The distant strains of triumph/Burst agonized and clear!" Helen, with an eye toward grammatical perfection, felt that the word *agonized* described the dying man's emotions and not the "strains of triumph," so she changed the phrase to "agonizingly clear." And Higginson, who edited the selections for the anthology, further compounded the desecration by his pompous opinion that the word *burst* was too harsh and explosive, so the last line came out in print: "Break, agonizingly clear." Emily herself was not consulted. Although she did not protest audibly, she was obviously outraged and hurt, for she denied all further requests from her friend for possible publication of poems. She went on writing, principally as an outlet for her own pent-up emotions and the pleasure of a small circle of people she loved and trusted, but even this select circle saw only a fraction of the enormous number of poems she created in the privacy of her bedroom.

Viewed from the outside, there was little to distinguish the life of Emily Dickinson from that of any other American spinster of her time and circumstances. Born into a genteel, nineteenth-century New England family of Puritan heritage, about midnight on December 10, 1830, she might well have passed into history unnoticed, like most unmarried, dutiful daughters of prominent families in a society soon to be dominated—and designated—by the strict morals of the British queen who ascended the throne seven years after Emily was born and reigned on for nearly twenty years more after she'd died. Add the stern code involving daily life and "the hereafter" handed down by her Puritan ancestors, and it is small wonder that Emily Dickinson in her life and work remains the most mysterious and unique literary figure of her time, if not of all time.

Until she was six years old, she lived in the house where she was born—her grandfather Dickinson's handsome brick Homestead on Main Street. As the town's leading lawyer, pillar of the church, founder of Amherst College and its subsidiary Academy, Samuel Fowler Dickinson thought it only fitting to build himself a substantial home. And when his son Edward, Emily's father, brought his bride, the former Emily Norcross of Monson, to Amherst after their marriage, they moved into the Homestead to live with the family. Here their three children were born: their first-born and only son, Austin, whom Emily loved to the point of idolatry; next Emily, who was given the second name of Elizabeth, after Mrs. Dickinson's older sister, known in the family as "the only male relative on the female side." Perhaps it was the influence of the flinty quality of this militant aunt, whose visits exhausted them all, that later enabled her namesake to steel herself against the disappointments of unrequited love, to renounce the love she might have possessed if her Puritan heritage had not forbidden illegitimate sexual joy. Emily's psyche was pagan as well as Puritan; out of the conflict between the two came the miracle of her poetry.

After the birth of their third child, Mrs. Dickinson was so ill she could not take proper care of the two other children, so Emily was sent to spend a month in Monson with her mother's family. There she was under the special care of her mother's younger sister, Lavinia, after whom the new baby was named, a woman as tender and loving as Aunt Elizabeth was energetic and domineering. During that stay, Emily, at age three and a half, probably received more demonstrative affection than at any time in her life. Her parents rarely showed outward signs of the love they undoubtedly felt for their children. During this stay, her aunt reported Emily a lively and lovable little girl who entertained them all with her bright remarks. The child mentioned her mother and father only a few times but spoke frequently of Austin. She was acutely aware of all that went on around her; they would miss her when it came time to bring her back.

By then all was in confusion at the Homestead. Squire Fowler, as Emily's grandfather was known, had squandered his money and energy to build up Amherst College and establish Amherst Academy. He was ahead of his time in fostering education for "females," but in his zeal for civic pride, his law practice was neglected. His income was dissipated, and he was suddenly forced into bankruptcy. He was selling the Homestead and moving his family out to Ohio, where he had accepted a minor position at Lane Theological Seminary. Several of Edward's unmarried sisters and two of his brothers still lived at home, and the household was bustling with the upheaval of moving.

Emily's father, however, decided that he would stay in Amherst with his family. He was a partner in his father's law firm, and as a young attorney, he resolved to rebuild the practice. He could not save the Homestead just then, but his letters—and his behavior—indicate that he was a deeply determined man, as devoted to civic duty as his father, but with greater practicality and self-interest. Within a few years he bought a pleasant house on Pleasant Street, which was to be the family home for the next fifteen years. Here Emily grew up, experienced her first worshipful love, suffered her first deep sorrow in the death of a dear mentor, and drank in a phenomenal store of knowledge concerning the natural world around her. The outdoor openness in summer was like a heady wine to her. As she was to write later, "Inebriate of Air—am I—/And Debauchee of Dew—/Reeling—thro endless summer days—/From inns of Molten Blue—"

It soon became evident, once Edward Dickinson was on his own, that he was more than qualified to assume Squire Fowler's place in the community. Besides lawyer, he became congressman, treasurer and chief trustee of Amherst College, and in his turn "Squire Dickinson" to the villagers. Above all, he was the dominant figure in his family. Emily's mother was like a dove, hovering over her nest, hoping to keep it quiet and peaceful, but hardly making her presence felt. Emily's father was like an eagle, foraging for the young, fiercely protective, fixing with his eagle eye any child he felt was in error, then delivering a lecture to the culprit or ordering as punishment, "Go to your room for the next hour." Yet somehow he was remote from them all. When the children were little, the household undoubtedly revolved about him. Emily regarded him with admiration and awe. With some exaggeration and theatricality, she wrote to Colonel Higginson of those early days: "I never had a mother. I suppose a mother is one to whom you hurry when you are troubled. . . . I always ran Home to Awe when a child, if anything befell me. He was an Awful Mother, but I liked him better than none."

As she grew older, however, her admiration mixed with the irrepressible humor and gift for mimicry that all the young Dickinsons possessed, Emily came to refer to her father's tirades as "Vesuvius at Home." And of his remoteness, she observed, "Father is too busy with his Briefs to notice what we do." She could have meant—at the time she and "Vinnie" were attending Amherst Academy and Austin, a boys' preparatory school—that they were reading "new" books that would have caused Father to frown with disapproval. (Squire Dickinson more than once gave Emily books as presents, then told her not to read them for fear the contents would "joggle" her mind.) If he had not been too busy with his briefs, he might have noticed the copy of Longfellow's *Kavanagh* that Austin smuggled into the house and hid under the piano cover. Then what a volcanic eruption of anger would have filled the house!

He might have been even more disturbed, however, if he had been aware of the books that the young apprentice in his law firm, Ben Newton, surreptitiously placed under the syringa bush for Emily to "discover" and devour in the privacy of her bedroom. These were the slim volumes of Emerson dealing with Transcendentalism, the heretical—in Squire Dickinson's eyes—new thought just then transforming religion for many people in the Western world. To Emily it must have come like a revelation, the answer to many doubts. Though she listened to her father reading a passage from the Bible every night and accompanied her parents to church twice every Sunday, she seems to have been born a skeptic. She could not accept the basic tenet that life on earth was simply a preparation for the hereafter, a test of one's worthiness to meet the Maker. She was grateful to Ben Newton for introducing her to Emerson's philosophy, and when he sent her a volume of the sage's poems, she was ecstatic. It was to Ben Newton that she showed her earliest attempts at writing poetry of her own, lines which not only revealed her grasp of Emerson, but held the promise of a mysticism beyond his. Ben encouraged her to continue writing, and his words came at a time when she sorely needed them. She had just failed in her only venture away from home, the better part of a year at Mount Holyoke Female Seminary in the neighboring village of South Hadley. The studies gave her no trouble, but she missed her life in Amherst, as she admitted freely. "I have such a dear home, you see," she wrote, a remark at odds with the description of the dark psychopathology of the Dickinson household, dictatorially ruled by her father. Of greater significance is that Emily could not in all honesty confess to being a sinner whose soul needed saving. Miss Mary Lyons, founder of the Seminary, tried in vain to persuade her to repent and receive salvation, as most of the girls did. Emily did wrestle with her own conscience. Ironically, she felt guilty at not being able to declare herself penitent, but she was a truth-seeker and could not affect an emotion she did not feel. This does not mean that she had no capacity for feeling—on the contrary, her emotions ran deep. Though she did not articulate it until later, she concluded, "*My* business is to love," emphasizing the pronoun. The upshot of her dilemma at Mt. Holyoke was that she became ill with a bronchial cold she could not shake. Her father came and whisked her back to Amherst, where the family put her to bed until she was strong enough to return to school—but not to the Seminary.

She took a few courses at Amherst Academy again and learned to cook and bake with an artist's touch. (Her father said no one else baked gingerbread as good as Emily's, and from then on he would eat only hers.) She and Austin had many good talks out by the barn in the morning, or by the kitchen hearth at night after the others had gone to bed. She once said that it was her life work "to make everything pleasant for Father and Austin." She may have been half joking, but she was probably more serious than not. She was inclined to hero worship, both male and female, particularly the former, although she had crushes on a number of her girlhood friends at school. She and Vinnie had no dearth of friends of either sex. There is ample evidence that Emily was not the neglected wallflower who turned to poetry for solace, as some of her biographers have claimed. She wore her reddish hair in smooth bands, and if her features were plain, they were attractively strong, especially her chin, and her remarkable, compelling eyes, which matched her hair. "The color of the sherry the guest leaves in the bottom of the glass," she described them with wry humor. Though they gave her trouble, probably from reading by candlelight late at night, those sherry-colored eyes were intensely alive and penetrating. They often flashed in amusement or anger, or shone with pleasure or with compassion if someone were in trouble. Later in life, according to a young neighbor, her eyes seemed to glow with some far-off vision that only she could glimpse.

She admired, and was admired by her tutors at the Academy, in particular one Leonard Humphrey, the young librarian and instructor in Shakespeare. On February 14th, she gave out valentines she had written; to Leonard went ardent and playful verses, which he promptly printed in the *Academy Bulletin*. His untimely death from consumption the following year was one of Emily's early sorrows, bringing into focus her sense of loss and the awareness of death as a part of life.

Within the confines of a Puritan community, the young Dickinsons led a simple but busy social life. They often attended taffy pulls, and they enjoyed sleigh rides in winter and hay rides in summer. In addition there were the two big annual community events, Cattle Show and Commencement, at which Squire Dickinson shone as the leading orator of the town.

In spite of such light-hearted activity, the inner struggle for the salvation of her soul continued, and Emily was grateful to Ben Newton for showing her Emerson's path toward peace of mind through transcendentalism and helping her to comprehend its full meaning. Ben himself was still in the process of learning, and, she was sure from the doubts he expressed during talks on country walks they took when the day was fine, that he too was troubled by the Puritan concept of total surrender to Christ. Even the honorable Squire Dickinson, for all his exalted position as a contributor and administrator in its financial affairs, did not officially join the church until the early 1850s—it was not unusual for people to "ponder and pause" before taking the final step. But he was a remote, if concerned, benefactor, the awesome head of the family, and Emily could not speak freely with him on subjects deeper than the surface of daily events. True, her father once surprised them all by a prolonged loud ringing of the church bells on a weekday at sunset, summoning the villagers out to view the exceptional display of color brought by the northern lights, but he rarely unbent to such a degree. She felt much closer to Ben Newton.

There is no way of knowing what might have come of their relationship if her father's assistant had decided to stay in Amherst when his apprenticeship was over, but, perhaps because he was not well, he went back to his home town to set up practice. He continued to send Emily books, and they kept up a steady correspondence. He confided to her that he had tuberculosis, but assured her he was under the care of a good doctor. She must not worry about him. Soon afterwards, he married a woman much older than himself, but he kept up the correspondence with Emily. If anything, the tone of his letters was warmer. Then came a nostalgic note that ended, "If I live, I shall come to Amherst in two weeks. If I die, I certainly shall." Emily puzzled over his cryptic message, trying to convince herself that it was one of Ben's humorous references to transcendentalism, which he sometimes made to keep from sounding too serious. But slightly more than two weeks later, without further warning, she read in the evening paper that Benjamin Newton had died of tuberculosis. The shock was so great she felt faint, and her father carried her up to bed, where she stayed for several days, ill with grief. The story of her near collapse may have been exaggerated; but her grief is documented by a letter that Emily painstakingly composed, asking Ben's pastor if he knew whether her friend was "at peace" in his soul when he died. It is a troubled letter, perhaps because she felt she had not treasured Ben's friendship for its true value, and now he was gone. Much later she immortalized their friendship in the phrase, "an amethyst remembrance." Now she could only vow to fulfill the prophecy he had made—that she would be a poet. And she would never cease her search for truth—and "tell it slant," for she knew instinctively that "The Truth must dazzle gradually/ Or every man be blind—"

So the pattern of her inner life was set. In a few years, her father, through steady industry and singleness of purpose, was able to reclaim the Homestead. Here Emily Dickinson lived out her life, in the house where she was born, staying within the immediate family circle, which was expanded by Austin's family when he married and moved into the house the Squire had built for him "a hedge away." The circle was diminished by her parents' death, then expanded again by addition of the little family of Austin's beloved mistress, Mabel Loomis Todd. She was later to become Emily's first editor and an ardent advocate for her poetry. It was a tightly drawn circle, fraught with tensions and strange passions, at whose center, Emily, involved, yet removed by her objectivity and her own secret passion, brought into being some 1775 poems.

There were of course other influences than Ben Newton

outside her family that caused her to write poetry of such magnitude and intensity. Her friendship with Susan Gilbert, the scintillating, brash classmate who eventually, with Emily's encouragement and early blessing, became Austin's wife and, for a time, her beloved "Sister Sue," was undoubtedly a major force in her poetic development. She showed her poems to this vivacious yet viciously assertive sister-in-law, who advised Emily on which of the various versions of a poem was best. Emily, though she accepted Sue's advice at the time, nevertheless preserved all versions, even seven or eight alternatives of a single word, for posterity to discover, an indication that she was more self-reliant than Sue ever realized. And when the fact emerged that his marriage was a bitter disappointment to Austin, though the incompatibility was kept secret for a long time, Emily did not hesitate to sever the relationship with her erstwhile friend and sister-in-law. Austin's happiness came first, and Emily, as well as Vinnie, stood staunchly beside her brother.

The inspiration for Emily Dickinson's sheer, distilled love poetry has been the object of speculation on the part of her biographers since the beginning of the century. After Ben Newton left her father's law firm, the apprentice who followed him, George Gould, like his predecessor, formed the habit of stopping by the mansion for tea on Sunday afternoon. Like Ben, he enjoyed talking to Emily, who found him agreeable, but by no means the mentor she had discovered in Ben Newton.

She may have gone for a carriage ride with George occasionally, but it is doubtful that he proposed to her, or that, if he did, her father broke up the romance, as has been suggested. One recent biographer, Richard Sewall, points to Squire Dickinson's own struggle as a young attorney as likely to make him tolerant of meager financial status, especially in regard to his apprentices. He probably would have considered Gould's proposal, if it was made, a perfectly respectable offer of marriage for his elder daughter. He was no Mr. Barrett of Wimpole Street, one parallel that has been drawn. Nor was he like Clara Wieck's father, who violently opposed her marriage to the struggling musician-composer Robert Schumann, a former pupil of his. Wieck felt that Clara's career as a concert pianist, which he was exploiting to the hilt, would be destroyed by marriage no matter how much promise Robert Schumann showed as a composer. Squire Dickinson, on the other hand, did not seem to perceive even remotely that his daughter possessed the germ of genius, or to care so much as to inquire about the nature of her writing in the privacy of her room. Or if, like Barrett, he had feelings of incest toward Emily, they were far more latent than Mr. Barrett's for his daughter Elizabeth. The Squire was too involved in his public career to notice what Emily did. He expected her to attend to his surface needs and pleasures: to bake his gingerbread, to play the piano for him after supper in the evening—as she was more than happy to do—and to entertain the faculty at the Commencement Day teas the Dickinsons gave every year. He never tried to make an invalid of her.

Although Genevieve Taggard in her biography has tried to make a strong case for George Gould as the lover/suitor for Emily's hand whose romance was broken by a possessive father, it is more likely that Emily herself made the decision. She was still under the shadow of Newton's death and too near the threshold of artistic creation to accept a proposal of marriage just then. Her remark, often cited, that her father was "in the habit of her," and she could not leave him may have been just an excuse for turning down a man who did not move her sufficiently or measure up to the high standards she had set.

She had already begun to cherish solitude—time to meditate, to watch the changes of nature in its seasons as she roamed the hills, to tend her garden or the plants in her small herbarium and greenhouse-room in winter. She wanted time to read and write—and think. Her sister, Vinnie, the most outgoing of the three Dickinson children, put it bluntly, "Em's business is to *think*, and that is what she has to do." Emily did not let her father's being "in the habit of her" stand in the way of refusing to go to Washington during his first term in Congress, although during the second she did accompany her mother and Vinnie for a visit of several weeks in the capital. While she rather enjoyed the whirl of Washington society and was able to hold her own in conversation with senators and officials of state, she was glad to leave for Philadelphia to visit old friends before returning to Amherst. It was here that she met the man who was to become her second mentor, and, according to her niece, Martha Dickinson Bianchi, the one who brought on the crisis that caused her to become a recluse.

This man was the Reverend Charles Wadsworth, minister of the First Presbyterian Church, noted for his spiritually persuasive sermons. Emily, who attended his church with her family and their hosts one fine Sunday in spring, was so impressed with the minister's sermon and his moving delivery that she was shaken with ardor and sought a private session with him. The result of that meeting was an exalted and supposedly mutual love, both spiritual and physical. Emily had never before found a teacher who gave such promise of being able to answer her questions on immortality and who was at the same time a man who might fulfill her desire. The minister had never found such a willing and apt pupil, one who asked such extraordinary questions. There followed an ardent correspondence, extending for years. Twice during that time Wadsworth came to Amherst to see Emily, the second time to ask her to leave her home, as he was leaving his, and go out west with him, accepting a call to a new church. But he was a married man with a family—divorce for a "man of the cloth" was unthinkable in those days—and her Puritan conscience would not allow her to accept. It was then that Emily Dickinson is supposed to have renounced love and gone into reclusion to write poetry; ever afterward she wore white dresses as a sign of celibacy and the purity of her self-denied love.

This long-lived legend, begun by her niece, but later discounted by half a dozen different biographers, is still supported by lines from a good many poems, allowing a certain amount for poetic license. With superb brevity she told the story in general:

> Proud of my broken heart, since thou didst break it,
> Proud of the pain I did not feel till thee,
>
> Proud of my night, since thou with moons dost slake it,
> *Not* to partake thy passion, *my* humility.

These words apply to anyone who might have been the object of her love; but other poems, particularly one of ten five-line stanzas, seem to indicate the minister:

> I cannot live with You—
> It would be Life—
> And Life is over there—
> Behind the Shelf
>
> The Sexton keeps the Key to— . . .

In the first three lines of the sixth stanza, we find:

> Nor could I rise—with You—
> Because Your Face
> Would put out Jesus'— . . .

And the eighth stanza reads:

> They'd judge Us—How—
> For You—served Heaven—You know,
> Or sought to—
> I could not—
>
> Because You saturated Sight—
> And I had no more Eyes
> For sordid excellence
> As Paradise. . . .

Such overwhelming adoration expressed in religious terms provides a temptation to believe the Wadsworth legend even now, although several biographers have discarded Wadsworth in favor of Samuel Bowles, editor of the *Springfield Republican,* as the inspiration. Emily had met Bowles through Austin and Sue, and was on more outgoing, familiar terms with him than with Wadsworth. Bowles once called her "Rascal," summoning her downstairs when she tried to seclude herself in her room during one of his visits. She wrote to and received letters from both men; and both left on long journeys by ship at about the same time. The poem beginning,

> I got so I could take his name—
> Without—Tremendous gain—
> That Stop-sensation—on my Soul—
> And Thunder—in the Room—

and continuing,

> I got so I could walk across
> That Angle in the floor,
> Where he turned so, and I turned—how—
> And all our Sinew tore—
>
> I got so I could stir the Box—
> In which his letters grew
> Without that forcing, in my breath—
> As Staples—driven through—

contains elements of her emotional state, and the circumstances surrounding her relationship to both men make the poem applicable to either. However, not even legend claims that Bowles urged Emily to go to Europe with him, and the correspondence between them seems to have dealt with her poems and her professional advice rather than the sort of spiritual counsel she received from Wadsworth, which might more easily have deepened into an all-enveloping love.

One of her chroniclers, Rebecca Patterson, in *The Riddle of*

Emily Dickinson, tried to solve the mystery of her love by citing poems that might be interpreted as homosexual, naming Kate Scott Anthon as the lover/beloved. But it is stretching one's credulity to accept even a handful of the poems as homosexual, and the factual evidence is flimsy indeed. The author may prove that Mrs. Anthon, whom Emily met also through Austin and Sue, had definite lesbian tendencies, but in doing so she leaves Emily behind, forgotten in Amherst. The reader must voyage to Italy with Kate in hot pursuit of a young girl—she apparently sailed at the same time Bowles left for Europe and Wadsworth for the far West—and not till the last chapter does the history return to Emily Dickinson's life and poetry. It is true that Emily admired Kate, as she admired more than one woman who showed intelligence and wit during the conversations that took place in the salon-like parlor of the Evergreens, her brother's home. And, in the manner of that era, she wrote fond notes to Kate, as well as to other women friends.

The overall tone of the love poems in any case is definitely heterosexual—that of a woman who has renounced the love of a man. The identity of the man may never be known—Sewall brought to light three "Dear Master" letters, more emotion-wracked than any previous discoveries, but was not able to furnish a clue as to the person for whom they were intended, though she greeted both Wadsworth and Higginson as "Master" at various times. (Two of these letters were rough drafts, not even copied for mailing.) Whoever the object of her heartfelt emotion may have been, it seems certain that some critical moment in her life occurred early in the 1860s, shaking her to the core, yet strengthening her creative powers tenfold. In poem after poem she deals poignantly with her decision to renounce love, but not life: "I dreaded that first Robin, so,/But He is mastered, now," she sets the theme mournfully in one poem, recording her reaction to each sign of spring that appeared after her love was gone. In a fine conclusion, she wisely observes: "They're here, though; not a creature failed—/No Blossom stayed away/In gentle deference to me—/The Queen of

Calvary—" They salute her, so she lifts her "childish Plumes" in "bereaved acknowledgement/Of their unthinking Drums—" Rarely has the inevitability of the springtime been drawn with such power and drama. Though a few of Emily's early critics objected violently to such far-fetched rhymes as *plumes* and *drums,* most of them conceded her individuality and strength. Gradually, the joys of Nature and the everchanging seasons returned to her in their intrinsic value, and she was able to celebrate them with undiluted pleasure. She drank deeply, "the little Tippler/Leaning against the—Sun—"

Other sorrows came, but she was able to withstand adversity by viewing it objectively in her poems. Death and immortality almost outdistanced nature and unrequited love as themes for poems. The passing of those dear to her seemed irreparable loss; the unexpected death of her father in 1874 was shattering. (The Squire had gone to Boston and was speaking before the state legislature when he felt faint; he had to leave the rostrum and died a few hours later in his hotel room.) By then Emily had a third mentor, Colonel Thomas Wentworth Higginson, editor of the *Atlantic Monthly,* to whom she sent some of her most vital verses, and from whom she received ambivalent praise with meretricious advice. To him she wrote a revealing letter, unconsciously depicting the sort of serenity that had developed over the years between the Squire and his daughter, whom he never really understood. "The last Afternoon that my Father lived," she wrote, "though with no premonition—I preferred to be with him, and invented an absence for Mother, Vinnie being asleep. He seemed peculiarly pleased, as I oftenest stayed with myself, and remarked, as the Afternoon withdrew, that he 'would like it not to end.' His pleasure almost embarrassed me, and my Brother coming, I suggested that they walk. Next morning I woke him for the train—and saw him no more." From the vantage point of her mature poetic vision of her awesome parent, she added, "His Heart was pure & terrible, and I think no other like it exists."

From this point on, she stayed more and more within the

confines of the Dickinson grounds for several reasons. The most urgent was that her mother, made invalid by a stroke after the Squire died, required constant care, and it was up to her daughters to look after her. Although they had help from Maggie and Tom, the domestics who had been with the Dickinson family for years, Emily still did the baking and put up jams and jellies besides keeping up her beloved gardening. Every other moment was spent at her writing, and there were not many hours to spare during the day after Mrs. Dickinson became ill. Often Emily sat at her desk at night, perfecting her poems according to her own lights. No matter how much Colonel Higginson might admonish her against unorthodox rhymes and her use of dashes and capital letters to begin a word she wished to emphasize wherever it fell in the line, she had to follow her own judgment. She searched the dictionary for the exact word. It was said that she actually read the "lexicon" as one might read a novel, lapping up information and storing it away for later lines.

In spite of her reticence, her strong will made itself felt in her refusal to alter her ways, and in the electric shock of her personality on those who met her. Higginson, who visited her twice in the years they corresponded, reported a marked reaction: "I never was with anyone who drained my nerve power so much . . . I am glad not to live near her." His description is hardly that of the old-maid recluse of legend, and, according to recent biographies, her reclusion came gradually. Her vast correspondence alone is proof that she did not shut herself away from the world entirely or abruptly. Friends who were ill or had a birthday might find themselves the recipient of a carefully iced cake or a jar of wine jelly (her specialty) delivered with a poem scribbled on a scrap of paper in her fine but almost indecipherable script. Occasionally a poem was sent with a flower or a bouquet arranged to look like one large blossom from her garden. Such thoughtfulness is not typical of a closeted recluse, as some claimed the Squire's queer "elder darter" had become. Her constant wearing of white may have expressed theatricality as much as eccentricity. A late love came along when Judge Otis Lord, a friend of the family who lost his wife, responded warmly to Emily's condolence note, and an exchange of letters led to a mellow romance. This time Emily not only felt love for but was loved in return by a man she respected and enjoyed as her peer. Apparently marriage was considered, but again the poet in her would not let the woman triumph. In one letter she wrote: "Oh, my too beloved, save me from the idolatry which would crush us both." And in speaking of their life together, "Oh, that I had found it sooner! Yet Tenderness has not a date—it comes—and overwhelms." But in the end she did not allow it to overwhelm her; she chose to remain on the solitary path the dedicated poet must take. Her vocation could not accommodate more than one person; even the consideration of marriage seemed to crowd out the poet in her, which reasserted itself as soon as she made her decision. "Renunciation—is a piercing Virtue—/The letting go/A Presence—for an Expectation—" she wrote. Yet in this case the decision may not have been so difficult. She may have felt more reverence than passion for Judge Lord, who was in a way a father figure. In fact, he had been a friend of her father's from the time Emily was a girl, and was close by in Boston when the Squire died. The judge probably was a vivid reminder of her father, with the added appeal for her of a wit and vein of humor that Emily called "the Judge Lord brand." She could not have objected to the age difference between them, but she must instinctively have feared that he, like her father, might be seized with some fatal attack at any time. And indeed, within a year of their love correspondence (1877–1883), the judge was gone. Emily wrote mysteriously, "Abstinence from Melody was what made him die." The year before, Mrs. Dickinson had slipped away in her sleep, relieved at last of the painful paralysis that made her an invalid. It may have been then (if not earlier) that Emily, who had come to feel more affection for her mother in tending her uncomplaining parent than she had at any time before, wrote one of her most touching, profound poems:

The Bustle in a House
The Morning after Death
Is solemnest of industries
Enacted upon Earth—

The Sweeping up the Heart
And putting Love away
We shall not want to use again
Until Eternity.

She and Vinnie were alone in Homestead. But they were
not quite alone, for Austin, who had more than taken their
father's place as the town's leading lawyer and public citizen,
began coming over every day for relief from the hostility that
kept mounting in the Evergreens. His barely concealed, burning love for the dashing young Mabel Loomis Todd was at its
flood-tide, and he needed the support of his sisters—Vinnie as
the practical go-between, and Emily as his confidante, a sister-
confessor, as it were. She wrote frankly in one of her letters to
Higginson, "My brother is with us so often each day, we almost
forget that he ever passed to a wedded Home." And Austin,
during Mabel's brief absence on a visit to her family in
Washington, wrote her the same thing in one of his love notes,
adding, that they spoke of nothing else but her. "I see Vin and
Em more than I did, and you are the constant theme." His love,
in contrast to Emily's carefully guarded passion, was like a
rushing stream, renewing itself in a burst of freshets at every
turn. But Emily, in whose fine restraint lay the seeds of a powerful creative flowering, understood her brother's need to let the
flood waters run off as they might. She probably felt partly
responsible for Austin's unhappy home life, since it was she
who had encouraged his marriage to Sue. Mrs. Todd's daughter, Millicent Todd Bingham, recorded in her diary that her
mother felt that "Emily was glad that Austin had found some
comfort after his all but ruined life," and quoted Mabel as saying, "Emily always respected real emotion."

She also respected real talent, and apparently Mabel Todd
was enormously talented. She had a fine soprano voice and

frequently sang for Emily in the evening. The poet, who listened from an adjoining room or the stairway landing, would send a little poem by way of appreciation. Mabel was an ardent painter as well. Once when she presented Emily with a watercolor panel of Indian-pipes, Emily's favorite wildflower, she received a message of thanks that read: "I cannot make an Indian-pipe, but please accept a humming-bird." Attached was Emily's brilliant word picture:

> A Route of Evanescence
> With a revolving Wheel—
> A Resonance of Emerald—
> A Rush of Cochineal—

followed by the playful yet far-reaching conclusion:

> And every Blossom on the Bush
> Adjusts its tumbled Head—
> The mail from Tunis, probably,
> An easy Morning's Ride—

Surely Emily must have known that a many-talented person like Mabel (who sometimes wrote poetry herself, played leading roles in local theatrical productions, gave piano lessons, and led the choir in church in addition to following her other artistic abilities) would recognize the value of such lines. It seems obvious that if Emily Dickinson was no longer interested in publication, she still craved appreciation, and Mabel was unstinting in her praise, probably more generous than Sue had been. It is likely, too, that Emily wanted to make life pleasant for Austin, and as he was so overwhelmingly in love with Mabel, his sister accepted it whole-heartedly.

The complex situation can only be called bizarre—a melodrama that would test the credulity of a seasoned soap opera viewer today. Mabel's husband, David Todd, an astronomer and recent graduate of Amherst College himself, had returned to the college to head up the science department and observatory, bringing his bride and baby daughter. Austin Dickinson, as secretary-treasurer of the college, usually welcomed new faculty members, so he and Sue were among the Todds' first callers. The young couple were both impressed with Austin—in her diary Mabel called him "a magnificent" figure of a man, adding that it was apparent already on that short call that his marriage was not congenial. Sue was so taken by Mabel's charm that she immediately invited the Todds for dinner. Within two months the young couple were accepted by Amherst's academic circles and the villagers in general. The initial complication was that Austin's twenty-year-old son, Edward (the "little Ned" of Emily's letters a decade earlier), fell head over heels in love with Mabel. When she realized how serious he was, she managed to cool his ardor, but in the meantime she and Austin discovered their mutual love. Ned, in a jealous rage, complained to his mother about the attention Mabel was paying Austin. Whether she put his anger down to puppy love, or whether she no longer cared what Austin did, Sue did not break off relations with the Todds, although the invitations to them became less frequent.

Austin, however, did nothing to stem the tide of his love. He gave Mabel and David a plot of ground on Dickinson land and aided them in building a house, the Dell, just a meadow away from the Homestead. The three households maintained a precarious balance between harmony and dissonance. Austin swung between ecstasy and frustration, going to his sisters' for solace and practical help. As for Todd, he seems to have vacillated between admiration for the fifty-four-year-old treasurer of the College (through whom he had hopes of getting a new observatory) and jealousy toward this same dignitary who, though twenty-seven years older than she, was his wife's lover. At first David may have thought the affair merely a passing infatuation, but when it continued and kept the fever pitch of a total commitment, he, too, was torn by conflicting emotions. He turned to other women but never found the fulfillment that Austin and Mabel knew. He once admitted, "Adultery ruined my life," but on the other hand, observed after Austin's death, "I loved him more than any man I ever knew." Todd ended his days in a mental institution, a victim of his vacillation.

Just how much the poet in Emily Dickinson was affected by this explosive situation is hard to say. Certainly she was involved in the family melee, not only because of Austin's feelings, but because of her own. Less and less frequently she sped along the "little path just wide enough for two" that led to the Evergreens, and by the time the Dell was built for the Todds, she hardly ever left the Homestead. She kept herself removed, but not aloof. She could view life objectively for all its deep sorrows. "I can wade Grief—" she wrote, "Whole Pools of it—/I'm used to that—But the least push of Joy/Breaks up my feet—" One of her great joys was to note the changing seasons. She showed an uncanny awareness of spring: "An altered look about the hills—/A Tyrian light the village fills—" and was equally sharp in limning the passing of summer, using a familiar motif: "As imperceptibly as Grief/The Summer lapsed away—" She captured the stillness of late summer: "Nature spending with herself/Sequestered Afternoon—" She made an original commentary on society from observing a bee: "The Pedigree of Honey/Does not concern the Bee—/A Clover, any time, to him,/Is Aristocracy—." Because she was as much pagan as Puritan, she understood Austin's rapture at having found fulfillment in love—in his words, "the perfect soul-mate for time and eternity." Over and over in his letters to Mabel the words "I love you" are repeated with little variation. But at one point he injects a thought that might well have come from one of his talks with Emily: "Conventionality is for those not strong enough to be laws for themselves or to conform themselves to the great higher law where all harmonies meet."

There is little doubt from the quantity and quality—the content—of her poems that Emily had conformed herself to the "great higher law," forming her own concept of God, death, and immortality. Long before her father died she had stopped going to Sunday services. As she wrote:

> Some keep the Sabbath going to Church—
> I keep it, staying at Home—
> With a Bobolink for a Chorister—
> And an Orchard, for a Dome—

She concluded,

> So, instead of getting to Heaven, at last—
> I'm going, all along.

In a more powerful poem she proclaimed:

> I'm ceded—I've stopped being Theirs—
> The name They dropped upon my face
> With water, in the country church
> Is finished using, now, . . .
>
> Baptized, before, without the choice,
> But this time, consciously, of Grace—
> Unto supremest name—
>
> . . . this time—Adequate—Erect,
> With Will to choose, or to reject,
> And I choose, just a Crown—

She never joined the church, but in the faith of her own forming was more religious than those who, out of sheer conformity, attended services twice every Sunday.

The poems of the last few years of her life were largely concerned with that self-developed faith, which enabled her to rejoice in the gift of life. One of her chief delights lay in the little band of children that played in the Dickinson yard: Austin's three and a few neighborhood girls and boys. She joined in their games in a conspiratorial way, offering treats from the pantry by way of a slowly lowered basket on a long cord from her bedroom window. She let them watch when she baked gingerbread or her huge "black" (molasses) cake. Once, when Mac Jenkins, the minister's son, asked why she took such care in measuring, she told him with the merest twinkle, "Because I don't want to get a quarter-teaspoonful of Eternity in by mistake."

No matter how deep her grief as those closest to her passed away, she did not lose the will to live, but one blow was well-nigh unbearable: In October 1883, her nephew Gilbert, Austin's late-born son, by all accounts an extraordinary child who possessed a brilliant mind and sunny disposition, was seized by a deadly fever and died at the age of eight, after three days of delirium. Of the three Dickinson children, he was closest to Emily in spirit, and indeed, judging from the only published photograph, bore a marked physical resemblance to her. Little "Gib" had been the remaining link between the two households for several years, and after his death Emily did not set foot in the Evergreens again. She became seriously ill. The doctor pronounced it "nervous prostration," but she felt that it was Gilbert's death: "The crisis of the sorrow of so many years is all that tires me," she claimed, writing to Judge Lord.

He, however, suspected the truth, and in a letter to his sister paid tribute to one of Emily's sterling traits. "Knowing how entirely unselfish she is," he said, "I fear she has been more ill than she has been willing to tell me." As Emily knew, Otis Lord himself was ill, and he died the following year, 1884, while she was still trying to regain her strength. She had to stay "in a chair," as she put it, but she managed to write a few letters and work over her poems. She had devised a typically complex system of preserving them, tying together six or eight sheets of note paper, each bearing a copied poem, to form little "fascicules," as Mabel Todd called them. These in turn were strung one to another with loose ends of the strings binding each cluster of poems.

Emily did not sign, date, or give a title to any of her poems, but she exulted as the number grew. In the two-stanza verse beginning, "This is my letter to the World/That never wrote to Me—" she made sure that her identity as author would be acknowledged. In 1884, however, she could make few additions to her canon. She was suffering from Bright's disease, which slowly sapped her energy during the next year and a half. Vinnie watched over her with grave concern, and Austin continued to stop in every day. By May 15, 1886, she was bedridden. Austin silently sat with her, holding her hand. She was only semiconscious, but she seemed to know he was there. Then she apparently fell asleep, so he left.

She never wakened from that peaceful sleep. She never wrote more prophetic lines than these:

> Because I could not stop for Death—
> He kindly stopped for me—
> The Carriage held but just Ourselves—
> And Immortality.

2

AMY LOWELL:
Imagism and Surrealism

On the night of March 31, 1915, the Poetry Society of America, with headquarters in New York, scheduled a program that aroused a good deal of interest, producing a large turnout. One of the attractions was the announcement that Miss Amy Lowell of Brookline, Massachusetts, had requested and been granted permission before the close of the meeting to give a reading from the forthcoming volume *Some Imagist Poets*. She was introducing the "new poetry," as defined in the works of several poets in the recently transported Imagist movement, which Amy herself had brought over from England, the leadership of which she had wrested from the equally volatile expatriate poet Ezra Pound. Tonight she intended to read poems by John Gould Fletcher and the mysterious H.D., both, like Pound, Americans living in England; D. H. Lawrence, although he would not be categorized as an Imagist; F. S. Flint; Richard Aldington; and maybe one or two others. And, of course, she would read her own. She would include some of her latest

poems, in addition to a few from her second and startling volume *Sword Blades and Poppy Seed.* Published six months earlier
by Macmillan, it had caused a furor of combined approval, dis-
may, and downright disapproval among the critics, depending
on their preferences and feeling for the avant-garde in poetry.

Following as it did her first fairly acceptable but purely
conventional volume, *A Dome of Many-Coloured Glass,* the second offering was all the more astonishing. It had brought its
author a phenomenal rise to fame. Louis Untermeyer, then a
bright young critic making a name for himself in literary circles,
had damned Amy Lowell's initial volume with the faintest of
faint praise. After the second volume was published, he proclaimed that "a wholly new poet, and, what was more, a new
epoch" had appeared. *Sword Blades and Poppy Seed* sounded
some of the first notes of the controversy which raged about the
new poetry.

There was considerable stir in the auditorium. Everyone
craned to see Miss Lowell as she majestically rose from her
front-row seat, took the papers and book handed to her by the
serene-faced woman beside her—Ada Russell, her beloved
companion—and ascended the few steps to the podium. Those
who had only read her revolutionary volume or her earlier tame
verses, who had not heard any of the legends about the author,
were astonished to see a woman of square proportions, almost
as wide as her five-foot height, come on stage. Somehow she
managed to carry her enormous bulk with dignity and grace.
She wore a severe blue serge suit with a long flowing skirt and a
longish flared jacket over a man's shirt with high collar and
stock. Her outfit concealed her size to a certain extent, and
behind the podium her girth was hardly remarkable at all. She
fixed the audience with an open if rather imperious gaze. Her
intelligent hazel eyes were set in a face that was large and
round, but her features were well-formed and small. Her hair
was combed high off her forehead in a pompadour under which
a switch of hair was hidden—to give her added height—and the

pince-nez perched on the narrow bridge of her nose gave her a professorial air.

She began with a stinging statement of the 1915 Imagist credo as set forth in the provocative preface to *Some Imagist Poets,* to the effect that most poetry of the last quarter of the nineteenth century had been stagnant, stale, and insipid. The aims of the creators of the credo were, she declaimed, counting them off on her fingers:

> 1. To use the language of common speech, but to employ always the *exact* word. . . .
> 2. To create new rhythms. . . . We do not insist upon free verse as the only method of writing poetry. We fight for it as a principle of liberty. . . .
> 3. To allow absolute freedom in the choice of subject. . . .
> 4. To present an image [hence the name Imagist]. . . .
> 5. To produce poetry that is hard and clear, never blurred nor indefinite.
> 6. Finally, most of us believe that concentration is the very essence of poetry.

Her tone of voice throughout this recital was so bristling that it stirred the Society's conservatives to action, gearing them for rebuttal.

She chose to read as her opening example a recent poem of her own entitled "Bath." It was the first of a series of five written in polyphonic prose, a medium she had learned from John Gould Fletcher, with which both were experimenting. This series was called "Spring Day" and formed a narrative describing the poet's activities from morning till night. A playful and sensuous poem, it was one of Lowell's most successful in the free flowing style she had evolved. In her resonant voice she began to read: "The day is fresh-washed and fair, and there is a smell of tulips and narcissus in the air . . ." The poet is in her morning bath, relaxing pleasurably, as the third stanza realistically describes:

> Little spots of sunshine lie on the surface of the water and dance, and their reflections wobble deliciously over the ceiling; a stir of my finger sets them whirring, reeling. I move a foot, and the planes of light in the water jar. I lie back and laugh, and let the green-white water, the sun-flawed, beryl water, flow over me. The day is almost too bright to bear, the green water covers me from the too bright day. I will lie here awhile and play with the water and the sun spots.

Before the bath scene closed with the short stanza, "The sky is blue and high. A crow flaps by the window, and there is a whiff of tulips and narcissus in the air," an audible ripple of laughter, barely suppressed, flowed through the audience.

In 1915, "Bath" was bound to be a shocker. The image of the poet's obese nude body in her morning tub-water brought gasps and chortles. She kept reading determinedly, leaving out most of "Spring Day," and turning instead to an entirely different kind of poem, the finely wrought love lyric "Venus Transiens," which she gave as an example of free verse. The lines were inspired by her beloved Ada Russell.

> Tell me,
> Was Venus more beautiful
> Than you are,
> When she topped
> The crinkled waves,
> Drifting shoreward
> On her plaited shell?
> Was Botticelli's vision
> Fairer than mine. . . .

The "controlled and shining beauty" of this passage, as John Livingston Lowes, professor of literature at Harvard, called it, was lost on most of the members at the March meeting of the Poetry Society. Nor did her audience pay close attention to samples of other Imagists' work that she went on to read. As soon as she stopped, Amy was showered with a deluge of questions, most of them concerned with her "Bath." Many were from conservatives needle-sharp with hostility. Some of her attackers demanded to know if this was supposed to be poetry. Some accused her of deliberately destroying time-honored tradition.

Amy rose to the challenge with rapierlike brilliance. Single-handedly, she justified her poetry and defended the poets of her persuasion. She stood her ground firmly, perhaps too firmly. Her listeners could not know—and many of them never did know—that hers was a highly intense, nerve-wracked, passionate nature, inwardly, if not outwardly, extremely fragile and sensitive.

Born on the morning of February 9, 1874, she was late coming into the family, and her early childhood was essentially lonely, as she had no playmates among her siblings. Her brothers—Percy, nineteen, and Lawrence, seventeen and a half—were at Harvard when she was born. Her older sister, Katie, at sixteen, was already a young lady preparing for her debut, and Bessie, the closest to her in age and usually charged to "look after the baby" on family outings, was an adolescent by the time Amy was talking and "running wild" in the nursery.

Her father, Augustus Lowell, was known as a "hard man of business." His sole outside interest was horticulture. By the time Amy came along, he was devoting many hours to his garden, a pastime that became an ardent passion and unlimited source of inspiration in his youngest daughter's development as a career poet. Her mother, Katherine Lowell, née Lawrence, was a semi-invalid for much of her married life and could not cope, even with the help of a nurse, with the care of a new baby.

A precocious child, the future poet and flamboyant literary personality was both petted and patronized by her elders. She quickly learned to take advantage of her position. She was a difficult child to discipline. Although she was fond of her governess-nurse, she teased and tormented the poor woman to distraction, obeying orders only when she chose. She did observe the rules Augustus Lowell laid down for the daily routine at Sevenels, the name he gave to his home, signifying the seven Lowells of his domain; but even these regulations Amy managed to circumvent within a few years. The only person whose orders she obeyed unhesitatingly was Burns, the coachman. At the age of four, when asked why she deferred to him instead of her sister Bessie, she said seriously, "Oh, Burns was born to command." Her remark brought a howl of laughter from her brothers and sisters, so Amy, sensing she had scored, followed rapidly with, "Now can I stay up an hour longer at night?" She wanted desperately to be like the grownups.

Her favorite place on the ten-acre estate of Sevenels was the stables, where she spent hours watching Burns curry the horses, learning equestrian lore from this former jockey who served the Lowell household for years. To a child who had no friends her own age until she was eleven, he was a source of exciting information and a steadfast companion. When the Lowells went out in the family carriage, Amy's place was on the box beside Burns, who let her take the reins early on. Before she was nine she could actually drive, and he declared that she "handled the horses like a man," which she considered a high compliment.

She adored her brothers, particularly Percy, and she often expressed the wish to be a boy so that she could grow up to be just like him. He was a crack polo player, but it is notable that as much as she tried to emulate him, and for all her love of horses, Amy never liked to ride them, only to drive them. Long after she owned a maroon Pierce-Arrow, with a hired chauffeur in livery, she chose to drive her horses when traveling to and from her summer home overlooking Dublin Lake in New Hampshire. She preferred carriage drives through country lanes to her luxury automobile.

Before she was twelve it was evident that a glandular disorder was causing Amy's childish plumpness to balloon into obesity. Eventually she learned to make a joke of it—"Lord, I'm a walking sideshow!" she would say, then turn to other subjects so that people forgot her size at once. Until she reached that stage, however, she suffered the adolescent pangs of a wallflower. Once, with remarkable insight, she wrote in her diary: "If I were not so self-conscious, I would be much better. . . ." She also viewed herself as a "great, rough, masculine strong thing."

In the private girls' school she attended from her eleventh to her seventeenth years, Amy Lowell was the clown of the class. Because of her ability to entertain, she made friends easily, and several of those during her school years remained lifelong. She was a bright pupil, but not a studious one. The teachers and the curriculum, except for books that drew her interest, bored her. She later wrote that she could not be taught—she had to learn for herself.

The snubs she endured from the boys in dancing class finally aroused her to learn the steps. She overcame her clumsiness, and during her debut year in 1891 was a popular partner at no less than sixty balls. It was a hollow victory, however, for none of the partners *she* liked took a serious interest in her, and the suitors who came to call did not appeal to her. She felt they were fortune hunters, nothing more. Probably because Amy worshipped her brother Percy, who had gone off to the Orient just after her ninth birthday, none of the few suitors measured up to her standards.

From the time she was fourteen, when Bessie, following Lawrence and Katie, was married, Amy was alone at Sevenels with aging parents. She left school at seventeen in part because her mother was visibly fading and her father felt that Amy, as the only child at home, should be around her mother more. Since Amy had already informed her parents that she did not care to attend "Miss Cabot's" any longer, it was easy to comply with "Papa's wish" for once, and it proved fortuitous. She began to educate herself.

Browsing through her father's library one day she came across a copy of Leigh Hunt's *Imagination and Fancy; or, Selections from the English Poets,* and it became her Book of Revelations. She went to the Boston Athenaeum (founded by Lowells, among others) and brought home the volumes of these poets, ignoring the fact that her father wouldn't allow "that atheist Shelley" in the house, and read them avidly, both to herself and aloud to her friends. Among the poets represented there, Keats became her idol—like him, Amy was a moon-worshiper. He expressed her inner emotions as no other poet. Although she had always admired and stood in awe of her great cousin James Russell Lowell, whom she saw at family gatherings, and with whom on one occasion she had had a brief but awkward conversation, he was on too exalted a plane in the family hierarchy for her to feel at ease with him. Keats, on the other hand, could have been her alter ego.

In one of those coincidences of fate, at the point that Amy Lowell was finding herself in poetry, her cousin James died (in August of 1891). Her brother Lawrence was asked to be one of the pallbearers at the state funeral for the prominent figure in the literary, academic, and diplomatic worlds. In later years, at the height of her own fame, Amy was annoyed by frequent references linking her name to her eminent cousin's—just as the late Robert Lowell eschewed any but the most distant connection with Amy's; but in 1891 as she stood with her parents watching her brother move in the solemn procession accompanying the bier, she hoped that she could some day be one-tenth as famous a poet as James Russell Lowell. She never dreamed that for at least a decade her fame would exceed her cousin's, or that she would write the book he had planned but did not live to write, a biography of John Keats.

After the excitement of her debut was over, Amy continued her self-education. She divided her days among studies of literature and language, social engagements, and, when the nurse was off-duty, staying by her mother's side. The frail woman who had never been much of a mother to Amy now became her charge. However, there was little Amy could do for her mother as the disease that had plagued Mrs. Lowell for years became progressively worse. She was either delirious with pain or drugged into semiconsciousness from the morphine to deaden it. There were times when Amy, listening to the incoherent cries from the sickroom, began to fear she would lose her own mind. It was only her self-imposed habit of self-education that enabled her to maintain her sanity, she felt.

When Percy returned from the Orient in 1893 and announced that he was going to live in Flagstaff, Arizona, where he planned to continue his work in astronomy and build the Lowell Observatory, Amy could not help feeling deserted. It was two years until they saw him again, and by then this remarkable brother had established himself as a noted astronomer, about to publish his book *Mars*, revealing his startling discovery of features he mistook for canals on that planet. The book created a sensation in scientific circles. Small wonder that Amy drove herself to match his achievements.

On this first visit home Percy came to attend their mother's funeral. Mrs. Lowell's condition had suddenly become critical, and she died on April 1, 1895, two months after Amy's twenty-first brithday. Mr. Lowell, concerned though he had been about his wife, had only looked in on her morning and evening, and went about his financial and civic affairs or his gardening with grim stoicism. Now that she was gone, he was morose and gloomy but maintained his strict routine. Except for his interest in horticulture, which Amy had begun to share with him, Mr. Lowell was withdrawn, living a life remote from his daughter's.

Such an atmosphere was hardly congenial to one of Amy's ebullient nature whose inner sensibilities were just beginning to awaken the urge for poetic expression. Unless she had a friend visiting, as she was free to do, her home life was staid, lusterless. But as her friends were tapped for marriage, there were fewer available, and whether the truth was that Amy Lowell was jilted by a near-fiancé, or whether she simply felt left over because of her size, she made up her mind to try to lose weight. She chose "banting," the latest fad, which prescribed a strict diet of tomatoes and asparagus while taking a riverboat trip up the Nile. She organized a party of seven women for the venture in the fall of 1896, arranging the entire travel plan herself. But the diet proved a disaster to her health: She suffered a severe nervous breakdown on her return, having lost little weight and acquired chronic gastritis. For the next two years she was an invalid, spending the winter months on a secluded ranch in southern California, and the summer in Devonshire, England, trying to regain a modicum of health. Her nerves remained ragged.

In 1900, just as she was beginning to emerge from the grisly effect of her health experiment in Egypt, her father died suddenly. Even as the family gathered for the funeral in the front parlor, Amy resolved to buy Sevenels from the estate, which was left to the five children. Her brothers and sisters agreed to the purchase, which was easily arranged, and once in sole possession, Amy remodeled the mansion to suit herself. The project was not complete until about 1907. With the aid of architects, she created a baronial library by combining the front and back parlors into one immense room, with floor-to-ceiling built-in bookshelves. An avid reader, she had a passion for books, rare and fine volumes, which was to result in a notable collection over the years, including original manuscripts. Not only was she successor to her father as the sole owner of Sevenels, but she stepped into his shoes in civic life as well, serving on several boards. She was the first Lowell woman ever to make a speech in public. At the same time she pursued her own artistic bent.

Her principal source of solace during adolescence had been the theater. Then she'd attended a matinee every Saturday afternoon with a group of girls. It was a recreation that she continued by herself. It became her initial inspiration in 1902, on the opening night of Eleonora Duse's third and triumphant American tour. Amy had seen the great Italian star on previous occasions and been moved by her acting, but on this occasion she sat in the Lowell box enthralled throughout the play. At home, still in a state of emotional turmoil, she was impelled "with infinite agitation" to express her feelings in poetry. It was near midnight. She poured out her soul in a fervent flow of "seventy-one lines of bad blank verse," as she admitted later, but the poem, such as it was, marked a lifelong commitment to poetry. She was twenty-eight years old and would be thirty-eight before her first volume was published—thirty-six before her first poem appeared (in the *Atlantic Monthly*). But the vision that Duse had given her always spurred her efforts.

Duse became her idol, her tenth muse. Amy attended all the performances of the Duse Boston run, then followed the tour to Philadelphia, where she managed to arrange a visit with the actress at her hotel. It was an awesome moment for Amy Lowell when she was received. The tragedienne was resting in bed, clad in a filmy negligee. Though neither could converse in the other's tongue, they spoke the language of the spirit. It was a communication that lasted throughout their lives. Amy's tender adoration for Duse never wavered, and it was the source of a series of poems and sonnets, some considered too intimate to publish till after the death of both.

It was perhaps inevitable that a person of Amy Lowell's temperament should turn to women for romantic fulfillment. It is notable that the two women who had the greatest influence on her life and work were connected with the theater. The woman who accompanied her to the Poetry Society meeting, who from 1915 was always at her side, had been a well-known character-lead, a seasoned trouper. As Ada Dwyer, she had trod the boards since the 1880s, and she only left the stage at Amy's coaxing in 1914 when an illness forced her to give up the tour she was making in one of her hit portrayals. They had met at a crucial moment in Amy's life, just before her first volume of poems was published in 1912. Ada was starring in a dramatic vehicle, *The Deep Purple,* and during the Boston run was guest of honor at an informal luncheon in the home of Amy's school friend Bessie Ward Perkins, who shared her love of poetry and the arts.

Amy had seen and admired Ada's performance, but she was not prepared for the delightful, warm, and cultivated off-stage personality who charmed them all. A handsome person, whose calm, luminous brown eyes radiated compassion, humor, and intelligence, Ada Dwyer had a literary and adventurous background that complemented her acting ability. There was immediate rapport with Amy. They "recognized each other at once," as Ferris Greenslet, Amy's editor at Houghton Mifflin, later wrote. Ada's father had established the first bookshop in the far West. His daughter read books of her own choosing, and had developed an unusual love for poetry. She had been sent to the Boston Latin School for her high school education, and there showed such acting ability in the Shakespeare plays that she received offers to go on the stage, which she gladly accepted. At eighteen, a brief marriage to British actor Harold Russell ended in a year, after the birth of a daughter, Lorna. Ada had never remarried. Her love was for the theater and literature.

Amy, quick to sense a kindred spirit, asked Ada to go over the poems she had selected for her first volume. She was uncertain of some, and she felt from Ada's knowledge of poetry that the judgment of her new-found friend would be sound. Ada proved to be both discerning and firm in her decisions and advice, and after only a few meetings, reinforced by a visit to Amy's country home in the summer, Ada found herself being persuaded to leave the theater and live with the poet. Although she did not consent until 1914, the relationship, with Ada as devoted companion, literary adviser, research expert, and efficient manager of Amy's households, worked so well that Amy wanted to dedicate her first volume—and all that followed—to her friend. Ada would not allow it. Although there were a few tense scenes—Amy at one time became so possessive that she objected to Ada's visits to her family in Salt Lake City—the relationship was in general so harmonious that by 1915 everyone accepted Amy and Ada as a pair.

It was Ada who introduced Amy to Mrs. August Belmont, the former Eleanor Robson, the famous actress with whom Ada had performed in her theatrical days. Amy's volume *Can Grande's Castle* was to contain narrative poems based on tales told by both the Belmonts, and "Nell" Belmont was to be the inspiration for Amy's free verse lyric "Portrait (E. R. B.)."

Between the advent of Eleonora Duse and Ada Russell, a man appeared in 1908 who was as great an influence on Amy Lowell's life and work as any member of her own sex. This was Carl Engel. He had just come to town to head the Boston Music Company, a branch of G. Schirmer's, the noted music publishing house in New York. He was a pleasant man—urbane, witty, and a talented musician himself. He had been French trained and knew the music of early twentieth-century composers Debussy, Fauré, and Erik Satie—and knew as well many notables in the American music world. Moreover, he knew the work of the modern French poets who formed the symbolist movement around Mallarmé. Amy and he got along famously from the first; he became her mentor, her adviser in all things musical, and her most encouraging ally in poetry, as well as a sympathetic friend.

In 1909 a mysterious fire destroyed the stables at Sevenels. Amy's beloved horses burned to death before the volunteer fire department could rescue them. None knew how the fire started, but it was followed by some terrifying letters from a religious fanatic, expressing wild glee at the fate of Miss Lowell's horses and implying that she herself would burn in hell if she did not mend her hedonistic ways. The experience was traumatic in the extreme. If it had not been for Carl Engel, Amy might have regressed to her state of nervous prostration. As it was, she took to her outsize bed—with its sixteen down pillows over the mattress and under tightly stretched sheets—for several days. Curiously, when Amy made over the mansion, she had not moved down to a second floor bedroom, but kept the third floor—the nursery—as her private domain, wiring it for electric light and installing a modern bathroom with the immense tub that figured in her poem.

Carl Engel sympathized with Amy over loss of her beloved horses and soothed her fears of attack. He also suggested that she translate a play by Alfred de Musset and produce it in a program of home theatricals. He would play Le Marquis and she La Baronne. The idea appealed to her, and it was all she needed to restore her energies. She decided not to rebuild her stables, but while she was working on the translation of the Musset verse drama *A Caprice,* she and a school friend started a kennel for the breeding and raising of shaggy sheep dogs. This in turn started another Lowell legend. There were always at least seven of these dogs—for Sevenels—as Amy's pets, indeed as her "children." Actually, she chose the breed, known for fierce barking, as protection against prowlers, for she never lost her fear of another attack on her citadel. At dinner parties, each guest was furnished with a clean white towel to put over dinner clothes that might get stained from the affectionate caresses and pawings of the animals.

As soon as Amy had finished translating it from the French, production of *A Caprice* began. In the course of rehearsals, the friendship between Carl and Amy increased, and she grew dependent on him, demanding of his company. The fact that she requested in her will that his letters as well as the correspondence between Ada and herself, all of which she kept in a locked drawer of her desk, be burned at her death is indicative of deep feeling between them. Engel, for his part, culled his letters from Amy, but judging from those still extant in the Library of Congress, it is evident that Amy, hungry for love, had overwhelmed and embarrassed him with attention. Toward the end of 1911, after highly successful performances of their play, he went to Paris, ostensibly for vacation, but quite possibly to escape her emotional demands. Yet he sent concerned advice about her poems, urging her to put together a volume, since she had been published in the *Atlantic Monthly,* which had accepted four poems, beginning in 1910. And again he advised her to read the French symbolists, for which she later acknowledged her gratitude. At the moment, she felt lost without him, dubious about her work, though her editor, Ferris Greenslet, saw no indication of uncertainty from the way she took command of their first interview. Two months later, in February of 1912, she met Ada, and her whole outlook on life changed. There can be little doubt that Amy Lowell was androgynous, and a manic-depressive. But she was extremely levelheaded when it came to business matters, whether they dealt with poetry or real estate. It was not without reason that T. S. Eliot called her "the demon saleswoman of poetry."

In 1912 Harriet Monroe in Chicago launched her landmark publication *Poetry, A Magazine of Verse,* which announced that it would pay contributors whose work was accepted. Amy had been pleased to receive an advance notice of the venture, asking her to submit some of her poems, except that the accompanying letter included a request for funds backing the project. Experience had already taught Amy that her wealth and social position comprised "one of the greatest handicaps that anyone could possibly have," as she wrote later. "I belonged to the class which is not supposed to be able to produce good creative work." She wanted to be an activist, but not a patron of the arts *per se.* Wary of Monroe's motives, she sent a token contribution, a check for twenty-five dollars. Later she submitted a few poems, but Miss Monroe, though she accepted Lowell's work, made no move to publish it. However, it was in *Poetry* that Amy found the kind of creative expression she was striving for, set forth in a few poems signed simply, " 'H. D.,' Imagiste." The poems were spare, exact in word choice, heavily freighted with meaning, classic in subject matter. A later issue of the magazine carried an article by Ezra Pound stating the principles of Imagism much as they were later listed and read off by Amy from the preface of *Some Imagist Poets* at the meeting of the Poetry Society.

Excited, and with an overpowering curiosity to know more about the Imagistes,* as Pound had designated the group, Amy went to England in the summer of 1913. There she studied the new method that had been born out of the theories of T. E.

---

* For a more complete outline of Imagist tenets and sources, see *Amy, the World of Amy Lowell and the Imagist Movement.*

Hulme, an English philosopher who was more of a poetaster than a professional. He examined the esthetics of poetic expression in an effort to find a way to slough off the conventions of the immediate past and establish an entirely different technique. He and a few others, including Ezra Pound, met over tea and scones in the cheap cafes of Soho to formulate their ideas, which were drawn from the modern French *vers libre* and various ancient forms created by the Greeks and Romans, the Chinese and Japanese, and the Hebrew historical poems of the Haggadah. The outstanding features of the Imagiste method were the paring away of all unnecessary words, as Pound emphasized over and over; the emotional impact on the viewer of objects seen or of inner visions, expressed in unusual metaphor; and composition in the musical phrase instead of the metronome. In Amy's terms, when she took over, this was "cadence instead of meter."

That first summer Amy was a rapt listener. She was surprised and pleased to discover that H.D. was the pen name of a young American girl, Hilda Doolittle, a tall, willowy blonde from Pennsylvania who was serious, sensitive, and incisive in her thinking.

Pound never enjoyed a more willing disciple than Amy Lowell proved during the summer of 1913, though there were moments when she challenged his precepts with ideas of her own. Each sensed a domineering streak in the other that was to cause an open break during the following summer, when, accompanied by Ada and fortified by her friend's calm presence, Amy went to England again to find Pound involved with still another group, the Vorticists, an even more avant-garde circle than the Imagistes. True, he had achieved publication of a small anthology, to which he gave the French title *Des Imagistes* and in which he had included Amy Lowell, but he seemed to feel that this discharged his responsibility toward the movement, if such it could be called. Yet he did not want to release his hold of the leadership when Amy started to take over the reins.

Gathering a group of the faithful around her, and persuading D. H. Lawrence to join them, Amy formed a nucleus of her own with which to launch a full-scale campaign for new poetry in America. Lawrence was loath to lend his name to any group. He was just beginning to prove his individuality, and he considered Imagisme "an advertising scheme of Pound's." Besides, he hated French poetry, he said. Amy assured him that it was not her intention to bind, but to free poetry and to see that it had a place in modern literature. She would anglicize the name by dropping the *e*, and Lawrence, if he didn't like them, need not accept the tenets that Pound insisted upon. Hers was to be a cooperative publication venture. Any profits would be shared by all. For Lawrence it would mean a possible outlet for his poetry, and even income.

She had won him over. Lawrence enjoyed her straightforward manner, Johnsonian humor, and "the buccaneering maleness of her." * An instant, genuine affinity of spirit sprang up, a seemingly unlikely alliance between two disparate personalities. Each had enough insight to recognize the problems and the extent of the other's genius. Amy sensed that Lawrence had a far greater share of the latter than she—for all her bravado, she had enough humility (though few were aware of it) to appreciate his gifts and want to learn from them. She and Ada, detained in London by the outbreak of World War I in Europe, exchanged several visits with Lawrence and his wife, Frieda, a volatile German-born woman who had left her husband and children to elope with Lawrence.

Shortly after Amy finally secured return passage, her second volume appeared in England and the United States. It was practically overlooked in England because of the war, but at home the poems created a sensation, and Amy Lowell became the voice of the future in poetry. The noted contemporary poet Ann Stanford, who edited the anthology *The Women Poets in English*, published in 1972, has this to say of her:

* The phrase is used by Elizabeth Sergeant in her chapter on Amy Lowell in *Fire Under the Andes*, 1926.

[She] did not confine herself to Imagism but moved on to other kinds of verse. Notable were her translations and adaptations of Chinese poetry and experiments with what she called "polyphonic prose," a form in which line as a unit is abandoned, but the other qualities of poetry remain—i.e. recurrent patterns of sound, repetition of syntactical units, strong and colorful images. One of her finest pieces is "The Basket," which contains passages of surrealism and others of sexual symbolism modern enough to have been written today.

It is small wonder that, in September of 1914, Amy's second volume, *Sword Blades and Poppy Seed,* had the impact of an explosion.

Her speech at the Poetry Society meeting in 1915 split the membership wide open. Waves of "Bath" inundated the gossip columns the next day and, indeed, provided entertaining copy for some time. However, the truth is that "Bath" is neither as innocuous nor as sensational as her defenders and detractors claimed. Amy Lowell knew her legends too well not to intend the significance of narcissus and the water. Both flowers she picked to mention—tulips as well as narcissus—have sexual meaning here, especially since she says "no flowers are in bloom anywhere." Anyone who has a physical deformity or handicap loves as well as hates the body that causes so much misery. Amy's background had given her a generous portion of self-love, and this poem is an example of it. She could also describe a woman's body in the tender terms of a lover:

> Her breasts point outwards,
> And the nipples are like buds of peonies.
> Her flanks ripple as she plays,
> And the water is not more undulating than the lines of her
>   body.

And a moment of self-hate comes out in "The Bungler," an example of early Imagism:

You glow in my heart
Like the flames of uncounted candles.
But when I go to warm my hands,
My clumsiness overturns the light
And then I stumble
Against the tables and chairs.

"The Taxi," a poem often quoted among her free verse lyrics, was cited by D. H. Lawrence as one he found most revealing of her true self, of the "bitterness" he berated her for denying in much of her poetry. Probably written at one of those times when she saw Ada off on the train, after much protest, the poem maintains strong imagery throughout.

When I go away from you
The world beats dead
Like a slackened drum.
I call out for you against the jutted stars
And shout into the ridges of the wind.
Streets coming fast,
One after the other,
Wedge you away from me,
And the lamps of the city prick my eyes
So that I can no longer see your face.
Why should I leave you,
To wound myself on the sharp edges of the night?

Amy did not take offense at Lawrence's candid criticism of her "posturing," for she was pleased that on the whole he had praised her work. She respected his judgment and in return did all she could to place his poems, outside those included in *Some Imagist Poets*. Because of all the publicity she received, that little anthology sold more copies than anyone had expected, and Amy, true to her word, having divided the profits six ways, was gratified to receive ecstatic letters from the small band of contributors who had cast their lot in with her. H.D. and her husband, Richard Aldington, were overjoyed, especially since they were launching a new "little magazine," *The Egoist*, which they hoped to keep going in spite of the war. Amy gave them moral support and advice but little financial assistance except for the anthology royalties.

She had the additional foresight to realize that Robert Frost's second volume, which had come out in England to excellent notices, was going to be equally recognized in America; and she was the first to give *North of Boston* a major review in the second issue of an important magazine making its initial appearance, *The New Republic*. Her piece, featured on the front cover, served as a welcome-home greeting to Frost and his family, who also had been detained in England by the war.

A few days later, Amy received a call from "the uncompromising New Englander," as she had referred to him in the review, and she immediately invited him to dinner at Sevenels. Their meeting was the beginning of a kind of sparring friendship—a mixture of admiration, rivalry, and wit—between the two poets, which was soon extended to include the whole Frost family. Amy never could convince Robert Frost that he was as revolutionary in his own way as any Imagist and so should join their ranks. He was as firm with her as he had been with Ezra Pound, who had tried his damnedest to win Frost over. As for Ezra, he was furious over the success of the Imagist anthology in America, and over the public's growing acceptance of Amy Lowell as leader of the Imagist movement. He at first threatened to sue her. Then, realizing from a brilliant reply she made that he had no case, he scoffed and called the movement "Amygisme," purposely adding the *e* to show that it derived from his original title.

Shortly after the Imagist anthology was out, Amy published a book of essays, *Six French Poets,* issued in England and America at the same time by Macmillan. Drawn from a series of lectures she had given on the French symbolists, the book did much to establish her authority in America both as critic and poet, since most American readers had known little about the symbolists before then. But the British intellectuals would not grant her that distinction, and a scathing, politely sarcastic review by Lytton Strachey in the London *Times* sent her to bed with a raging headache, angry, frustrated, and hurt. But with the calm counsel of her friend Ada and the strength of her own common sense, she recovered. As she was to do time and again after losing a skirmish, she plunged into battle again, not only with verbal retaliation, but producing another volume of poetry. *Men, Women, and Ghosts,* published in 1916, contained some of her best work, including "Patterns," perhaps the most quoted of her poems in anthologies. The conclusion speaks of "a pattern called a war," and the final line, "Christ! What are patterns for?" a shocker in 1916, still carries considerable impact in the last quarter of the century.

With the appearance of *Men, Women, and Ghosts,* and because of the interest aroused by many of the poems besides "Patterns," Amy Lowell became the acknowledged leader of Imagism in America and as such was invited to give lectures. She was the first woman ever to appear in the Harvard Poetry Club series, and after her talk, she answered questions the college men fired at her through a cloud of cigar smoke. She was asked to give readings, and young poets asked her for advice. She entertained all manner of poets—from the rag-tag Bohemian Maxwell Bodenheim to the shabby-genteel, correct Edwin Arlington Robinson, the romantic Sara Teasdale, and the sophisticated, beautiful Elinor Wylie. And in the watches of the night, after the guests had left, she wrote and rewrote more and more of her own poetry and prose. She rarely got more than five hours sleep or rose before one in the afternoon, following breakfast in bed. She kept two secretaries busy typing her manuscripts and taking dictation of letters for the wide correspondence she maintained.

All this would have been enough to wear out a strong, healthy person. Although Amy gave the impression of being a fortress, she was not well or as strong as she herself thought. In the summer of 1916, a strange accident took a heavy toll on her already precarious health. She and Ada were in Dublin and had gone for a drive in the rig Amy kept in the country. On this particular day, a thunderstorm blew up when they were on the way home, and the rear wheels of the buggy went off the shoulder of the road. Handing the reins to Ada, Amy lifted the back end of the vehicle onto the road again with a tremendous heave. She always overestimated her strength and now she felt such a terrible pull on her stomach muscles that she groaned aloud.

The outcome of her feat was that she suffered an umbilical hernia, which eventually proved fatal. From 1916 on, the pace of living, which involved writing at least one published book a year in the more sanguine stretches between jagged peaks of pain before and after a series of operations, became a frenzied race with time. Some inner compulsion forced her to keep up her multiple activities on behalf of poetry, the new poetry, beyond the production of verses of her own that came pouring out in what she called a "poetry-burst." She published a book of essays, *Tendencies in Modern American Poetry*, which, like the work on French poets, discussed six important figures shaping the trend of American poetic literature. They were presented in three pairs: Frost and Robinson, representing "Evolution"; Masters and Sandburg, representing "Revolution"; and H.D. and Fletcher, representing the full-fledged modern technique contained in the Imagist creed. The book was widely accepted as an important critical study and did much to enhance Amy Lowell's reputation as an authority on American poetry. Next came *Can Grande's Castle*, her cinematic version of historic events and personages, written in polyphonic prose and "charged with enough electricity to burn your hand off," as Van Wyck Brooks said. And in 1919, her *Pictures of the Floating World*, the most personal of all her volumes, became a bestseller, with—and no doubt because of—its section of tender love poems, some of them passionate outbursts, written to Ada.

Through all the hours of daytime work, when she was not actually writing, or when she was supposed to be resting, the research for a biography of John Keats served as a bright thread of inspiration for her creative experiments. As early as 1916, when overactivity had aggravated the hernia so that she was in great pain and was ordered by her doctor to stay in bed, she decided to begin reading about her literary hero, so Ada went to the library and brought home an armload of books. And at tea parties in her bedroom—the poet's disability did not keep her from entertaining—Amy's main topic of conversation was Keats, Keats, Keats. Her preoccupation with him took on the intensity of fanaticism at times. On other occasions she held forth on Imagism and the new poetry while lying in her outsize bed, smoking a cigar. At one of these informal teas, to which she had invited Robert Frost's daughter, Lesley, then a freshman at Wellesley, Amy, after introducing the girl to other guests, reached under her pillow and pulled out a box of her famous Manilas. Lifting the lid, she offered, "Will you have a cigar?" When Lesley, startled, refused politely, Amy lit one for herself, pausing between puffs to ask, like an Inquisitor, "What do you think of Keats?"

With the entry of the United States into the war, Amy experienced public attacks and triumphs, and personal tragedies in addition to her physical sufferings. At a time when her pain was so severe that she was kept under morphine, the tragic word came that her adored brother Percy had died suddenly of a cerebral hemorrhage. He had been forced to take long periods of rest ever since his discovery of the Planet X, later named Pluto, which he located but did not live to see. Amy was too ill to be told of his death for several days. When Ada broke it to her gently, she said, "I knew something terrible was happening to Percy that night. I saw streaks of red and white lightning flashing through the room, and for some mysterious reason thought of my brother."

Food rationing during the years 1917–18 brought another loss, for Amy's famous sheep dogs grew so sick from the diet of horse meat they were forced to eat that they had to be "put to sleep." Again it was Ada who softened the blow by arranging for the chloroforming. "Don't tell me about it till afterward," Amy pleaded. Even so, she could not work for a week, mourning the loss of her "children."

She was still under attack from the conservative camp of the Poetry Society. The strongest attack was the hoax of the Spectrist movement, hatched by Witter Bynner and Arthur Davison Ficke, who published poems meant to satirize free verse. These were presented seriously under spoof pseudonyms—Anne Knish was Ficke's—and for a period of almost two years fooled a great many people, including Harriet Monroe, but not Amy. When Bynner was cheeky enough to ask her what she thought of the Spectrists, she snapped, "Bynner, I think they are charlatans." Surprised by her perception, he was silent, but the hoax continued. It was finally exposed, however, prompting Amy to write him a triumphant, sarcastic letter, crowing gleefully. Bynner, usually kind and considerate of people's feelings, retaliated by pinning on her the flippant epithet "Hippopoetess," which was picked up by all the columnists as a hilarious, juicy morsel to spice up their reportage. Amy was not only hurt but angry. But she silenced the clever columnists once and for all by attacking them en masse in an interview published December 27, 1919, in the *New York Evening Post,* making no rebuttal to their subsequent counterattacks. From that time on, they let her alone.

During the war, quite by chance, because of an ardent letter she had received from a training camp, Amy found herself in demand as an authority on poetry libraries. The letter was from Donald Evans, a young poet who had had the temerity to publish Gertrude Stein's *Tender Buttons* (written under the pseudonym Claire-Marie) in 1914, and who had won a reputation for his own *Sonnets from the Patagonian.* Out of their correspondence grew the idea of a poetry library in the camp. To everyone's surprise, the volumes proved immensely popular with the "doughboys." Before she knew it, Amy, at the request of the U.S. Army, was involved in furnishing poetry libraries for thirty-five training camps—a service that might well be cited as the forerunner of the USIS.

She was told that she must undergo surgery for the hernia. She was justifiably apprehensive about the results as well as about the operation itself, but this did not keep her from a myriad of activities. Some were connected with the war effort, others far removed from it. In less than three years, Amy submitted to four operations, each time suffering great pain, "like an animal raging for comfort not to be had," as she described it. She confessed to being a wretched patient, but with Ada's tender companionship she was able to bear the excruciating period lying flat on her back following each operation. In "A Decade," one of the love lyrics in "Two Speak Together," the section of *Pictures of the Floating World* devoted to her relationship with Ada, Amy drew an unmistakable image of both the passion and contentment she had come to know with Ada:

> When you came, you were like red wine and honey,
> And the taste of you burnt my mouth with its sweetness.
> Now you are like morning bread,
> Smooth and pleasant.
> I hardly taste you at all for I know your savour,
> But I am completely nourished.

Ada tried to prevent Amy from overdoing things, writing or working on some project as soon as she was able to sit up; but in vain.

In the spring of 1920, hearing that British poet Siegfried Sassoon was in the United States for a lecture but had been stranded by a shady manager, Amy immediately offered to sponsor a reading by him at the Harvard Union. Sassoon was, in her words, "the first important voice to protest the sentimental glorification of war." As patriotic as she had been, Amy was fully aware of the horrors of the war and the falseness of glorifying it.

Paying a third of Sassoon's fee herself, Amy gave a dinner at Sevenels before the reading on April 29, then the whole party drove to the Harvard Union, arriving in good time. Sassoon's reading of his poems was a great success. It was Amy's first outing since the doctor had informed her she must rest pending a possible third operation for hernia, yet no one guessed that she had climbed out of a sick bed. In his book, *Siegfried's Journey, 1916–1920,* the English poet later spoke of "the presiding presence of Miss Amy Lowell" at his address to the Poetry Club at the Harvard Union, and added, "She was mainly responsible for my being there at all." He went on to describe "a memorable evening spent in her beautiful library."

Amy, exhilarated by the whole affair, invited him and Harold Laski, with whom Sassoon was staying, to Sevenels a few nights later. Though he enjoyed himself, Sassoon hardly got a word in. "Listening to her and Laski," he wrote, "I felt almost nonexistent as a talker. They were a remarkably contrasted couple—he, small, boyishly brilliant, provocative in argument, and essentially generous and idealistic; she, stout and masculine, jocularly downright and dogmatic, smoking a long Manila cigar, and completely confident that 'Imagism' was the poetry of the future." Such was the picture almost everyone outside her intimates had of Amy Lowell, and it is accurate in portraying the forthright, domineering male in her. Few ever saw the female side of her androgynous psyche. In all probability, Sassoon never knew that she was in pain during those evenings, or that she was tenderhearted toward her loved ones and maternal toward the young poets who came to her for advice. But in fact Evans, grateful for her letters of encouragement, had dedicated a long poem to her, and D. H. Lawrence his new volume, *Coming Awake!* The latter was a mark of true esteem. Lawrence was actually one of the few who realized that hers was an "impassioned heart," concealed by bombast. Because of his own bisexual tendencies, he felt that there was "a sort of odd congenital understanding" between them.

The third operation, presided over by five doctors and three nurses, took place in October of 1920. As she had predicted, the period following the operation was "sheer hell." Not till late December could she come downstairs.

That year, 1920, was the only one in which she did not have a book published. As if to make up for the lapse, however, two came out in 1921. *Legends,* a series of narrative poems based on

Indian tales and ceremonials, appeared in May. In December, *Fir Flower Tablets* was issued. She and Florence (Wheelock) Ayscough had chosen the title for the latter, a book of translations from the Chinese. Both books were published by Houghton Mifflin, the firm Amy had dealt with originally, to which she had returned—from Macmillan—with publication of *Pictures.* She herself prepared the dummies for both books and summoned a committee from the Riverside Press, Houghton Mifflin's printers, to her bedside so that production would follow her instructions. Early in January 1922 she accepted an invitation from Yale to deliver the centenary lecture on Keats (February 23rd). At the same time she agreed to give a lecture on Walt Whitman at Brooklyn College. She tried to override the nagging pain of the sagging incision, but was alerted by the doctor that she would have to undergo another operation, probably in the spring.

News of the fourth surgical ordeal was grave, and many friends sent words of comfort. The gesture that touched her most deeply was a letter that D. H. Lawrence wrote to Ada, requesting her to buy a fuchsia tree for Amy with his next share of the anthology royalties. As soon as she could sit up, Amy dictated a letter to him thanking him for the "sweetness" of his thought. "The bond between us is intensified by your picking fuchsias, as they are one of my favorite flowers," she said. In the letter she included the royalty check, now only a pittance. She also commented on his *Women in Love,* which she considered his finest novel to date. She reported on the progress she had made in placing a few of his poems, and ended by telling him she was sending him a copy of *Legends,* just off the press. "I hardly know whether you will like it or not," she added to cover her own uncertainty about the book.

To her astonished delight, these largely Indian legends struck an echoing chord in the English poet's atavistic psyche. He wrote at once, "I read *Legends* last night—and again this morning. I like them best of all your poems. . . . I like best "Many Swans" which I have read twice and which I feel really speaks inside my unexplained soul. I should not like to try to explain it, because of the deep fear and danger that is in it. But it isn't a myth of the sun. It is something else. All the better that we can't say off-hand what. That means it is true. It rings a note in my soul."

Lawrence's words in regard to *Legends* gave her one of the great satisfactions of her literary life. In answer to his letter she wrote, "That you see what you do in 'Many Swans' makes me very happy, because it was exactly what I tried to put into that poem." Still scarcely recovered from her latest operation, she went on, "Sometimes I wonder whether I shall live long enough . . . to be able to put into my poetry what I want to have there. . . . The technique of poetry is easy, very easy to anyone born that way; life is not easy, and it is still less simple to express in words the real throb, and misery, and gusto which it has. That is what you do, and that is what I wish I could learn of you."

A more self-revelatory analysis or one with more humility toward her work could hardly be expressed by any poet, let alone the Amy Lowell most people knew or thought they knew. Some relentless force made her drive herself even during convalescence. The doctor warned her that she must not strain herself in any way, so Amy amused herself by hatching a plot for a hoax of her own—a modern counterpart of her "great-cousin" James Russell Lowell's "A Fable for Critics," which her brother had read aloud to her and Ada the evening before she went into the hospital, perhaps to divert her from anxiety. The result was a series of satirical verse portraits, catching the essence of all the important poets of the day—including herself—just as her cousin had done in his time. If they were good enough, she planned to publish them anonymously. She called her series of verses *A Critical Fable.* From the samples she sent, Ferris Greenslet, editor-in-chief at Houghton Mifflin, thought the book would be a good item to follow *Fir Flower Tablets,* even if Amy's authorship remained a secret.

The book was hardly off press in 1922 before Amy noised

about a rumor that Leonard Bacon, whose piece of light verse "Banquet of the Poets" she had enjoyed, was the "brilliant" author of the *Fable*. She wrote a long letter to John Farrar, then editor of *The Bookman*, speculating on the authorship, implying that she had not the faintest idea who was responsible. When she herself was accused by Louis Untermeyer, she pointed the finger back at him, and for about a year and a half it was a sort of literary game to guess the author of *A Critical Fable*. She stuck to her masquerade of anonymity, enjoying the light-hearted mischief it provided as relief from the arduous task of writing her biography of Keats during this period of precarious health. Amy finally exposed herself as author of the *Fable* in a letter to John Farrar, who preserved it in the Farrar Collection at Yale University.

From 1922 on until early 1925, although she accepted certain invitations to appear in public—like one from Robert Frost, in May of 1922, to open the Poetry Festival that his students at the University of Michigan organized and raised money for—Amy's principal project was her biography of Keats. She felt she had to get down on paper all the facts and feelings she had been storing up about her idol. She had stopped hammering on Imagism, *vers libre*, or even the new poetry since the end of the war. Now she dwelt more on the freedom of the individual poet to express a thought or mood in the manner best suited to it.

Amy's last extended lecture tour came early in 1923, when she interrupted her work on the Keats manuscript to give readings in New Jersey, New York, Ohio, Indiana, Illinois, Wisconsin, Minnesota, Nebraska, and Ontario, Canada—an exhausting schedule for a well person, and she was far from well. She traveled with a powerful reading lamp, which had to be plugged in ahead of time, and she came onstage bearing a basket, containing, besides her books, half a dozen pairs of eyeglasses, each tied at the temple with a different colored silk thread to denote the strength of the lenses, each progressively stronger than the ones she started with. The lamp more than once blew a fuse, causing some commotion, as it did most notably the spring before in Ann Arbor, when 2500 people sat in darkness enjoying the ad lib exchange between Frost and Amy until the fuse was replaced.

Some said Amy Lowell used these devices as diversions, to make her delivery more dramatic, but she could not have read at all if it had not been for the powerful lamp and the change of glasses—they were props in the literal sense. As soon as the tour ended on March 10 of 1923, she settled down to work on her Keats manuscript. She wrote like one possessed, as if hypnotized by her subject. She was sometimes still at her library table when Ada came down at eight o'clock in the morning. She seemed to be in a kind of frenzy to get the book finished. Then in October an exciting interruption occurred: Eleonora Duse returned to the United States during the 1923–24 season and expressed a desire to see Miss Lowell! Amy cancelled all of her appointments and shifted her entire schedule. Even the Keats biography was of secondary importance. Duse was touring in *Lady from the Sea*, which opened in Boston. She came out to Sevenels after a performance and "fell in love with the place." She said she would like to come back to visit when the tour was over. Amy, ecstatic, wrote a poem, "To Eleonora Duse, 1923," revealing her deep joy.

Amy and Ada followed the production to New York. While Amy was there, she arranged with the headwaiter at the Belmont Hotel, where she and Ada always stayed in the corner suite on the eighth floor, to procure champagne for her idol. She also smoothed the way for Duse by arranging with friends in the cities where the production was booked to put her up and take good care of her so that she would not have to stay in hotels. During this time the poet wrote six sonnets to Duse.

It was an exciting, emotional experience, perhaps too heady for a person with high blood pressure and severe eyestrain, for Amy suffered retinal hemorrhages in both eyes and fell into a state of sheer exhaustion that sent her to bed again for several weeks. While recuperating, she wrote another poem, "To Eleonora Duse, In Answer to a Letter," saluting the actress

as "Dear Lady of the great compassion/All tenderness en-
meshed in withes of truth. . . ."

She sent telegrams to friends in the cities that Duse's second
tour included, and when she was able to get around, saw to it
that champagne was delivered to Duse again. She also prepared
for the promised visit by modernizing the main guest room,
having a tile bath installed, everything included, to make things
more convenient for the actress, who was also ailing. Then she
settled down to work again on the biography of Keats, which
seemed to grow longer the harder she worked. February 9 was
her fiftieth birthday, but she did not want the formal celebration
her friends and colleagues suggested because she was too deeply
involved in completing the manuscript.

Two months later, without warning, word came that Duse,
now at the end of her tour, was desperately ill with pneumonia,
stricken while playing in Pittsburgh. Nightly phone calls informed Amy that the doctor had prescribed injections that at
first seemed to help, but after a brief rally Duse faded rapidly.
She died before dawn on Easter Monday, April 21, and was
brought to New York for the funeral. It was a sorrowful close to
a period of high expectancy. Amy and Ada went to New York
for the moving memorial services held in St. Vincent Ferrer
church.

Back in Brookline, Amy and Ada concentrated on the Keats
manuscript once more, Ada taking meticulous care to see that
day-to-day life was made smooth for Amy. She wrote steadily
through the spring, summer, and early fall, taxing her eyes to
the point where she was forced to dictate the manuscript page
by page to her secretaries, who often worked overtime tran-
scribing and typing until the copy was letter perfect. The strain
began to tell on her by way of a flareup of the double hernia, but
she kept on, doggedly, desperately. "Keats is nearly killing
me," she wrote to Louis Untermeyer in the midst of her labors,
but she did not give him any details. Prior to the fourth operation, she had written him, "Do try and get here as early as
possible before they have quite minced me to pieces and swept

me up in the dustpan," but she didn't mention the cause. She never let her colleagues, even close friends like the Frosts and the Untermeyers, know how ill she was.

Early in November the manuscript for her biography of Keats was completed at last. Yates, her chauffeur, delivered the monumental package of 1160 pages to Ferris Greenslet, who was to have exactly ten days to read it and give the doughty poet-biographer his expert opinion. In order to keep from fretting over his evaluation, she accepted an invitation from the Frosts to speak at Amherst College. She could give a lecture or a reading; she and Ada and her maid could stay at the Frosts', who would make her more comfortable than she would be in the hotel at Holyoke. She chose to give a reading, which the students applauded loudly, and she and Ada and the Frosts all enjoyed the brief visit. Yet as soon as she was home she began worrying about the verdict from her editor. She feared she had left something out, though Ada assured her she couldn't have squeezed in one more intimate detail of Keats' short life. Ada was concerned about her.

On the day of her appointment with Greenslet, Amy's bandages seemed to take forever to be properly adjusted. She was an hour and a half late, yet there was no sign of her inner agitation when she entered the editor's office, "apologetic and as always completely disarming," according to Greenslet.

"Well, Ferris, what about it?" she demanded as she took out her cigar case and lit up a Manila, offering him one at the same time.

"Amy, it's a great book," he began, "but . . ." He tried to point out tactfully that it needed pruning, but she cut him short.

"Ferris, you are a dear good boy, but you don't know a thing about biography, not a damned Thing!" she told him flatly. Though they discussed the matter for an hour and more, it was to no avail. The upshot was that not one word of the 1160 pages was deleted. Amy left the office triumphant, and, now that she was sure of publication, stone dead-tired. The doctor said she must take it easy. Yet she could not rest for long. She began to collect another book of lyrics and short pieces. She wanted to bring together all her poems of a personal nature without delay. She felt more than ever that there were not too many hours left in store for her. Like Richard III, she kept asking herself, "What's o'clock?"—the title she had already chosen for the book.

It was a disturbing autumn, ominous. Her sister Bessie's husband, William Lowell Putnam, died, and Amy, accompanied by Ada, attended the funeral. On December 10, tragic word came from New York: August Belmont, husband of Ada's old friend former stage star Eleanor Robson, had died suddenly and unexpectedly. Ada got ready at once to rush to her friend's side, and Amy sent along a heartfelt note to "Dearest Nell," urging her to come to them as soon as she could, and always to consider Sevenels another home. Only Ada and Nell, who knew Amy's possessiveness toward her companion, could realize fully how generous this note was.

The publication date for *John Keats* was set for February 10, 1925. As soon as Ada returned from New York, Amy and she got busy on the galleys, checking and rechecking to be sure they missed no typos. It was to be a two-volume work, and for once the whole family was interested in the biography that had occupied so much of Amy's time. Her sister Katie could hardly wait till it came out. Then, on February 4, tragedy struck again, unexpectedly, as before. Katie, who was president of the Women's Municipal League in Brookline, was watching a parade she had organized from the window of Hotel Vendome. Leaning over the balcony, she was seized by a dizziness and fell. She was killed instantly.

It was almost too much to bear. In her weakened condition, Amy was sure she could not have stood the shock and confusion if Ada had not been with her. Ada's calm, serene presence was like a rock for her support—indeed, Amy's nickname for her companion was Peter. She was especially comforting when the advance copies of the biography arrived. As Amy wrote to

"Dearest Bibi"—her old friend Carl Engel—who had called from Washington as soon as he heard the sad news of Amy's sister, "Katie died like a captain on his quarter-deck, serving her beloved Municipal League. It was almost horrible to receive advance copies of my book the morning after her death. She was waiting for it so eagerly. . . . I can't write, Dear. I am so tired. They brought Katie here, to her old home, and there was much to do. . . ."

With Ada's help, she got through it somehow. The two "stout red volumes" of *John Keats* were released on schedule, February 10; on the same date, a second printing, not yet available, had already sold out. Three more printings were ordered within five days. She was glad she had insisted on the dedication. Ada had at last given Amy her consent to dedicate this work to her, and Amy had taken advantage of the opportunity to do what she had wanted to do for years. She added a phrase to the initials, so there would be no doubt in anyone's mind about the extent of her friend's share in her life and creativity. The dedication reads: "To A. D. R., This, and all my books. A.L." Ada was more pleased and touched than vexed, and, as the work seemed to be the most successful of all Amy's books, she must have felt more than a little proud of her share in it, which was considerable.

Reviews in America were uniformly good. The critics could all agree about this book by Amy Lowell on at least one level: The biography of Keats was a "monumental" work, a scholarly contribution as a reliable source book. And many commended her interpretation of Keats—her self-identification with his "cult of the moon"; her clarification of Fanny Brawne's behavior; and her treatment of Keats' relationship with the men who formed his circle, particularly Joseph Severn. Amy and Ada thought this was one book that would be free of controversy. But when the reviews began to arrive from England, they were shocked. Almost without exception, the critics were hostile. They seemed to feel that Amy Lowell had invaded English literary territory. She had had the effrontery to negate

Sidney Colvin's long-accepted theory of Keats' life. How did she know so much?

Amy was angry and heartbroken. She did receive a good review from A.E.—George Russell, the Irish poet—in the *Irish Statesman;* she also received invitations to speak at Oxford and Cambridge and at Keats' residence, Wentworth House, which had been bought and restored largely through her efforts. So she planned a trip to England to speak on Keats' and her own behalf. The doctor told her that a sea voyage might be dangerous because of the risk of strangulation of the hernia, but she was willing to take the chance. She and Ada made plans to sail on the *Berengaria,* due at Southampton on April 21.

In the meantime, she wrote tributes to celebrate the fiftieth birthdays of Robert Frost and Percy MacKaye. (Actually, Frost was going to be fifty-one, the same as she, but he didn't bother to correct the error in his birth records—if people wanted to make him a year younger than he was, it was all right with him.) Though Amy's fiftieth birthday had been more or less ignored because of her work on Keats the year before, this year, because of Katie's death, there was no thought of a celebration on February 9. However, her many associates and friends decided that a "Complimentary Dinner" should be given early in April as a mark of recognition for her contribution to modern American literature. She and Frost received invitations to each other's parties. His was on March 26 at the Brevoort in New York. She did not feel well enough to attend Frost's evening, but she did send along the fine tribute she had prepared to deliver in person, which was read by one of their colleagues at the Brevoort.

She had not revealed to the Frosts or any of her friends just how weak she was feeling. A strange pride kept her from admitting how ill she was. Ada had confided to Nell Belmont that she was extremely anxious about Amy's health. But Nell, who had hesitated because of her deep mourning to attend the Lowell affair, coming only after the two convinced her that this would not be a social gathering in the usual sense, was not prepared for the alarming change in the poet within the two months since she had seen her. Amy was pale and her eyes were darkly circled. She was near the point of collapse with fatigue, and she was, for her, thin—down to 159 pounds. Dressing for the event was a terrible strain. But when she was ready at last, she somehow managed to look regal, almost like her usual self by the time they reached the ballroom of the Hotel Somerset in Boston, already filled with over four hundred guests. Poets, novelists, editors, composers, and theater people were all there to do her honor.

It was nearly 1:00 A.M. by the time Amy herself was called upon to respond to the paeans offered her. She stood up—with some difficulty, though few noticed—and observed that she hardly recognized herself in the evening's speeches. After several more remarks, she recited "Lilacs" and "A Tulip Garden." Tired as she was, she read in her best style. Exhausted, but thoroughly happy, she left with Ada and Nell for Sevenels, carrying like a priestess holding a chalice the gift that had been presented to her, a silver bowl of orchids. That night she did not sit up writing, but went to bed when the others did, she and Ada first accompanying Nell to the guest room that had been remodelled for Eleonora Duse.

After no more than a day's rest, she began to make detailed plans for the coming tour in England, lining up a total of sixteen lectures. Ada tried in vain to dissuade her from the venture. Amy seemed determined to go through with it, although she was losing weight—involuntarily. It was puzzling, frightening. And then on April 10th, the hernia flared up flagrantly. Surgery was necessary, but it had to be deferred. The continued weight loss made it risky. Absolute quiet was ordered. The sailing had to be cancelled.

In terrible pain, Amy dictated a letter to Ferris Greenslet with a list of corrections for the next edition of *Keats*. "I have two nurses now, and am no good at all for anything," she told him. "The sooner we get through these corrections, the better."

The operation was set for May 13. On the twelfth, she woke

up in despair. "Peter, I'm done," she said wearily to Ada. "Why can't they let me alone?" Her friend said she might feel differently when she got up, for, miserable as she was, Amy insisted on being up part of each day. While she was trying to pin the bandage the nurse had wound around her, however, she noticed that her hand felt numb. Suddenly, catching sight of herself in the dressing-table mirror, she saw the right side of her face drop. At once she recognized her tragic fate. "Pete," she gasped in a low voice. "A stroke." As she sank into semiconsciousness, Ada hurried to call the doctor. An hour and a half later, at 5:30 P.M., May 12, 1925, Amy Lowell died, at the climax of her career. Three months after her death, the volume she collected, *What's O'Clock,* was published. In May of 1926 it received the Pulitzer Prize.

Amy Lowell was a phenomenon, a force in the liberation of prosody from conventional forms. A propagandist, barker, and ballyhoo artist, she pushed the new poetry faster than it was ready to go, or than it would if allowed to evolve naturally. She did so to the detriment of her own reputation as a poet. As famous as she was at the time of her death, she was forgotten from 1935, when the first big biography *Amy Lowell, A Chronicle,* was published, until 1955, when the *Complete Poetical Works* came out. Since then, both critical and narrative biographies have appeared, and recent anthologies have devoted more space to her poetry, because it relates to contemporary expression.

3

GERTRUDE STEIN

AMY LOWELL and Gertrude Stein were zodiacal twins. Whether one believes in astrology or not, the parallels in their lives are too startling to be ignored. They were born in the same week in the second month of the same year—Gertrude Stein on February 3 and Amy Lowell on February 9 of 1874. Both were born in the early morning.

Their family constellations were surprisingly similar. Both Stein and Lowell were the last children to be born into large families. Although Gertrude's brother Leo was close to her in age, both of these last-borns had siblings nearly a generation older than they, and in both cases two children had died in between. The births, in each case coming late in their mothers' lives, were precarious and difficult, causing both matrons to become semi-invalids unable to take care of their daughters much of the time. Both fathers were remote figures preoccupied with their own affairs.

Both the Stein and Lowell families were well-to-do, but the source of their wealth differed widely. And there could be no sharper contrast in ethnic backgrounds. The Lowells descended from English Protestant, early Yankee settlers who came to America in 1639, and their history can hardly be separated from that of New England cotton mills, courts of law, and education. The Stein heritage was German-Jewish. Both sides of the Stein family had been fairly successful in Europe, then became part of the melting pot of America as immigrants in 1848, escaping the religious persecution of that era suffered in Europe. They soon rebuilt their fortune in the United States.

Gertrude was born in Allegheny, Pennsylvania, and she never forgot her birthplace, although she lived there only the first six months of her life. There followed three years in Vienna, and when the family returned to the United States, they settled in California, where Gertrude grew up. But Stein always was explicit about recalling her place of birth. One reason for doing so, she said after she eventually decided to live in Paris, was for the pleasure of "seeing the various French officials try to write 'Allegheny, Pennsylvania.' "

Life in California was pleasant enough during childhood, but before she was twelve years old, Gertrude lost first her mother and then her father. The five Stein children, orphaned, left Oakland and the family home with its surrounding eucalyptus trees for San Francisco. That city seemed a great metropolis to the adolescent Gertrude, but even though they attended the theater frequently, she did not enjoy life there.

Like Amy Lowell, Gertrude was a precocious child. She was already prattling away in German at the age of three when the family lived in Vienna; she easily acquired French the following year, which the family spent in Paris. When they settled in California, in no time at all she was equally voluble in English. Then she also began to read—she read and absorbed Shakespeare from the time she was eight years old—and she read in English, which remained her only reading and writing language. Though the greater part of her life was lived in France, she never had French books on her library table.

The California years ended when Gertrude was seventeen

and she went with her sister Bertha and her brother Leo to live in Baltimore with her mother's family, which included a number of "little aunts and uncles" living cheerfully together. The atmosphere of a pleasant large family dispelled the lonely lost feeling that had come with adolescence. As with Amy Lowell, puberty brought a tendency toward obesity, which Gertrude resented but could—or would—do nothing about. She was short, square, and stocky from the beginning, and while she never was as flabby as Amy Lowell, at one point in her life she weighed almost as much.

After a winter in Baltimore, "having become more humanized and less adolescent and less lonesome," she went to Radcliffe, though she did not pass all the entrance exams. She did not intend to study for credit. She enjoyed her life and herself.

At Radcliffe the most important person in her life was William James, the eminent psychologist. He influenced her thinking and, to a certain extent, her career as well. She was his favorite student. On the day of her final exam, a very lovely spring day, Gertrude, who had been going to the opera every night, just sat there with the paper staring her in the face. She simply could not face answering the questions. Finally she wrote at the top of the paper, "Dear Professor James, I am so sorry but really I do not feel a bit like an examination paper in philosophy today." And she left. The next day she received a post card from James saying, "Dear Miss Stein, I understand perfectly how you feel. I often feel like that myself." And underneath he gave her the highest mark in his course.

In her last year at Radcliffe James asked her what she was going to do. When she said she had no idea, he advised her to take up either philosophy or psychology. He warned her, however, that for the former she would need higher mathematics, which bored her. The latter required a medical education, but as she was interested in biology that should pose no problems. So, after making up the Radcliffe entrance exams she had never taken, Gertrude went to Johns Hopkins. She was a brilliant student, but became bored with the Hopkins curriculum. She was more interested in a servant girl, Lena, whose story she took as the basis for her early novella *Melanctha*, contained in her book *Three Lives*.

Gertrude Stein spent her summer vacations during the years at Radcliffe and Johns Hopkins in Europe, since her brother Leo, after a year or so at Harvard, spent most of his time abroad. While she was at medical school, he settled in Florence for two years. He kept writing her of the art treasures to be found in both Italy and France. The brother-sister relationship was a close one from the time of their childhood in Oakland, and when Gertrude decided her medical career was definitely finished, she joined Leo in Florence. For some reason, they chose to spend a winter in London, but it was not a happy time for Gertrude, although they had interesting connections—the Berensons, Bertrand Russell, the Israel Zangwills—who could introduce them to people in the world of art, theater, and philosophy. However, Gertrude was not "much amused" by the people they met, and the theater did not interest her. She preferred to read Shakespeare rather than attend performances of the masterpieces she had digested years before. The one benefit of that winter in London was her discovery of the works of Anthony Trollope at the British Museum, where she began reading every day for hours. She delved deeply into the Elizabethans and bought a complete set of Trollope, which later became an integral part of her library in Paris.

When in the British Museum she was completely absorbed in her reading, but the rest of the time she found London dreary. To her it was Dickens' London, and she found it frightening and sinister. It would be many years before she learned to like London, not until she went to consult the publishing firm of Lane about bringing out *Three Lives*. Now she was more than ready to leave the sooty city on the Thames for the "City of light" on the Seine.

It was Leo's suggestion that they go live in Paris. Here, in an apartment on the rue de Fleurus, with an attached atelier, Gertrude began to write immediately, both poetry and prose, in a style completely her own. There she and Leo, who had studied art and galleries and gallery dealers in Florence to know how to buy paintings, began the salon that was soon to become famous—not only for the paintings they acquired, but as a gathering place as well for the avant-garde painters who created the canvases. In Florence Leo had seen some works by Cézanne and been given the name of a Paris dealer who handled this artist and several others—M. Vollard, whom Gertrude later described in her best-selling book, *The Autobiography of Alice B. Toklas.* After some hesitation, Vollard let the brother-sister team browse. Though they laughed a lot at many of the paintings, they bought two Cézannes as their first purchase. They bought more: works of Gauguin, Matisse, Derain, and, most important of all, Pablo Picasso.

Probably no patrons are more beloved of struggling artists than the first to take a chance on new, relatively unknown work. So it was that within a few years Gertrude Stein and her brother had become fast friends of most of the artists whose works they owned, Picasso in particular. In his rag-bag studio in Montparnasse, he painted her portrait. She was portrayed seated in a broken-down chair, and it required ninety sittings before he was satisfied. Every day Gertrude walked across Paris to the rue de Ravignon, where Picasso lived with his mistress, the beautiful Fernande, who often came with him to the Steins' for dinner. By 1907, Saturday evenings at the Steins' atelier were an established custom: people were invited to come and view the paintings, and some—special friends such as the Matisses—were invited to come for dinner first.

Early in 1907, a guest who was invited for dinner became a permanent fixture in the rue de Fleurus establishment, and in the life and career of Gertrude Stein. This was Alice B. Toklas, a native Californian, who had been lured to Paris by the sight of two Matisse paintings brought back to California by Gertrude's older brother and sister-in-law, who also lived in Paris from time to time. They had hurried back to San Francisco to protect the family finances in the upheaval that followed the great earthquake of 1906. When things were in order, they returned to Paris, urging Alice to visit them. It was at their house that she first met Gertrude Stein, and, as in the case of Amy Lowell and Ada Russell, there was instant recognition between wispy, wiry little Miss Toklas and stocky Gertrude Stein. According to her own account,* it was Gertrude's deep, golden laugh that particularly attracted this native Californian whose background and ancestry were similar to Stein's. The two made an appointment to take a walk across Paris the next day. Alice arrived late. Although she had sent a note advising Gertrude of the delay, the latter was white with rage at the inconvenience. Like Amy, she was quick to anger, but she was always as quickly restored to good humor. As later behavior showed, Gertrude was not prone to forgive and forget, a trait she inherited from her mother.**

In this case, however, Alice calmed her after about half an hour, and the two went on a long, long walk as promised. The anecdote is one that Gertrude did not include in her "autobiography" of Alice. It is significant that her new friend was one of the few people whose tardiness she forgave—Picasso was another. Soon Alice was a regular visitor, and before many months elapsed she informed the friend with whom she had come to Paris that she was moving into number 27 rue de Fleurus. This action caused a breach between Leo and Gertrude. While there has never been any hint of incest in the brother-sister relationship, there was undoubtedly emotional jealousy over the inclusion of a third person in the bachelor

---

* Alice B. Toklas, *What is Remembered,* written after Gertrude's death; published in 1963.
** For example, Mrs. Stein stubbornly refused to forgive or forget a quarrel she had had with her sister-in-law and thereby broke up the business partnership that Gertrude's father had with his brother. Gertrude claimed to be grateful to her mother, for if the partnership had not broken up, the family would have had to live in New York and become oppressively rich instead of just comfortably so.

household, especially one treated as a member of the family, or, more accurately, a mate, to be regarded as an in-law. The schism began with arguments over paintings, which was not unusual—the reason they often bought two pictures at a time was because neither would compromise on choosing a single canvas. But when Gertrude began asking Alice's opinion of her writing instead of his, Leo was offended. He sulked, he stayed away, and finally left for good, moving to an apartment of his own.

After Leo, who eventually became an art critic, was gone, Alice B. Toklas occuped the same place in Gertrude's life that Ada Russell did in Amy Lowell's. It is not surprising that both of these literary personalities took female companions as mates; but it is curious that the given names of their respective friends both began with the letter *A*. It is an even more curious coincidence that when Gertrude Stein wrote her first "portrait," a sketch of Alice, she called it "Ada." There could hardly be a greater contrast than that between the scrawny Alice, whose sallow face was marked by a thin line of mustache above her upper lip and who was known for her succinct, dry wit, and the almost Junoesque, warm and gentle Ada, with her quiet humor and great love of people. But both companions completely filled the multiple needs of these two masculine women. Both smoothed the paths of their respective careers. Just as Amy always tried out her manuscripts on Ada, so Gertrude read her pieces to Alice. And each writer abided by her companion's approval or disapproval. In both cases, the harmony of the relationship was truly remarkable, socially and professionally.

At the time Alice came to live with her, Gertrude was concentrating on the trilogy of novellas eventually entitled *Three Lives*. She was also writing poetry—strange, repetitive, staccato, rhythmic lines not unlike the abstract and cubist art she had been studying and collecting under Leo's tutelage. A number of her poems had been accepted and published in literary magazines, most notably in Margaret Anderson's *Little Review*, which appeared in midwestern America after Harriet

Monroe launched *Poetry*, but which soon acquired an international reputation for experimental verse. It was not until 1914 that a slim volume of Stein poems, entitled enigmatically *Tender Buttons*, was brought out almost surreptitiously by Donald Evans, a young hopeful among the poetic experimenters. It was issued under the imprint Claire-Marie, the pseudonym he chose as publisher. He circulated copies of it around Harvard, where it found a surprising circle of interested readers, among them Edward Estlin Cummings, a literature major who was already writing poetry. But he had not yet taken his lower-case, double-initialed professional name or initiated his practice of using principally lower-case letters in his evocative lines. Cummings was attracted by Stein's emphasis on such simple words as *and, or, is, as, a* to denote abstract values, and of participles to suggest continuity of action. In her portrait of herself and Leo, she repeated over and over, "they were talking," and "they were laughing," "they were walking." The reader is nearly saturated, but still compelled to go on and left with the sharp impression of two young people in constant companionship, as she and Leo had been through childhood and youth.

Cummings enjoyed the quixotic observations that showed Gertrude's keen insight, as "in the midst of our happiness we were very pleased." But a few months after his graduation, when, as a graduate fellow working for his master's degree in literature, he chaired a lecture that Amy Lowell gave before the Harvard Poetry Club, he hesitated before asking her if she liked the work of Gertrude Stein. He waited until after the meeting and put the question to her privately, as he was seeing her to her car. Amy, wary, countered with "Do you?" Cummings, almost as wary, answered slowly, "Ye-es, I do . . ." In her response, an emphatic "Well, I don't!" Amy left no doubt of her disapproval.

It was inevitable that the author of "Patterns," who spoke of walking up and down the garden paths where "the daffodils/are blowing, and the bright blue squills," should object to a rival poet who chanted, "Rose is a rose is a rose is a rose." Even more objectionable was this bit of drollery tossed to the reader from the author of *Tender Buttons:* "A table means does it not my dear it means a whole steadiness./Is it likely that a change. . . ./A table means more than a glass even a looking glass is tall." Such quirky lines placed beside the quiet eloquence of "Venus Transiens" or the roar of "Bombardment," the definite design of "Patterns," or the strange sexual symbolism of "The Basket," could not be reconciled, no matter how unorthodox Amy Lowell was at the time, with her Imagism and polyphonic prose, or how tolerant of all new poetry she considered herself. And the feeling was mutual. These two opposing regal personages of the hour were too much alike ever to accept each other.

An indication of the similarity was evident in their lifestyle. Like Amy, Gertrude preferred nocturnal hours for writing. In each case, once the last guest had left—usually between eleven-thirty and midnight—these two literary leaders, in their respective salons on either side of the Atlantic, would settle down with copybook or manuscript paper and pencil for a night's work, while Alice Toklas and Ada Russell, who were early risers, usually went to their respective rooms for a night's rest. The two writers set down their thoughts with amazing speed and were capable of tremendous output, though both claimed to struggle with words. Despite their own unconventionalities, both objected to obscenities or pornography in the literature of the day, particularly to James Joyce's *Ulysses.* Amy Lowell withdrew her support from the *Little Review* because Margaret Anderson published the work serially; Gertrude Stein broke away from Sylvia Beach's bookshop because that famous proprietor sponsored publication of *Ulysses* in Europe. Amy subsequently continued to contribute to the magazine in America, but Gertrude never went back to the Shakespeare Bookshop.

Gertrude, like Amy, objected to Ezra Pound's edicts in regard to poetry, as well as those of T. S. Eliot. She was even more vehement in voicing her distaste for the attitude that today's women's movement calls male chauvinism. Amy never really broke with Ezra, though he mocked her unmercifully. Gertrude, on the other hand, found him so obnoxious that she made it plain that he would not be welcome at 27 rue de Fleurus after his one and only visit. She responded to Eliot's command for her most "current" piece, to be printed in a magazine he was launching, by writing a malicious portrait of him, titled with the date of his visit to her salon, so there would be no doubt of its currency, she said. He was furious and tried to get out of publishing the odious portrait, but Gertrude would not let him. Indeed, because of her abstract style and the title "November 15," no one but himself and those who knew of the visit could recognize Eliot, as she was quick to point out. The catch was that everyone in the Paris world of intellectuals knew of the encounter.

Gertrude Stein did not approve of movements in general, whether suffragist or Imagist. Her principal objection to Amy Lowell was that she tried to make the new poetry a *cause célèbre,* and with a good deal of success, which may have been the real reason for Gertrude's antipathy. Jealous or not, whether she sanctioned movements or not, Gertrude gathered a sizeable circle around her, and she probably did not care for competition from another American, even an ocean away. Winfield Townley Scott, who includes a comparison of these two figures in his essay "Amy Lowell of Brookline, Mass.," * observed, "Both had a dynamism which was basically rare ego-centricity; and it exercised compellant dominance, not only in the women themselves but over most people who ventured near them, and even over a good many who merely read their books." He ends with the fillip, "However they differed in intellectualisms, the two were so much alike we should be grateful they set up shop on different continents."

* Winfield Townley Scott, *Exiles and Fabrications* (New York: Doubleday and Company, Inc., 1961).

In another comparison, Robert McAlmon contended that Amy preferred to surround herself with "second-raters" who would flatter her, while Stein attracted giants like Picasso and Hemingway. One wonders if McAlmon considered D. H. Lawrence or Robert Frost "second-raters," or if he was even aware that they were part of Amy's circle, since he knew her mainly through reports from his short-term wife, Bryher, and H.D.—and did he discount the latter's genius? Before his quarrel with Gertrude over publication of *The Making of Americans,* he thought Stein "a much better specimen than Amy Lowell, though they were species of the same family: doubting and spoiled rich children, hurt only when they discover they can't have the moon if they want it." His parting shot was that "one thing was certain: Amy did weigh a good deal more than Gertrude." But this was not true in their early years, nor in Amy's last.

Tender Buttons attracted a sizeable following at Harvard among upper classmen and graduate students like Cummings who were alert to any new trend in poetry. One of these was S. Foster Damon, who wrote an award-winning paper on Imagism, which led Amy Lowell to track him down. Though he became a devoted member of her circle and was to be her official biographer, he also maintained his admiration for Gertrude Stein. By 1919, as a young English instructor, he introduced Virgil Thomson, just entering Harvard to study music, to her poems. It proved to be one of the most important introductions in the careers of both composer and poet, for Virgil was so taken with the unique tempo and satiric content of *Tender Buttons* that he determined to meet the author when he went to Paris in the late twenties to study with the late Nadia Boulanger. At Harvard, Thomson had studied music with the French-trained composer, E. B. Hill, who was a good friend of Amy Lowell's—with his wife, Alison, he was often at her home for musicales, and he set to music a number of her poems. Most notable was an oratorio of "Lilacs," one of her most famous and successful creations.

Thomson, however, was inspired by the work of Gertrude Stein. At their first meeting they sat and talked together like a couple of old Harvard grads about all manner of things, including *Tender Buttons* and music. He soon felt familiar enough to suggest that she "write an opera" for him. After some discussion as to the subject matter, Gertrude decided to do the story of Teresa and the surrounding saints in her own inimitable way. The result was *Four Saints in Three Acts*, which she wrote in Spain, she and Alice taking the trip there for that purpose. When it was finished, Thomson composed the music.

The opera was produced in 1934. Though they did not work together, there was a fine synthesis of music and libretto. Gertrude Stein's lines, especially a delightful lyric like, "The Pigeons on the grass/alas!" seemed appropriate for Thomson's witty, at times impish, but never impious handling of religious themes. The production, done with an all-Negro cast of singers, because Thomson felt that they had the best voices for spiritual singing, was highly provocative, but nonetheless successful. And it came at a time when Gertrude's fame was at its height. Her book, *The Autobiography of Alice B. Toklas*, had proved a surprise best seller, and her reputation as an avant-garde literary leader was unrivalled, for by then Amy Lowell had been dead almost ten years. Although Foster Damon's monumental *Chronicle* of Lowell's life appeared in 1935, and three volumes of her work had been posthumously published, Imagism as a force had been on the wane even in her own writing several years before her death.

All during the twenties, American artists in all fields flocked to Paris and sought the advice of the strange literary seer at 27 rue de Fleurus. The stories of Stein's volcanic friendship with Hemingway, erupting in fierce arguments every so often, with periods of calm in between, were legion. The friendship ended after one violent outburst that caused irreparable damage.

Her 1000-page novel *The Making of Americans*, which was based on family history and published through McAlmon's efforts in 1928, was recognized as monumental for its length, if not for its intelligibility—few people could wade through the overflow of words to the solid ground of the story. More novelists than poets came knocking at her door, writers like Fitzgerald and Sherwood Anderson. Sculptors like Jo Davidson and photographers like Man Ray haunted her atelier. Jo persuaded Gertrude to pose for him, and the result was an alabaster seated figure of her that resembles a benign Buddha. Man Ray's photograph of her at her desk with Alice standing in the studio door is also well known. When *The Autobiography* . . . became a runaway best-seller, it was inevitable that Gertrude find herself in demand as a lecturer. She was invited to tour the United States at about the same time that *Four Saints in Three Acts* was opening in 1934.

She and Alice were eager to see the opera produced. They had heard the score played by the composer himself on the piano and had applauded Thomson's music enthusiastically. The performances and the tour were triumphal, if puzzling to many people. It was evident, as one commentator said, that Gertrude enjoyed lecturing. She gave a performance, delivering her talk in a kind of chant that cast a spell over her audiences. When she left the podium she spoke in her normal manner, which T. S. Matthews, for years editor of *Time,* described as "downright and plain-spoken, with her middle-western voice."

In 1934, Gertrude Stein was sixty years old. She wore her hair cropped very short, like a man's "crew cut." Alice had clipped it all off one day on an impulse they both had, to see what the effect would be. It gave her head a sculpted look. When Picasso saw it, he said it was good, so she never let her hair grow out again. Allanah Harper, writing in the *Partisan Review,* related, "The first time I went to tea with Gertrude Stein at 27 rue de Fleurus, I thought I had never seen a more magnificent head—she looked like a bust of a Roman emperor and at the same time like a Buddhist monk." Amy in her time had also been compared to an emperor or a general, but in neither case was the description quite accurate. Virgil Thomson thought Gertrude resembled a "medieval abbot"; and Amy, with her high forehead, her intelligent eyes behind the pince-nez she always wore, looked more like a judge than a potentate.

Like Amy, Gertrude dressed to conceal her size. Both women wore mannish suits with loose-fitting jackets and long skirts, but Amy's were of blue serge, fitted with a high collar and stock, and she had dress suits for evening. Gertrude was all for comfortable garb. She sometimes wore a long, loose robe for receiving people in the atelier, but she was usually clad in "no-nonsense, rough-spun clothes," as Matthews said. She preferred brown or tan corduroys. Her one decorative garment was a vest, of which she had a vast assortment in different designs and fabrics. The Museum of Modern Art once had an exhibit of Gertrude Stein's collection of hand-embroidered and appliquéd vests or waistcoats, some thirty in number. Matthews described her further as "a solid, elderly woman . . . with deep black eyes that make her grave face and its archaic smile come alive."

This was the image she presented during the lecture tour of 1934. She was accompanied by Alice everywhere. To those who did not know them, they were a strange-looking pair, as a reporter in Toledo, Ohio, discovered. The lecture there, under the auspices of the Town Hall Series, was sold out weeks in advance. The response was enthusiastic, and afterward Miss Stein told the reporter that she found Americans warm and friendly audiences. She had little else to say; she did not think it necessary to go into detail. Later she and Alice found they had a few hours to kill before train-time, so they wandered around the town awhile. They finally went into an exclusive jewelry and art shop. Gertrude wore very little jewelry and did not care for gems, but she was fond of fine coral; a handsome coral brooch she wore at her throat had drawn Alice's attention at their first meeting as much as Gertrude's deep laugh—the laugh seemed to come from that warm, glowing coral. Gertrude also liked enamels and fine porcelains. She and Alice went immediately to

the second floor where such items were on display. They took
their time, walking slowly around, looking at different objects,
picking up a porcelain here, asking the price of a pin there,
laughing and talking in low tones. The clerk finally got
suspicious—she had never seen two such odd-looking women.
At last she called the proprietor and told him he had better come
up and find out what they were doing there. He was a man of
some taste and a knowledge of current events. He had seen
Gertrude's photo in the local paper heralding her lecture and
knew at once who the two "suspicious characters" were.

All through her career Gertrude Stein wrote her own peculiar runelike verse, satiric in tone and repetitive in form. Her
volume *Geography and Plays,* published in the 1920s, contains
typical Steinian mockery toward the times, as in the passage
from Scene VIII from *I Like It To Be a Play:*

> You were astonished by me.
> All of us complain.
> You were astonished by me.
> Don't you interested trying.
> Don't you interested trying to stammer.
> No indeed I do not.

It was this sort of serio-comedic nonsense that caused
Sinclair Lewis to ask, "Was Miss Stein crazy . . . joking, or was
she contributing new rhythms to an outworn English style?" He
concluded that she was "conducting a racket." In today's idiom,
he would have called her style a "put-on," but the general reaction was the same on the part of many writers like Lewis. However, J. Hyde Preston observed that Stein was "the foun-
tainhead for all young Americans writing in Paris after the first
World War." During that war, she, like Amy Lowell, had been a
loyal patriot. Amy established poetry libraries in training
camps and gave readings, both of which proved surprisingly
popular; Gertrude volunteered to drive a Ford truck taking
supplies to the trenches, with Alice perched in the cab beside
her. She read some of her plays, but for the most part she

mingled and made friends with the "doughboys." When the second world war broke out, she and Alice remained in Paris as long as they dared. Even then they did not leave France, but stayed in the village of Culoz, suffering the hardships of the occupied country. When the American army entered Culoz in 1944, and three months later when she and Alice returned to their Paris apartment at 27 rue de Fleurus, Gertrude was surrounded by American GIs, for whom she was both a legend and a friend from home. The feeling of warmth and ease in their conversation was reflected in "Brewsie and Willie," as well as in "Wars I Have Seen," Gertrude Stein's account of life in occupied territory during the war.

By 1945 Stein was suffering from intestinal illness, undoubtedly brought on by the hardship of the war years when they frequently had next to nothing to eat, but illness did not stop the Steinian flow of words—frequently it was the source of both wit and wisdom. Her *Last Operas and Plays* contained some of her best verse and quite possibly her major work: *The Mother of Us All*, her opera championing the life of suffragist Susan B. Anthony, a unique form of biography. After all her talk about not wishing to be part of the women's movement—the "Cause," as it was called—Gertrude Stein chose to portray this outstanding figure in American history. The dialogue in rhythmic verse delineated the characters and story with a humor and tenderness one would not have thought possible in dealing with such a subject. And Virgil Thomson, who composed the music for the opera, caught the ambience of the libretto as he had in the score he wrote for *Four Saints in Three Acts*. The counterpoint in the courtroom scene of Miss Anthony's confrontation with the judge and the playful dialogue on balloting and marriage of the young couple who are supposed to be engaged are delightfully realized in the music, and the final scene, featuring a closing aria, sung by the ghost of Susan B. Anthony, is sensitive and touching.

Production of the opera was planned for the year after the war. Gertrude hoped to return to the United States for the premiere, but her illness became worse. After a brief stay in the

American Hospital in Neuilly, she died, on July 27, 1946. The opera was not published or produced until 1947. It was then, and in revivals throughout the years—the most recent in 1976—successfully performed. *Four Saints,* most recently revived in 1974 with choreography and costumes by the Alvin Ailey Dance company was equally successful.

Gertrude Stein is an acknowledged influence on American novelists, but the point was at first often made that she exercised little influence on poets. However, midway in the sixties, with the reissuing of several volumes of her plays, Stein became immensely popular with young poets and composers. Even now poems are written to her and about her. Anne Sexton's "Transformations," versions of traditional fairy tales touched with madness, bear the Steinian stamp of satire and repetition. A trilogy of Gertrude's one-act plays has been set to music and produced under the title of the couplet she wrote on all her manuscripts: "When this you see/Remember me." It was preceded by a highly successful setting of "In Circles," her spoof of the literary circles in Paris during the twenties, including, perhaps based on, her own salon. The composer, director and producer, Al Carmines also set to music selected portions of her giant novel, *The Making of Americans,* transforming the material into an oratorio. Audiences for these productions, as well as her readers, consist largely of college students and contemporary poets. Perhaps because of the gay liberation movement, Gertrude Stein's poetry is to the younger generation of the sixties and seventies what Edna St. Vincent Millay's sonnets of flaunted free love were to the "flaming youth" of the twenties.

Gertrude Stein outlived Amy Lowell by two decades and a year. If the latter had lived and the two had met, it is likely they would have clashed in person as they did in their work. Each was too individualistic, too monumental in personality and physical size to give way to the other or to stand together on common ground. But both in their separate ways contributed to the freedom of modern American literature, and, by the lives they led, to the liberation of women, lesbian or other, the world over.

E. O. Hoppé

4

SARA TEASDALE

SARA TEASDALE was another last-born child, and a seven-month baby besides, frail and in delicate health from the beginning. Like Amy Lowell and Gertrude Stein, she came from a well-to-do family, had siblings almost a generation older than she, and was the "unexpected fruit of her parents' old age," as Louis Untermeyer put it. The daughter of Mary Elizabeth née Willard and John Warren Teasdale, she was born on August 8, 1884. Because of her extremely frail health, she was nurtured, like a rare orchid, rather than petted and pampered, like the two poets who preceded her by ten years. Her sister, Mary Willard—always called Mamie—seventeen years her senior, adored the baby of the family and showered her with affectionate, sheltering care from the first.

Named Sarah Trevor Teasdale for her Puritan grandmother and great-great grandmother on the maternal side—both her parents were descendents of early American Puritans—the poet changed the biblical spelling of her given name when she began to publish, and she dropped the middle patronymic because she considered triple names pretentious in her profession. Modesty, without a trace of false humility, was one of Sara Teasdale's most attractive attributes. She had that rare quality, a true sense of her own worth, and she neither aggrandized nor apologized for her creative output. Equally important, she possessed an ample share of the saving grace that kept her lyrics from becoming sodden with sentimentality or self-pity. Her subtle sense of humor was ever present in her lines.

The circumstances of her birth, the anxiety of her family over the mere survival of such an infant, and the fact that they had every means to assure survival and a life of comfortable luxury, led to a pattern that was set within the first six months of Sara's babyhood. Although she came through the critical period, she was far from strong. She was easily exhausted and seemed to need an enormous amount of rest. She was susceptible to colds that hung on, often confining her to her bed. So she was watched over by a nurse, waited on hand and foot, indulged in her every wish—for toys, for books and music and pictures—and was never required to assume even the slight responsibility for household care that wealthy girls were taught as a rule. There were maids, a cook, a seamstress, and a housekeeper, all supervised by Mrs. Teasdale, to tend to the large home the latter had helped to design, built in St. Louis soon after the Teasdales' marriage in 1863. Mr. Teasdale, a prosperous businessman (president of J. W. Teasdale and Company, wholesale dealers in dried fruits, beans, and pecans), kept a full stable of fine horses, and there was a coachman to take little Sara for a drive when she was feeling well enough. For all of this, Sara was not a spoiled child or one given to temper tantrums like Amy Lowell and Gertrude Stein. Rather she was a dreamy little girl who lived in her own inner world much of the time. Her friends at a later age delighted in citing a line from one of her poems as a self-portrait: "I was the flower amid a toiling world."

Because of her unpredictable health, Sara, nicknamed

Sadie by the family, was educated at home, largely by her sister Mamie, until she was nine. Her sister read to her a great deal. Among other books besides history texts and geographies, she read aloud the poetry of Christina Rosetti, which made a lasting impression on the future poet. She was enchanted by the rhythmic beauty of the words. She identified with Rosetti even as a child, a link that held her to lyric poetry throughout her life. In addition, she always planned to write a biography of her model, but it was a manuscript that never got beyond the notebook stage.

At age nine little Sadie went to Mrs. Lockwood's school for small children, which was only a block away, close enough for her to go there by herself. In her final year—the fifth form, equivalent to the eighth grade—the Teasdales let their delicate daughter try attending Mary Institute, the fine school for girls from which Mamie had graduated. It had been founded by the grandfather of T. S. Eliot, attended by the latter's mother and four sisters, and, during the poet's boyhood years, was located next door to the Eliots' home. Speaking at Mary Institute's centennial in 1959, Eliot observed, "If not for a matter of sex, my brother and I would also have attended Mary Institute." He recalled that when the girls left for the weekend, "their playground and their gymnasium became his." Sara usually was one of the last to leave school, so she could avoid the crush on the streetcar and not have to stand amid her chattering schoolmates, which wore her out. The daily trip finally proved too strenuous, so after one term she was enrolled at Hosmer Hall, an exclusive private school for girls, named for American sculptor Harriet Hosmer and one of the earliest college preparatory schools for women.

The Hall was closer to the Teasdales' home than the Institute, and the streetcar was not so crowded, but the family carriage more often than not brought Sara to school. Her parents were taking no chances on having her frail health undermined again. If her father felt for any reason that the horses should not be taken out, the girl would occasionally miss school or some school event. She was a good student, however, well liked by her classmates, one of whom was Zoë Akins, the writer who in 1935 won the Pulitzer Prize for her dramatization of Edith Wharton's novella *The Old Maid*. It was at Hosmer that Sara came to know the poetry of Heinrich Heine, whose lyrical quality, like Rosetti's, was a major influence in shaping her own poetic genre. Her teachers were quick to recognize her literary talent, and in her senior year suggested that she be represented on the commencement program with a poem. She was too shy to agree to read her work in front of an audience, so Miss Mathews, the founder and Head of Hosmer, decided that the graduation class must instead have a class song, and Sara should write the lyrics for it, which she was happy to do. *The St. Louis Republic* for May 28, 1903, carried the following detail in its description of the graduation program: "The hundred undergraduates dressed entirely in white will participate in the exercises and will help the graduates sing the class poem, the work of Miss Sadie Trevor Teasdale."

At eighteen, her formal education was finished, for her parents would not countenance the idea of her going on to college, considering her questionable health. Sara Teasdale continued to develop her gift in an unusual but probably more effective medium than the halls of academia. The summer of 1903 she spent with her family at their beautiful summer home near Charlevoix, Michigan, where her father had bought an estate, Altasand, on a high cliff overlooking Lake Michigan. The property included ample stables for Mr. Teasdale's horses, which were shipped up first every spring so all would be in readiness when the family arrived. They often went for country drives, but Sara's favorite spot was a small summer house among the pines, set on stilts and reached by a narrow footbridge. The place afforded a fine view of the "sky-blue water" below and provided the peaceful atmosphere that Sara loved for her work—writing poems, taking care of correspondence, or reading. If she had a house guest, they spent many hours talking in this retreat. Hers was an idyllic existence, and she made the most of it within the limits of her strength.

In the fall of 1903, Sara joined a group of intellectual, artistically talented girls who called themselves the Potters. The group produced a monthly manuscript magazine called *The Wheel*. Their activities, abundantly detailed in the biography of Sara Teasdale by Margaret Carpenter (1960), were so rarefied as to border on the precious or the consciously clever. But they were all bright young women who thoroughly enjoyed themselves, and there were sufficient resources in the city of St. Louis at the beginning of the century to stimulate their creativity. Besides Zoe Akins, who was Sara's friend outside the Potters' circle, and T. S. Eliot, St. Louis produced what was to be an amazing array of stars in the creative and artistic firmament. Such well-known names as Marianne Moore, Fannie Hurst, Orrick Johns, Emily Hahn, Alice Corbin (Henderson), John O'Hara, Tennessee Williams, Fanny Ward, Josephine Johnson, Martha Gellhorn, and the inimitable Eugene Field were either born in or closely allied with the city during the first quarter of the twentieth century. The city's situation midway between north and south on the Mississippi and position as gateway to the West, made it a focal point for arts and letters as well as the shipping trades and industry.

Sara Teasdale's first published poems appeared in *The Wheel*, printed by hand, often on fine parchment. Among them were her sonnets to Eleonora Duse, which represented a passion more esoteric than Amy Lowell's had been for Duse, since Sara came under the spell of the Italian first lady of the theater merely through gazing at portraits of her in various roles. Julia Marlowe, whose acting Sara admired and who was herself a devotee of Duse, obtained the photographs the budding poet studied. The one that made the deepest impression showed La Duse in costume for *The Dead City*, a play set in ancient Greece. It was Sara's great interest in the poetic fragments of Sappho that led her to write the first and most ardent of the sonnets to Duse in *The Dead City* role. It was included in the March 1906 issue of *The Wheel*, and was one of the poems that attracted the attention of Will Marion Reedy, editor and publisher of *Reedy's Mirror*, who subsequently launched the professional career of Sara Teasdale, as he had that of many of her contemporaries. It was in *Reedy's Mirror* that Sara first saw the poems of John Hall Wheelock, falling in love with his poetry before meeting the man who was to be the great unrequited love of her life. Here, too, were names that were to become friends and, in one case, Vachel Lindsay, her ardent but unsuccessful suitor. Many more—Carl Sandburg, William Rose Benét, Babette Deutsch, and Edna St. Vincent Millay—were among those whom Reedy recognized as poets of real value.

Sara's mother, a woman of definite ideas and religious fervor, felt her daughter should see the Holy Land before she was twenty-one. Together they made the pilgrimage by ship in February 1905, with over six hundred passengers, many of them ministers. Sara fell in love with the sea, which, along with the stars she had loved from early childhood, were to figure in her poems frequently. Cold, rainy weather kept her confined to her cabin with a severe sore throat when they reached the port of Athens, the city she had most longed to visit. The doctor did allow her to come on deck for a few hours, so she had to be content with viewing it from "afar off." Though she was allowed to go ashore for three hours on the second day of their stay, the excitement of it sent her temperature soaring, and she spent the next few days in the ship's hospital. Her diary of the entire three months' journey (which began in Seville, an unexpected "fairyland," and after the traditional Holy Land visits, ended in Europe with the great cities of London and Paris) is reflective of her life up to this point and even beyond. It is full of youthful enthusiasm and the conscious quest for beauty ever-present in Sara's psyche. Her descriptions of the sea, the cathedral in Seville, the little chapel of Ste. Chapelle in Paris, and the statue of Venus de Milo in the Louvre are unusual in their display of a poet's selectivity. Although the journal is also overcast with the shadow of ill health, that she seems to have accepted by then as a condition of life, it is not despondent. Her entries imply that her fragility was a fact.

Curiously enough, although Eleonora Duse was playing in Paris in *Camille*, which Sara had hoped to see, "she was not able to do so," according to her biographer. She did experience great excitement in attending a performance of Wagner's *Tristan and Isolde*, reading the libretto in French beforehand, and one would expect her to have made a special effort to secure tickets and take in every performance of Duse's, as Amy Lowell had done. Perhaps she felt that seeing her idol in person would alter the image she had formed in the sonnets, and she was loath to put her own creation to the test of reality. The sonnet, printed in *Wheel*, begins,

> Carved in the silence by the hand of Pain,
> And made more perfect by the gift of Peace,

and is as much a song of praise for ancient Greece as it is for Duse's thespian ability. In another early poem, Sara paid tribute to Sappho as the

> Impassioned singer of the happy time
> When all the world was waking into morn . . .

Once her work was published in *Reedy's Mirror*, Sara began to expand her self-expression and aims for recognition beyond *The Wheel*. The magazine *Poet Lore* accepted one of her sonnets to Duse, and the Poet Lore Company agreed to print a volume of her poems if she would sponsor publication costs. She was ill for much of 1907, and her parents were glad to pay for an acknowledgment of her talent that would not strain her and yet give her a happy sense of fulfillment. She decided to call her first book *Sonnets to Duse and Other Poems*, since the sonnets were the most impressive part of the slim paper volume. She spent most of the summer at Altasand in 1907 correcting proofs, which she "threshed over" three or more times. The book came out in September. It was dedicated to Sara's mother and father; but the first copy given to anyone was sent to Will (Williamina) Parrish, the uncompromising editor of *The Wheel*, who insisted that the Potters stick to her high standards in all their work.

Sara Teasdale was not too secluded to be aware of the world of criticism and review. She began to meet other professionals and to extend her contacts beyond the confines of her home and the intimate schoolgirl society of friends personified in the Potters. In 1909, the Teasdales moved to a portly Tudor mansion (also designed by Mrs. Teasdale with an architect's aid), which they built in a newly fashionable neighborhood. Sara, who was sent to a sanitarium to spare her the upheaval of moving, had her own suite of rooms in the southwest corner of the house—it included a library, sitting room, bedroom, and bath—which she furnished and decorated according to her own needs and desires, and in which she might have settled down for the rest of her life. But a conflict which never left her lay in the neurotic attachment, yet deep discontent she felt for her family, the longing to be loved and the dread of assuming a responsibility her health would not allow.

Will Parrish wrote that she remembered being ushered into the parlor of the big house by the maid, who would go up and announce her arrival. In a moment a door would open—Sara's suite was shut off from the rest of the house by doors—and then steps would be heard on the stair, accompanied by the clear, firm whistling of the love music of Siegmund and Sieglinde, and the "whistling, twinkling-eyed Sara" would appear, beckoning her upstairs. There she would launch forth into thrilling accounts of the Wagnerian performance she had heard, or the book she was reading, or the poem she had just finished. More often, however, the maid would tell Will to come up, and her friend would find Sara stretched out on her bed, a pair of stockings that had been over her eyes to shut out light while she rested now shoved up in a band around her forehead—demonstrating the practical side of her poetic nature—and she would continue resting while they visited. Her life at home was that of a princess in her private tower.

The only thing she lacked was vigorous health. Her parents were probably overprotective, and their solicitude induced her own preoccupation for her physical well-being. She once admitted to Will, "I often wonder if I had been born into a family with no means if I would have had better health." And her friend, who led the Potters with a strong hand and seemed to have boundless strength, confessed in her memoir that she often wondered the same, since in the hours Sara was with the Potters singly or at a party/meeting she "did not seem frail or weak, and she burned up energy at a break-neck speed." Whether she had to conserve it as much as she did remains a moot question. Even at that early age, her friend related, "Her life was a fixed and ordered entity, into which other lives had to fit, if they invaded hers at all. It never entered her head to fit herself to others. This was, of course, a strength as well as a weakness." However, in the next few years that concern for her health was to approach a hypochondria that also attested to her complete inability to adjust to the maturity of marriage.

Her well-ordered existence did enable her to send her poems out regularly, and not long after *Sonnets to Duse* had been circulated, Sara's first acceptance from the *Atlantic Monthly* arrived, along with a check. Another member of the Potters happened to have an appointment to visit her that day, and she never forgot Sara's glowing face as she announced the news, waving high the letter and check. Her rich, throaty voice was full of exultation.

The Potters began to take leave of their Lesbian society (in the classic sense of the phrase) for marriage. One of the first to wed was pretty Bessie Brey, on whom Sara had had a crush, and to whom she wrote a number of early poems. Married to a minister, Bessie moved to Indiana. Sara went to visit her. During the three-hour train trip coming home, refreshed in spirit, she wrote the rough draft of a long, blank verse poem, "Helen of Troy," which became the title poem of her second volume.

This was published in 1911 by a bona fide publishing house, Putnam's. Many of the lyrics in this volume were written to another woman friend, Marion Stanley, who was teaching at the University of Arizona in Tucson. Marion, thinking the sun and clear, dry air of the desert might improve Sara's health, suggested that the poet from St. Louis occupy a little cottage near the Stanley home in Tucson for a few months.

After some persuasion, the Teasdales allowed Sara to go, accompanied by one of the maids as cook, companion, and nurse. It was a rich, rewarding experience. The two women had much in common as poets, and although Marion was busy with her teaching as well as writing, she came over every evening before Sara went to bed. They talked about poetry and read it and criticized each other's lines. And they studied the stars, the stars that seem so close to earth on the desert. One night spent out-of-doors brought little sleep because of the awesome sight. "I fled away from the desert and the night," Sara wrote in a poem, "back to a narrow room— . . ./I fled away that I might hide my soul from the wonder of the desert and the night,/That I might hide my Darkness from the Question in the eyes of the burning stars." The lines are revealing of Sara's reticence, her deepset, unconscious fear of cosmic passions. She was not afraid to speak of the warm spiritual love she felt for her new friend. Perhaps the best known of all her poems to Marion is the love lyric "Song," written in Arizona:

> You bound strong sandals on my feet,
>   You gave me bread and wine,
> And sent me under sun and stars,
>   For all the world was mine.
>
> O, take the sandals off my feet,
>   You know not what you do;
> For all my world is in your arms,
>   My sun and stars are you.

A piquant, strange poem for one woman to write to another, but it is doubtful if Sara Teasdale realized the sexual implications of its images. She had always discounted the erotic legends about Sappho, preferring to believe in an unalloyed love of the soul between women. As her life worked itself out, she may have wished that the same sort of relationship could exist with men.

Three men were soon to become of the utmost importance to her. She was restless in her lovely new home. She began going to New York in 1911 because Will Parrish and her sister were spending the winter there and wrote that she must come. They found a room for her at a boarding house near theirs, close to Gramercy Park. She was enchanted with her initial taste of the metropolis, the "magical city," and the people she met were enchanted with her, for shortly after she arrived, her name was put up for membership in the Poetry Society of America. Her poem "Helen of Troy," read in moving tones (to her delight) by Witter Bynner, gave her more than enough votes for membership, and through Jessie Rittenhouse, the efficient and discerning secretary, Sara met and became fast friends with a group of established poets that included the secretary herself. And when the *Helen of Troy* volume appeared in the fall, Sara could claim full poet status herself. Her friend Orrick Johns wrote in *Reedy's Mirror,* "Sara Teasdale as a maker of poignantly perfect songs of simplicity and love outranks all other American poets." The critic for the *New York Times,* whom Sara did not know, said that her poems had "the authentic accent of genius." Even the skeptical critic of *Smart Set,* H. L. Mencken, asked, "Who will miss the genuine feeling in it, and the genuine beauty? It is the very simplicity of the thing, indeed, that gives it its charm."

Among the many letters that poured in was one that meant more to the newly arrived poet than any other, especially after she came to know its sender, John Hall Wheelock. He had come upon a copy of *Helen of Troy* while browsing in a bookshop, and, as he said, "discovered that there was a new poet in the world. Out of the impulse of my excitement, I wrote her one of the few letters of this kind that I have ever composed. Her answer was characteristic in its unaffected pleasure and appreciation. Some time later, she came to New York from her home in St. Louis. We met, and this was the beginning of an intellectual comradeship that was to last until the time of her death." To Sara, the relationship might have been much more if John had given her a sign, but he never did.

At the moment, however, she had not yet met him, and she was full of the wine of excitement from the success of her second volume, meeting people who had been no more than names—poets whose work she knew but never expected to know in person. Through Jessie Rittenhouse, who took Sara under her wing, she became the object of attentions from several young men.

In May of 1912, Sara and Jessie sailed to Europe to enjoy the Italian spring, an annual journey of Jessie's. The latter's account of their pilgrimage to the beautiful islands in the Bay of Naples reads like an idyll—the calm crossing, warm enough for them to be on deck without wraps, to take their rugs to the upper deck and lie in the sun, Sara working on a long poem she had begun before leaving St. Louis. In Naples, they stayed at Bertolini's, where from their balcony they could see all the islands in the bay and the coastal towns along the curving shore. From there they made daily excursions to nearby points, returning each night to their charming rooms.

Indicative of the deep fear that she would lose the gift of life because of her frail health are the prophetic lines that came from their stay on the Arno in the ancient city of Florence. It is a night song, evoked by the late, "long, long chime" of church bells over the water:

> Here in the quivering darkness
> I am afraid of time.
> Oh, gray bells cease your tolling,
> Time takes too much from me,
> And yet to rock and river
> He gives eternity.

It was a theme introduced briefly here, but repeated over and over and in more somber tones in future volumes. Sara seems to have withstood the rigors of travel very well, perhaps because their wanderings were so leisurely, paced according to their own inclinations. And Jessie Rittenhouse was the perfect companion.

Shortly after their return from Italy, the anthology that was to become famous for the controversy it caused, *The Lyric Year*, appeared. It contained the one hundred best poems of the year 1912, bringing to the forefront, through a contest of selection, the poets most likely to endure. To everyone's surprise and the consternation of many, Sara's friend Orrick Johns won first prize of $500 for his poem "Second Avenue." The storm arose when the award was challenged by those who felt that Edna St. Vincent Millay's long poem "Renascence" deserved first prize. Sara, though acknowledging the high merit of "Renascence," did not enter the controversy because she was so happy for her friend Orrick, and she was content to have a poem of hers included. Called "I Shall Not Care," its charm and freshness is still valid, although it has been overquoted and misjudged because of its quasicomic treatment of a tragic theme.

> When I am dead and over me bright April
> Shakes out her rain-drenched hair,
> Though you should lean above me broken-hearted,
> I shall not care.
> I shall have peace, as leafy trees are peaceful
> When rain bends down the bough,
> And I shall be more silent and cold-hearted
> Than you are now.

Now she could not stand St. Louis for more than a few months. January 1913 found her back in New York to attend the annual meeting of the Poetry Society. There she met John Hall Wheelock, with whom she found complete rapport. To her he seemed the pinnacle of all she admired in a poet and a man, and that primary impression was an intaglio that never altered. Within a few days they established a friendship that lasted through many crises in Sara's emotional life in the next two years and that stood her in good stead through many illnesses and periods of depression later on. In these first few weeks their acquaintance ripened quickly into friendship as they went about New York together—the city seemed more enchanting than ever in Jack Wheelock's company. His poet's eye for pointing out things she might have missed, his thoughtfulness for Sara's health, and delightful sense of humor endeared him to her just as his second volume, *The Beloved Adventure*, had sent her into an ecstasy of praise for his poetry. Now she discovered that he was a tall, handsome, and delightful young man. In the spring she made a longer visit to New York. They took walks and fed the swans in Central Park, which went into a poem of Sara's, and spent many enjoyable evenings together.

That spring of 1913 held joyous moments with other poets as well as Wheelock. Through the Untermeyers, where she and Jack dined one night, Sara learned that Edna Millay was in New York, studying at Barnard in preparation to enter Vassar in the fall. She dropped the author of "Renascence" a note to ask if they could have a cup of tea together. The answer was an eager offer to set a date. They met and rode atop a Fifth Avenue bus all the way up Riverside Drive, talking shop as only poets who like each other can. They compared methods of composing sonnets and lyrics, the relative merits of blank verse and rhymed, and the new free verse, then just coming into print, agreeing that the last was not their cup of tea. They spoke of Orrick Johns' splendid behavior in refusing to attend the banquet honoring the prize-winners of *The Lyric Year*, because he felt "Renascence" should have won first prize. Later the two had dinner together and talked, as women will, of clothes and the men they knew.

Of course Sara saw Jessie Rittenhouse and her other friends in the Poetry Society, but John Hall Wheelock was the star in her eyes, the one who outshone them all. However, although he was obviously very fond of Sara and admired her poetry as much as she did his, he showed no signs of falling in love with her or wanting their relationship to be more than one of affectionate friendship. Alfred Kreymborg once wrote that "in Wheelock, love is a cosmic philosophy." William Rose Benét added, "At times he is a little too cosmic," a sentiment with which Sara would probably have agreed at this point. Jack must have known how deeply she cared for him. In the late 1950s, he told an interviewer he had intimated to her that he was already pledged to someone else. Either this was true and the engagement was broken, or he wanted to save Sara from the anxiety, the alternating hope and despair of an unfulfilled or an unknown quantity of love. Whichever the case, she was suddenly so besieged by ardent love from two different men—different from him and very different from each other—that she hardly had time to wonder what Jack's feelings toward her actually were.

With the advent of Harriet Monroe's *Poetry, A Magazine of Verse,* a new mecca for poets had formed in Chicago, where poets from the Midwest could gather without having far to travel. Included were Carl Sandburg, Edgar Lee Masters, Vachel Lindsay, Arthur Davison Ficke, Witter Bynner, Maxwell Bodenheim, Eunice Tietjens (who was soon to become Miss Monroe's assistant), Zoë Akins, Elizabeth Seifert, and, as a kind of extramural member, Sara herself. She went to Chicago in the early summer of 1913 and visited the office of *Poetry,* where Harriet Monroe told her she had just missed Vachel Lindsay, Harriet's pride and joy as a discovery of hers—she had just published "General William Booth Enters into Heaven," the poem which brought Lindsay his first taste of popularity, although eventually it left a bitter aftertaste. Harriet had tried to induce Lindsay to stay longer so he could meet the fair Sara, but he could not afford to stay. It happened that Zoe Akins was also in town. Through her Sara met Eunice Tietjens, married to Paul Tietjens, the St. Louis composer, but separated from him and on the point of seeking a divorce. The two became close friends through their talks on many evenings, and Sara asked her advice as to whether she should write to Vachel Lindsay, as Harriet had suggested. Eunice guardedly said she thought Sara would find him interesting if rather wearing; so a correspondence began that led to a burning love on Lindsay's part, and an overwhelmed, admiring affection in return on Sara's part. Through Eunice, quite by chance, Sara met the man who was to be the deciding factor in her marital fate.

After an exchange of a few notes, Lindsay was eager to meet her. At the invitation of her parents, he came from his home in Springfield, Illinois, to spend the night at 38 Kingsbury Place. On this first visit, there was some constraint, yet each left a definite impression on the other. Lindsay, the big, blond, evangelistic, eager-eyed poet with a broad streak of boyish humor in his makeup, nearly filled Sara's tiny study, and when he began to recite some of his poetry, it was like listening to a pipe organ in "an hermetically sealed safe-deposit vault," as Sara wrote the Untermeyers. " 'The Kallyope Yell' really *is* a *YELL!*" Her ears ached, yet she would not have him lower his voice. . . . "The fresh humanity of the man—his beautiful exuberance—fills you with delight. He is a real lover of mankind, with a humorous tenderness for its weaknesses. . . . He has, quite literally, clean hands and a pure heart."

As for Lindsay, although he claimed to feel no more than a Platonic interest, he was smitten. Within a month he was writing, "I wrote to your friend Untermeyer today. I didn't write to Wheelock. I am just a bit jealous of his place with you—and am not going to pretend. I don't want it—but am just mean enough to be a bit envious, and as I say, I am not going to go through any insincere motions. . . . your sweetness binds me. Try as I will, I cannot always remain cool with you, Sara. Yet I must be cold as the stars." By the end of March 1914, he was making contradictory statements like, "I don't pretend to be making desperate love to you, but I am certainly very hungry to see you." And the statements grew warmer as the weeks passed. The love letters from Vachel Lindsay to Sara Teasdale are a tragic novel in themselves. Her instinct must have told her that she should not let him continue to send such worshipful missives, but she could not bring herself to stop him.

In the midst of this stimulating, if exhausting friendship, she met, through Eunice Tietjens, Ernst Filsinger, a man as different from Lindsay as Lindsay was from Wheelock—indeed, more so, for the latter two were both verse makers. Filsinger was a shoemaker who ran a large, international shoe business. He later proved an expert on international trade in general, publishing several books on the subject. Eunice was visiting Sara. The last day she was in town, she had lunch with Ernst. When she mentioned her hostess's name, his face took on a tender look, and he began to recite Sara's famous lines, "When I am dead and over me bright April/Shakes out her rain-drenched hair," going on from there to most of the other poems she had published by then. He explained that he had loved her work and had been trying to meet her for years. So Eunice arranged the affair, which became a whirlwind courtship. Sara could not help being drawn to Ernst. Although a business man, he was deeply interested in the arts and had what she termed "the same philosophical temper" as John Wheelock. Physically, too, he reminded her of the latter: Ernst was tall and distinguished-looking, slender, yet well-built, with a quiet strength in his appearance. She enjoyed his company, but was not exhausted by it as she was by Lindsay's buoyant, strenuous attentions.

That ebullient, idealistic, but penniless poet had ceased to talk about Platonic love. Now, to his own vast surprise, he was voicing views on the possibility of marriage. But fragile Sara must have known that Lindsay was impractical, unrealistic, even dangerous for her. Still she did not prevent him from planning, nor did she tell him about Ernst, who was obviously in love with her, though he had not yet declared his intentions. Lindsay continued to be under the impression that John Wheelock was his rival, and she did not enlighten him. In the midst of her turmoil, her father had a slight stroke. Her mother was not well enough to care for him without the help of a nurse, and Sara realized that they were both getting really old, that she would be left alone if she did not marry soon. Vachel was clamoring to come to St. Louis again, but she could not have him at Kingsbury Place with her parents ill. She took herself off to Saxton's Farm early in May: it was a place she had often retreated to in the past, sometimes with the Potters for a weekend, or by herself when she needed peace of mind. The country air revived her, and here Vachel visited her, followed shortly by Ernst.

The dilemma continued. Both her parents improved enough to make their usual plans to spend the summer at Altasand. Sara decided to go to New York before joining them, and on the way she planned a stop in Chicago. She tried to persuade Vachel to come to New York while she was there—he could see the shady publisher Kennerly and perhaps collect the $250 due him, meet some of her literary friends who could be helpful to him in his career. But he was loath to go for several reasons, one of which he stated humorously: "*If* you want to go to New York just to study your spiritual barometer in regard to Wheelock weather, I do not see what business I have around disturbing the *observation* station." And again, "I am quite sure that you are going to New York to see Wheelock. I love you well enough to almost forget that. Remember, someday you may have to choose, and choose forever. . . ."

It is strange that Sara did not clarify the situation, to give him peace of mind at least in regard to Wheelock. But perhaps, in the light of her admission toward the end of her life, she was hoping that the New York poet would change his attitude toward their friendship and marriage in general when she was in New York again. Unfortunately, all of Wheelock's letters to Sara Teasdale were destroyed at her behest—she also stated that she did not want hers published—but he must have known about Lindsay's passionate pursuit of her. There are hints that he felt he should not marry until he had the means, although his financial position was better than Lindsay's. He was soon to become an associate editor at Scribner's, a post he kept for many years.

Harriet Monroe, who was always looking out for Lindsay's welfare, let him know that Sara was stopping by in Chicago for a few days and invited him to come there at the same time, offering to send him the train fare if he needed it. He did not, he answered at once, but, if she owed him enough for poems she had accepted, there was a present he hoped to buy for Sara while they were in town. To Sara he sent a love note begging her to meet him by the statue of Lincoln—his idol—in Lincoln Park and talk things over. "You have completely disarmed my heart. I am bare and open for any hurt or cruelty you may do to me. So deal gently," he urged. "You are the one person on earth for whom I could cheerfully and even joyfully betray him [Lincoln]. . . . I shall see half the world through your eyes henceforth, if I continue in this gentle slavery. Good night— pillar of gold, and moonlight."

One can easily understand how the poet in Sara Teasdale responded to such imaginative wooing and why she was loath to give it up. When she got to Chicago, the first thing she did was go to the little office of *Poetry* on Cass Street to sound out her two good friends Harriet and Eunice, who were both there. She sat down on the floor between them and asked their advice. (For a person with a reputation for reticence, Sara was amazingly open in seeking counsel on a matter of private concern. The editors of *Poetry* were only the first of a number of her friends she consulted.) Harriet did not hesitate to say that although she didn't know Filsinger, she felt that "when one had a chance to marry a great poet like Vachel Lindsay, one should accept it gratefully." Eunice protested vigorously, now about to receive her divorce from Paul, "But one does not marry the great poet! One marries the man, which is a very different thing!" She knew only too well the trials of being married to a creative artist—Paul was a gifted composer, later known for such compositions as the score for *The Wizard of Oz*. She did not think two poets should marry, especially when one, the husband, was penniless. Vachel was, moreover, too vibrant for Sara. She was exhausted after his visits as it was. Ernst, on the other hand, would always take care of her and appreciate her poetic gift as much, if not more, than Vachel. This, perhaps, was not true, but Eunice was supporting Ernst's case. Sara, who had confessed to being half in love with each of the men, left the office as undecided as ever.

And she remained uncommitted when she met Vachel beside the statue of Lincoln. He had bought the engagement ring and insisted that she promise to send for it as soon as she was ready to accept it if she would not take it right then. Under the spell of his ardor, she promised. She left for New York the next day. His letters of persuasion followed her. "I *want* you, and that is all there is of it. I want you for keeps. I gave you my *soul* with those kisses." He was trying to alter his life so he could keep her safe and happy. His mother and father would set them up in housekeeping, and he thought he could earn enough for day-to-day expenses. He was still worried about Wheelock: ". . . and whether you decide for me or the other man—I shall dearly, dearly love you and never be angry. I cannot but wish him good fortune in general. . . . I do not think anyone but a thoroughbred could have written The Human Fantasy. . . ." Every day the desk clerk at the Martha Washington Hotel, where Sara always stayed after her first New York visit, handed her another letter from Vachel Lindsay. "I only know that you fill my heart—that the very thought of you is like a breath of high mountain air." One remarkable passage ends, "I have done myself the highest possible honor in giving you my heart." This feeling would continue "whether I win you or not," he vowed. He was willing to give up his goal of changing the values of ninety million Americans if she would be his. Yet the ninety million haunted him day and night. "The 90 million are your rival, just as Wheelock is mine."

Perhaps Sara thought the best way to enlighten him about John, whose feelings were still an enigma to her, was to let Vachel see for himself, so she asked him again to come to New York. This time he accepted. They spent many happy moments together. Parties were given by Edward J. Wheeler and the Untermeyers, and Jack Wheelock was among the guests at both. He was genuinely glad to meet the author of "The Congo," one of Lindsay's recent poems, but when he listened to Vachel recite it at the Untermeyers' one night, chanting, "Boom-lay, boom-lay, boom-lay, boom!" to represent the beat of African drums still sounding in the Negro's soul, and when he heard Vachel's evangelistic ideas for reforming commercial America with his Gospel of Beauty, Wheelock must have decided that it would be a greater burden than Sara could bear to be married to a zealot like Lindsay. It might jeopardize her own lyric gift. Sara herself was in a quandary, and she let Lindsay know she was a "monument of indecision," as he wrote to Harriet Monroe.

When Eunice Tietjens learned that Lindsay was in New York evidently making progress with Sara, she notified Ernst in St. Louis, urging him to act. He took the tip and began sending a barrage of letters, telegrams, flowers, and candy to Sara's hotel room in New York. Vachel, who by this time must have realized that Wheelock was not his rival, could not have helped learning that someone more persuasive, and in a different way, was out to win his beloved Sara. From his letters after his return it was evident that she told him who it was. A few nights before he left they got caught in a thunderstorm, and Sara woke up with a heavy summer cold the next day. Running a temperature, she was forced to stay in bed, and she was still confined when he said good-bye. Her illness made him understand fully for the first time her constant struggle for strength. And it made her realize how exhausted she was from his visit, from being with him for hours at a time every day. She needed the long periods of rest and solitude she was accustomed to, but probably would not have if she married Vachel.

In this frame of mind she sent for Ernst, who came as fast as the Twentieth Century Limited could get him there. Sara appreciated his quiet company and concern more than ever. She saw to it that he met all her friends, just as Vachel had. And one day after she and Ernst had dined at the Untermeyers, she asked Jean's advice as to which of the two suitors she should choose.

The Untermeyers had been most taken with Vachel Lindsay. They regarded him as one of the genuinely new voices in American poetry; they found his company refreshing and delightful. However, Jean did not hesitate to say that in her opinion he would not be a good husband for Sara or that she was equally sure Ernst would be. Both Louis and she had been impressed by Filsinger's manner, his knowledge of the arts, his protectiveness of Sara. She had little doubt that in Ernst Sara would be making a wise choice. But Sara was still hesitant. She invited Ernst to visit her at Altasand, where she was going to join her parents. Her mother and father liked both of their daughter's suitors and sensed her dilemma. Her mother's practical, half-humorous note borders on the hilarious: "Now Sadie my child, I think you will be happier if you married to *suit yourself* and if you do that we will both be glad and we will always make the best of it. I think both are good men and you may never have as good a chance again. . . . you must have time to make up your own mind and don't get upset. . . . Try to get well, and then you can see your way more clearly about everything. . . . Be sure to take good care of yourself and be thankful 2 *good men* want you. (Remember some ain't got none) and we want you too. Love from Mama and Papa." She probably felt that Sara, who would be thirty in a few days, might be a spinster for life if she didn't marry soon.

Still Sara hesitated. Before she made a definite decision, there was one more person her heart compelled her to consult: John Hall Wheelock. If she had hoped that the ardor of her two suitors would arouse Jack's jealousy and latent love for her, she was disappointed. Holding to his "cosmic philosophy" of love, he remained the good friend and impartial observer, as he would to the end. And so, when she asked his advice about Ernst, whom she was fairly certain of choosing by now, he told her that he felt the choice would be a wise one, pointing out to her the inadvisability of marriage between two poets.

Lindsay, who could tell that Sara was turning away from

him, through her own judgment as well as the advice of others, kept sending her poetic letters pleading love even after she and Ernst had gone to Altasand. But Sara, after Wheelock's approval reaffirmed her own decision, finally had to tell Vachel Lindsay the news of her engagement to Ernst Filsinger before it was announced in the papers late in August. It was a blow and deep disappointment to him, but he tried to be brave and honorable in crying out to her. Her lines, "I found more joy in sorrow/ Than you could find in joy," now applied to him. He could not, however, give her up completely. He would always love her, but he wanted to love her "finely." He bombarded her with burning pleas of love.

Sara finally asked him to wait a full month before sending her any more letters, and he consented to try to curb his impulse till he was calmer. At the end of that period, while Sara was in the midst of preparations for her wedding, she received copies of Vachel's two new books, *The Congo and Other Poems* and *Adventures While Preaching the Gospel of Beauty*. The second one was dedicated to her, and the copy was followed by a note telling her that she really was the lady in "The Chinese Nightingale," a poem she had helped him revise and which he always considered his finest. "When you read that poem, find yourself. . . . I am a very very restless creature. I am perfectly willing to admit I am spending a heap of time with the ladies of Springfield. And I suppose, without really thinking about it, I am groping around for my Filsinger, so to speak. . . ." This was the closest Lindsay ever came to delivering a barb about Sara's choice. In the midst of preparations for her wedding, Sara overlooked it.

In October Vachel went on the reading tour she had helped him secure. Before leaving Springfield, he sent her the manuscript of "The Chinese Nightingale," which touched her. His trip was highly successful—the applause of enthusiastic audiences still rang in his ears when he returned, and he credited Sara for its success. He felt at peace when he thought of her and was able to send her a symbolic wedding present—a strip of old Chinese embroidery that his parents had brought him from a recent trip to the Orient. It showed two phoenixes rising from the sea.

Sara and Ernst were married December 19, 1914, at the Teasdale home in St. Louis. It was a traditional, full-dress formal ceremony, though only the immediate families were present. She wore a long, lovely white satin wedding dress, and from every indication, was radiantly happy. The whole whirlwind affair had taken place in less than a year, though the months had been such a mixture of exhilaration, anxiety, and sadness in regard to Vachel that it seemed much longer.

And during the early years of her marriage, Sara was as happy as she would ever be during her life, probably happier than at any other time in her life. She and Ernst lived in a hotel on their return to St. Louis, since Ernst did not want his delicate wife burdened with household cares when she could be writing poetry. Sara was perfectly satisfied with the arrangement. Ernst was consul for Costa Rica and Ecuador in St. Louis and associated with Latin American trade development, so he often had to attend conferences. Sara did not want the responsibility of running an establishment with servants until it was necessary—if they had a family. She hoped to have children if she could. But in October of 1915 she was in the hospital, evidently having suffered a miscarriage.

As if to compensate for her loss, her third volume, *Rivers to the Sea,* was published by Macmillan. The book was dedicated to Ernst, but the title came from a poem of John Hall Wheelock's. Marriage to Ernst had not diminished her love nor lessened her relationship with Jack, nor, for that matter with Vachel in the realm of poetry, once the latter had controlled his emotions. She managed to keep the friendship and high regard of both men, but significantly, she never consulted Vachel or asked his advice. He never submitted a poem or a collection for publication without consulting her. Wheelock, however, was her mentor and adviser throughout her career. She wrote many poems to him, and she consulted him before attempting a new work. One might say a round-robin of love and admiration passed from Vachel to Sara and from Sara to Jack, quite apart from her marital love and relationship to Ernst.

Rivers to the Sea won high praise almost universally, and with the success of her third volume, overtures came from Macmillan for another as soon as enough new poems were ready. But Sara did not like being pressed, and she had another project in mind: an anthology of the best love poems written by women. As usual, she sounded out Jack Wheelock before she began. He not only responded favorably, but offered a title, *The Answering Voice*, which she accepted without hesitation. Edna Millay, in answering her request for permission to include a Millay poem, implied Sara's independent spirit in her answer: "Sara—you sweet old thing!" she wrote from Vassar. "I would so like to see you! Whadda you mean by having husbands and anthologys at the same time like that *Vile Inseck the Emancipated Woman?*" Sharp "Vincent," as Millay's friends called her, was perceptive enough to see that Sara, for all her femininity and delicate physique, had an innate strength of purpose, and, as Vachel once said, a pride that kept her free. "You may do anything you like with my *Ashes*," Millay told her.

Ernst assisted her in the research as much as he could by bringing books home from the library, but his business kept taking him out of town. In 1916 he accepted a post that would require him to be out of the country as foreign sales manager of a large firm, occasionally for months. Sara might have gone with him—two of her retreats for rest, one in Florida and one in California, required travel, and she always enjoyed seeing new places on her trips to Europe. But she had to go at her own leisurely pace, and Ernst's position demanded that he move rapidly from city to city in one country and then on to the next. His job also required that they live in New York, a circumstance with which Sara was happy to comply. Many of her St. Louis friends were already living in New York, and she would be close to Jack Wheelock and the rest of her Poetry Society friends.

The pattern of hotel life had been set in St. Louis, and since Ernst would have to be away a lot anyhow, with Sara too deeply immersed in her creative life to think of setting up housekeeping, even if she had had the strength or desire, they settled at the Beresford Hotel. The residential hotel overlooked Central Park and the grounds of the Museum of Natural History. Here Sara could live as quietly as she wished and still see cherished friends as often as she wished. Jack Wheelock was a frequent visitor. He and Sara kept up an exchange of poems and ideas, and when she and Ernst entertained with dinner parties in their suite, he was usually among the guests, who also included Louis and Jean Starr Untermeyer, Edgar Lee Masters and his wife Ellen, Mr. and Mrs. Edwin Markham, Joyce and Aline Kilmer, Harriet Monroe, Margaret Widdemer, Jessie Rittenhouse, and, when they were in town, Witter Bynner, Eunice Tietjens, Carl Sandburg, and Amy Lowell with her beloved friend-companion Ada Russell. Sara and Ernst had met the formidable Amy, leader of the Imagist movement, and gentle Ada at a dinner party the Untermeyers gave for the Filsingers soon after the move from St. Louis. It was a pleasant surprise for Sara to learn that Amy was a devotee of Eleonora Duse, and the fact that both poets had found inspiration in the great actress created a bond between them which was to last. Sara discovered that Amy had a warm heart as well as an indomitable will, and there was an exchange between them every time either had a book published. Sara included one of Amy's love poems to Ada in the anthology she was compiling.

Vachel Lindsay was another out-of-town guest at Sara and Ernst's parties. He had been a lost soul since Sara's marriage to the other man and did not call on them when he was in St. Louis. But when he came to New York early in 1917, he let Sara know. As Ernst was eager to meet the poet who had been his rival, the Filsingers gave a party for him, inviting most of the above-mentioned friends. It was a delicate situation, but Vachel, who knew all of the people there from his previous visit to New York, put them all at ease. The next day he sent a warm note of thanks for the party. "Seeing these people last night was a sort of homecoming," he wrote. "I felt in harbor, among them." From then on, whenever he was in town, he saw Sara and Ernst. To his surprise, he liked Ernst and the two became good friends. When Vachel married unexpectedly in 1925, he brought his bride to meet Sara. He never really recovered from the loss of his "golden Sara"—one of his terms of endearment—but it was a prop to him to be friends with her and her husband.

For the first five years of her marriage Sara Teasdale was serenely happy. Except for Ernst's long absences because of his work, they led a pleasant life together. If Sara was exhausted after completing a book he saw it through the press, handled much of her correspondence, and never bothered her with financial matters. Both the anthology *Answering Voices* and a new book of lyrics, *Love Songs,* appeared in 1917. The former was well received, and had a continuing sale. In 1928, when a revised edition came out, she added fifty more poems and a foreword tracing the changes in the attitude of women toward love during the eleven years between the two editions. The "free love" practiced by the "flaming youth" of the twenties had made a difference in the outlook of many women, perhaps even of Sara herself, with her Puritan background. The second book of 1917, her own *Love Songs,* was a triumph and brought her not only critical acclaim but an important award, one that was the forerunner of the Pulitzer Prize for poetry; a section of the book, "Songs Out of Sorrow," shared the National Arts Club Prize of the Poetry Society.

Sara wrote a touching little poem to commemorate the fifth anniversary of her marriage to Ernst, but she was in Santa Barbara at one of her favorite resting places and he was in Europe on a trip that had been unexpectedly extended when the December 19 date arrived. He did not get back to New York till the end of summer 1920. Though they had a joyous reunion, and her new book, *Flame and Shadow,* which appeared in October, was dedicated to him with the usual tender inscription, a subtle change began taking place in their relationship. It probably began during his long absence, with Sara becoming immersed in her poetry and feeling an unconscious resentment toward marriage, even though hers had been quite harmonious.

Poor Vachel Lindsay did not fare as well as Sara. His new volume, also published in 1920, was a complete failure, and he himself felt "dead" inside much of the time, though he was at the height of his popularity as a reader on the poetry circuit. Creatively, however, he felt he had come to a dead end, and as usual, he turned to Sara for support. She buoyed him up as best she could, but she herself was retreating, in spite of her own success. She turned down offers of honorary degrees from several colleges because she could not face the fanfare that went with such honors. She did not entertain for Vachel when he came through New York on the way to England, where a tour, including lectures at Oxford and Cambridge, had been arranged for him. The two poets talked about their profession, Sara keeping the conversation on an impersonal level. She did introduce Vachel to Robert Frost, a poet Lindsay had long admired, which led to a stimulating friendship for him. The tangle of mixed emotions revealed in Vachel's letters from then on until his sudden marriage in 1925 point to his undiluted adoration of Sara, which he never completely relinquished.

The death of Sara's father in 1921 deepened the element of sorrow in her outlook. To keep from dwelling on her loss, she began to compile an anthology of poems for children, enlisting the help of her friends, who gave her the titles of their favorite poems during childhood. She credited them all in a short preface—the roster reads like a lineup of the progressives of the Poetry Society who represented the new poetry. This was her circle of intimates. Yet Sara herself rarely wrote free verse. She was objective enough about her work to realize that the song was her métier. The anthology, entitled *Rainbow Gold*, was published in 1923.

After *Rainbow Gold* came out Sara went with Ernst on one of his business trips. This was one of the few times she accompanied her husband. It proved to be the last. She thought he was working too hard and tried to get him to slow his pace, but he would not. He seemed to feel a compulsion to be constantly on the move. When he was home, he spent his time writing books and articles in his field. Sara could not keep up with him, and they gradually drifted apart emotionally.

Sara's behavior indicates that she was not up to Ernst's sexual needs. She wrote poems and letters expressing loneliness and a longing for love, but everytime Ernst came home, she would go to one of her retreats a few days after his arrival. She was torn between physical love and love of solitude. And always there was the silent love she felt for Jack Wheelock.

In 1924 Sara's mother died. She had to go through the sad, difficult task of helping her sister dismantle the big house in St. Louis. By the time they were through, she was exhausted.

Vachel Lindsay had been in a state of torment since his return from England, despite the fact that he had had a successful tour. He could not "be an orator and a creator" at the same time, and the struggle to be so was driving him crazy. He was once more writing Sara pages and pages, pouring out his soul, once more declaring his love for her. His father had died in 1918, and when his mother died in 1922, he, who had had violent disagreements with his parents, particularly his mother, felt bereft, entirely alone. He pleaded with Sara to help him bring back the days of "The Chinese Nightingale." He loved her, but wanted to love her "with honor." It was a sort of sado-masochism—he was torturing her with his own pain. He had a nervous breakdown, followed by severe physical problems. Then suddenly, in 1925, Lindsay married a girl he had met when he was on tour in Spokane, Washington—she was Elizabeth Connor, a high school teacher and daughter of a minister. He brought his wife to New York to meet Sara; the Filsingers entertained the couple. Both thought Elizabeth a fine girl, the perfect wife for Vachel, and for a time that problem seemed to be solved.

The following year Sara found someone she could love as

she had loved the friends of her girlhood. This was Margaret
Conklin, a student who wrote to her from Connecticut College
for Women. After an exchange of a few letters, Sara invited
Margaret to visit her in New York. Their meeting was all both
had hoped it would be. For the poet it meant a rejuvenation. It
was as if she were reliving once again the magical, carefree
girlhood of the Potters. She wrote in an unpublished poem to
Margaret in January 1927, "You had only/To open the door/To
bring me the self/I was before."

From then on, although outwardly the same, Sara and Ernst
drifted farther and farther apart as husband and wife. Her sixth
volume, *Dark of the Moon,* appeared in 1926 shortly before she
met Margaret. It brought her new praise for its austere beauty
and somber tone, with poems that exposed her unspoken feeling toward Ernst and Vachel, her preference for solitude rather
than either the servile love of Ernst or the pleading adoration of
Vachel. In "The Solitary" it is hardly veiled:

> Let them think I love them more than I do,
>   Let them think I care, though I go alone;
> If it lifts their pride, what is it to me
>   Who am self-complete as a flower or a stone.

In Margaret Conklin, Sara evidently found the perfect companion, for she decided quite suddenly in the spring of 1927
that she must see her beloved England with her new young
friend. The trip was a sheer delight for both of them, but the
return crossing was stormy. Sara, on the verge of a bad cold,
exhausted, was not up to the task of moving from the Beresford
to the Hotel San Remo, which faced her at her return. She went
to Connecticut while Ernst, with the help of Margaret, handled
the whole job, including the packing of books, manuscripts and
papers that had accumulated during their ten years' residence
in the Beresford. Ernst's concern for Sara's health and constant
protectiveness were almost as neurotic as her own. If he hoped
that the new surroundings would bring them closer together
when he was in town, he was to be disappointed. Her lassitude

grew so great that she did not even have the desire to go to the theater or concerts with Ernst. She suggested that instead of her he should take Margaret. It was an odd and constrained design for living, but Sara could not—or would not—bring herself to change.

In 1928 news came that Marguerite Wilkinson had drowned in the Atlantic. It sent Sara into a mild melancholia that she could not shake off. Marguerite had been a good friend to her, to Vachel, and to all those who had benefitted through Wilkinson's *New Voices*. After the unexpected death of Amy Lowell, whose passing had stunned them all in 1925, Marguerite had become, as Vachel said in his letter, "a stateswoman for us all, a friend and destiny maker. . . ." Citing the death of Marguerite and her husband Jimmy, and that of Amy Lowell, Lindsay went on to say, "I am tired of the critical dictum that the New Poetry Movement has grown careless, as though it were a matter of the fading away of technique, when it is a plain case of the death of your parents, the death of my parents and all such, and we must put on a far sterner and more solitary harness to go forward. . . ."

In September of 1929, Sara Teasdale, taking an assumed name, went to Reno with a friend and obtained a divorce from Ernst, who was in South Africa at the time. She had tried to talk him into agreeing to a separation, but he was shocked and would not even discuss it. The thought of losing her was more than he could bear, although they were hardly together for more than a few days at a time, and he must have known that such a marriage as theirs could not last. The only one who knew of her plan was John Hall Wheelock, whom she consulted, as always. If she thought he would encourage her or that her action would bring a declaration of love from him, she was disappointed, for he tried to dissuade her from going to Reno. Perhaps his attitude even precipitated her action.

When Ernst received the letter from her telling him she was adamant in her decision to get a divorce, he was heart-broken. He knew, however, that once Sara made up her mind, she capitulated to no one, so he directed his lawyer to take care of the proceedings. After the divorce, he wrote to Jessie Rittenhouse, "I know that you know, dear Jessie, that I love Sara today, more completely, more desperately, more tenderly than in all the time I've known her. Never for a moment did I cease to love her, to admire her—to respect her wonderful independence of spirit." One of the amazing facets of Sara Teasdale's history is that the men in her life remained constant, loyal in their devotion to her no matter what she did. Even Jack Wheelock, though he never asked her to marry him, did not marry anyone else while she was alive. As for Sara herself, she had written prophetically in a poem aptly titled "An End" the telling line, "With my own will I vanquished my own heart."

Vachel and Elizabeth Lindsay were "stunned" by the news. Vachel admitted that he had no comment to make about her divorce. It is likely that if he had had any idea that Sara was contemplating divorce, he would not have married Elizabeth. Now, with two small children and a devoted wife, he could say nothing of all he felt in his innermost being. Instead he told her that those "new" poets who were left must go on singing. And this Sara did, compiling a book of her poems for children, *Stars Tonight*, which was published in 1930 and dedicated to Margaret Conklin. Besides the trusted Jack Wheelock, her young friend was her mainstay now. Margaret helped her to move to a smaller apartment in Gramercy Park, and three or four evenings a week came from her job at Macmillan to be with Sara. As always, they read poetry together and talked out their hearts. Around this time Sara wrote a poem in tribute to Margaret. In it were the lines, "I shall find no better thing upon the earth/Than the wilful, noble, faulty thing which is you." They spent weekends together, sometimes taking short trips, once to Washington, D.C., another time to Old Lyme, Connecticut. One cannot help wondering if Sara would have divorced Ernst had she never met Margaret.

Wheelock of course continued as the affectionate friend and, indeed, the strong dominant figure in Sara's world. She made no secret of the fact that many of her poems were written to him, and in a distillation of her feeling through the years extolled his friendship in two eloquent lines: "It is enough of honor for one lifetime/To have known you better than the rest have known." Yet she was not blind to Wheelock's faults, as she recorded in "Appraisal," from *Dark of the Moon*, but she felt there was "treasure to outweigh them." Best of all was his "humor flickering hushed and wide/As the moon on moving water,/And a tenderness too deep/To be gathered in a word." This was followed in the same section, entitled "Portraits" and "Those Who Love," by an unmistakable portrait of herself in the cadenced lines:

> And a woman I used to know
> Who loved one man from her youth,
> Against the strength of the fates
> Fighting in somber pride,
> Never spoke of this thing,
> But hearing his name by chance,
> A light would pass over her face.

The presence of Jack Wheelock did as much as Margaret Conklin's young strength to help Sara over the wrench of divorce, and she began to think of taking up the biography of Christina Rosetti she had considered doing over the years. At this point, Vachel Lindsay turned to her again for spiritual help, repeating his old refrain, but on a more despondent, desperate note than ever. He and his wife were having terrible financial troubles. His creative power had ebbed away with the strain of constant recital tours, and he could not keep on performing like "a dancing bear," to use Amy Lowell's image. His prose book on Springfield and its Lincolnian background was a total failure. Once again he was writing "Darling Sara," his dear "Golden Eyes," pleading passionately for her to save him from the public, to bring back his old creative self. The worst of it was that his wife was helping him in a practical way far more than Sara could—Elizabeth was tutoring, writing reviews, and taking care of the household. But that only seemed to increase

Vachel's depression. He cancelled his speaking dates, but could not write. He poured out his heart in long letters to Sara, and he saw her once when he was in New York in November of 1931, spending an evening with her. Both felt strained and uncomfortable.

She was worried about her old friend and insistent erstwhile suitor, but she did not expect him to do anything drastic. And then the terrible news came: on December 5, 1931, Vachel Lindsay took his life in the early morning by drinking a bottle of Lysol. He had threatened before to commit suicide—in his nerve-wracked condition had even threatened Elizabeth and their children to save them all from a life of misery, as he saw it. Elizabeth had talked him out of it, but this time, in a crazed, impulsive moment, he downed the bottle of Lysol and died in horrible pain at his wife's feet. Sara felt as if she had been struck a shattering blow that "shook her to her very roots," as she said when she could write about it. Grief-stricken, she called Jack Wheelock at Scribner's, but she was in such a state of shock she could scarcely speak through her sobs. He called her back twice but could not make out what she was trying to tell him. In great alarm, he left the office and hurried down to her hotel. There, through her sobs, he learned of the tragic event and tried to comfort her, but in that crisis moment she was inconsolable. She ultimately found consolation in her own way, by writing a memorial poem to Vachel. She had been talking to the Untermeyers, who, like all his friends, were deeply saddened by Lindsay's suicide. Louis had written a poem, "Transfigured Swan," in memory of this man who was "not only one of our best poets but one of my best friends," as he wrote Benét. In her poem, Sara addressed Vachel as an eagle:

> Fly out, fly on, eagle that is not forgotten
> Fly straight to the innermost light, you who loved sun
>   in your eyes,
> Free of the fret, free of the weight of living,
> Bravest among the brave, gayest among the wise.

Sara never completely recovered from the trauma she suffered over Vachel's suicide. After some months she began working again on her biography of Christina Rosetti, to be dedicated, "To the Memory of Vachel Lindsay Who Loved the Poetry of Christina Rosetti." It is significant that, though he had dedicated most of his books to Sara and written countless poems to her, the only poem she ever wrote to him and the only book she ever planned to dedicate to him both came after his death—and the book was never completed or published. Research for the biography took her mind off Lindsay's tragedy and the sense of guilt she may have felt at not helping him to a greater extent than she had during his last months. She decided to go to England to interview Rosetti's nieces. It was the only time in her life she traveled alone, sailing in the early summer of 1932. She had an enjoyable, successful stay in London until she somehow developed double pneumonia after tiring herself out on a rainy day. She may not have realized that the climate of London, "this adorable, cold grey cosy darling city" as she wrote in a letter to Margaret, was too chilly even in summer for her delicate system. She was fond of wearing filmy chiffon dresses that never quite hid the long-sleeved underwear she had adopted to keep from catching cold, but the dampness of the weather probably required heavy tweeds, which she never wore. Her pneumonia reached a critical stage.

Dreading to stay abroad in such a condition, she managed to gather the strength to sail for home, although the ship's doctor later said he did not expect her to survive the trip. Her left lung was still clogged when she arrived in New York. Nervous exhaustion combined with her illness kept her in bed for weeks, and deep depression was inevitable. In December, hoping that a warm climate might help her recover, she went to Florida for two weeks to visit Jessie Rittenhouse. While there she consulted a doctor and learned that she had a heart murmur, along with very high blood pressure. She was sure a stroke was imminent.

After Sara came home from Florida in January of 1933, she

consulted seven doctors, but none could lessen her suffering or hold out any hope of improvement. When the blood vessels in her hands broke, a paralytic stroke seemed unavoidable. By January 29 whe was terribly weak and fading visibly, more passive than she had been during the past months. When Margaret Conklin came over in the evening she read to her and played a recording of Beethoven's Fifth—his "victory" symphony. The evening was quiet, unbroken by any seizure of coughing. Sara suggested that Margaret, who had twisted her ankle and was in pain, leave early and get a good night's rest— the nurse would be there if she needed anything. The next morning, when the nurse came to her room, Sara was not there. The nurse found her in the bathtub, apparently dead from drowning moments before—the water was still warm. But an autopsy subsequently showed that the poet had taken an overdose of sleeping pills. It was as if Sara Teasdale were echoing to those who found her, her own dictum: "Oh when my spirit's fire burns low,/Leave me the darkness and the stillness,/I shall be tired and glad to go."

With a heavy heart, but reverent care, Jack Wheelock helped Margaret Conklin arrange for posthumous publication of the twenty-two poems Sara had left in her notebook marked for her next volume, to which she had given the title *Strange Victory*—a title interpreted in various ways by her friends. Wheelock must have pondered its meaning, must have sensed that it related to him as well as to Sara's immortality of spirit through her poems. He had remained single throughout her lifetime, and he did not marry until 1940, nearly eight years after her death.

Strange Victory was hailed by the critics when it appeared in October 1933, eight months after Sara's death. And those who had been close to her all agreed that these last poems were her best.

Of the three men who formed the triangle of love around Sara Teasdale in her life, the most important was John Hall Wheelock, who died at the age of ninety-one in March 1978, himself a loved and honored lyric poet. In the introduction to her proposed biography of Christina Rosetti, Sara had written, "A lyric poet is always a contemporary." The observation applies to Sara herself.

One of the most endearing love songs from *Flame and Shadow* obviously alludes to Wheelock in its closing lines:

> In many another soul I broke the bread,
>   And drank the wine and played the happy guest,
> But I was lonely, I remembered you;
>   The heart belongs to him who knew it best.

She belongs, as Wheelock said, in the front rank of women who have contributed to modern American poetry.

5

ELINOR WYLIE

LIKE Sara Teasdale and Amy Lowell, Elinor Wylie was born with a "silver spoon in her mouth," as her friend Elizabeth Sergeant said in an overwritten character portrait three years before this high-spirited, high-strung, complex poet died. Obviously Sergeant could not supply names and dates of certain key figures who were all living or the shocking events in the fascinating life-story of Elinor Wylie, but without them biography becomes mere high-flown rhetoric. Elinor Wylie was born in Somerville, New Jersey, on September 7, 1885, the first child of Henry Martyn Hoyt—later solicitor-general of the United States—and Anne McMichael Hoyt. On both sides of the family she came from distinguished Philadelphia ancestors, and she was proud of the name Hoyt, although she never used it professionally. That was probably because, in defiance of family tradition, she took the name that made her an outcast in the rigid society circles of Philadelphia and Washington.

Most of Elinor's childhood was spent close to the Hoyt-McMichael heritage, for when she was two her family moved to the fashionable Philadelphia suburb of Rosemont, and she attended a private school at Bryn Mawr. It was a world that Edith Wharton or Henry James would have understood, as would her fellow poet Amy Lowell: a world of formal manners and "stiff, brocaded mores," a polite society of people whose households shone with polished silver and gleaming crystal. Elinor's closest playmates were her brother, Henry Martyn III, born two years after her, and sister Constance ("Connie"), who followed him by two years. They continued to be real intimates in Washington, D.C., where the family moved when Elinor was twelve—her father had become assistant solicitor-general and a year later was made solicitor-general, an important figure in the federal government. Here Elinor attended a private school again, as did Connie, and their brother a prep school. When the three were together during holidays, they tossed aside their textbooks and read forbidden poets. Elinor fell in love with the poetry of Percy Bysshe Shelley, a passion she never relinquished and always fiercely defended.

Two more children were born to the Hoyts in Washington—Morton, 1899, and Anne McMichael, in 1902. The baby, seventeen years younger than Elinor, was named after their mother, but, on Elinor's plea, was always called Nancy, their mother's nickname. It was Nancy who was to write the first biography of her famous sister in 1935, seven years after the poet's death. The telling subtitle was *Portrait of an Unknown Lady*.

By the time Elinor was eighteen, she had grown into a rare beauty—tall and slender, with tawny hair and perfect features and a merry malice in her amber eyes. According to custom, her grandfather took her and Connie to Europe for a season in Paris and London, then considered a necessary preparation for the debut and marriage of the daughters of Washington families in high government circles. As might be expected, Elinor was among the most popular of the debutantes to come out that season. Despite her scorn of both convention and family pride of position in society, there was a certain haughty elegance about Elinor that attracted young men in droves, adoring at her feet. One who adored her from afar at this time was her brother's roommate at Yale, a budding young poet with literary ambitions by the name of William Rose Benét. Henry brought him home from college a few times. Although he caught only glimpses of her as she was coming and going, and had little chance to talk to her, Bill Benét thought Elinor was the most exquisite and brilliant creature he had ever met.

However, she was so sought after by the eligible suitors in her set that he felt he had no chance of winning her. Indeed, she regarded him as a nice boy who was her brother's roommate, but hardly more than that, though she enjoyed talking poetry with him. She was in fact involved in a passionate romance with a young man, but it was broken off abruptly for some reason no one quite understood.

Elinor, piqued, feeling rejected, rushed into another affair on the rebound. "Without the knowledge of her parents, she became engaged to a nice-looking and well-born young suitor with a bad temper," Nancy wrote years later. The young man was Philip Hichborn, son of a rear admiral, whose family was wealthy and highly placed in government echelons. He was arrogant, conceited, and erratic in mood. As Elinor was to discover, his bad temper manifested itself in tantrums that were maniacal. Elinor's father disliked him on sight and was leery of the match. Her mother did not object to the marriage, but to Elinor's way of going about it, without the proper engagement announcement or a large formal society wedding. Her brother and sister stood by her—Henry was best man and Connie maid of honor at the quiet home wedding that took place on December 12, 1906, in the Hoyt residence on Rhode Island Avenue. Among the few guests was President Theodore Roosevelt and Henry's Yale friend, Bill Benét.

As a society matron, Elinor was, in appearance, the perfect hostess. She had beauty, a flair for fashion, a slim figure well-formed for the beautiful gowns she chose to wear, and a ready conversational wit. However, beneath her flawless appearance lay a restless, discontented heart. Elinor discovered too late that she was not in love with her husband, that there was more to marriage than "making a good match," to use her mother's terms. The round of high society parties bored her. When she found she was pregnant, she stopped entertaining until after the baby, a son named for his father, was born. She read much poetry during those months and tried to write a little, but she felt stifled. She could not express the feelings deep within her, at any rate not in the way she wished. Philip's fits of jealousy toward the baby and toward her interest in poetry, his shouting like a madman over minor details that were wrong in the household, which produced in him an incoherent rage, frightened and alienated Elinor. When she confessed her fears at home, her mother thought she was exaggerating and told her she must try to make the best of her unfortunate marriage. Her father, often away from home and preoccupied with matters of state, was more sympathetic when he finally learned the extent of her problem. He promised to try to secure a divorce for her quietly, without publicity. Elinor could do nothing but wait.

Then suddenly she fell hopelessly in love with a man fifteen years her senior. This was Horace Wylie, a distinguished Washington lawyer and himself married—a family man with four children. He had noticed her at various Washington functions and thought her "the most beautiful creature he had ever seen." Just how or when they met is not clear, but the attraction must have been instantaneous and mutually strong and compelling. There is a record of clandestine meetings in Rock Creek Park and of a rapidly mounting quest for means of a lasting liaison. Elinor hoped her father would help her start proceedings for divorce from Philip, but Hoyt suddenly became seriously ill and died within a few weeks. With her father's death, all hope for a divorce vanished, for her mother would not countenance such action to be initiated by her daughter. Admiral Hichborn, Philip's father, had died of a heart attack only six months before. If Elinor were to institute divorce proceedings while both families were in mourning, it would create a terrible scandal.

Elinor's reaction was to throw convention to the winds and elope with Horace Wylie. Her family was shocked and shamed, even Henry, who, at his mother's command went rushing after her with Philip Hichborn in an effort to stop her from boarding a ship in New York. But the couple sailed from Canada incognito, leaving no trace. Hichborn's family was outraged and vengeful—they vowed she would never have custody of her son, at the time scarcely more than three years old. They decided to take him to the elder Hichborn's home to be brought up in the tradition of the naval officer's code. Philip himself seemed bewildered and close to insanity. He did not quite know what had happened, but evidently he did realize soon after their marriage that Elinor was a difficult partner for a life such as he had always known. Her mind was far beyond his; there was something wild and elusive in her spirit that he could not get hold of, and he was not sure he wished to discover what it was. The amazing fact was that none of the three families involved—Hoyts, Hichborns, or Wylies—ever suspected the romance that was going on between Elinor and Horace, so well did they keep it secret.

As for Elinor, she was like one in a dream who scarcely knew what she was doing. She only knew that Wylie had stirred her senses as no man ever had and that she could not stand the vapid life of Washington society any longer. She was sorry to leave her child, but from the attitude of Hichborn's parents, they would not have allowed her to bring up her own child the way she wished anyhow. Later she would come back and see if she could claim him; Philip was going to give her a divorce, and Wylie was going to try to get a divorce from his wife. He had already asked her, but she had refused to consider it. Neither Elinor nor Horace Wylie wanted to wait for his wife to be persuaded to change her mind, so the two lovers lived in Europe for five years as Mr. and Mrs. Waring.

The first year all the dreams of a love-filled life were realized. They lived in England and on the continent; and if at times Elinor, like Jennifer Lorn, the heroine in the novel she later wrote, grew hysterical at having cut herself off from her former life, she was comforted by her love and by the fact that she was out of the trap into which she had willfully walked. She wrote some poems, tentatively, and had a little chapbook published in England unsigned. It would be years before she acknowledged this work, although some of the poems, notably "The Knight Fallen on Evil Days" and "Pegasus Lost," a strange, ironic fantasy, show the firm thought that is matched by the firmly formed line of her mature work.

In 1912 word came that Philip Hichborn had been found dead in the library of his sister's home—he had shot himself through the head. The news was deeply disturbing to Elinor. She had known her husband was emotionally unstable in his mad expression of love-hate feelings toward her, but she did not think he was deranged to the point of suicide. She learned from her mother, who managed to keep in touch with her—if only to berate her—that her little boy was being shunted back and forth between his two grandmothers, but that the Hichborn family was claiming the greater hold on him. She seems to have felt that her first-born was lost to her forever, though she saw him two or three times in the years that followed. She wanted to have a child by Horace, whom she loved, whether they were married or not, and she strove to do so, but her pregnancies miscarried. When she succeeded in giving birth to a seven-month baby son, who seemed fine in every way, he died after a week. Then another was still-born. Her inability to bear any more children was one of the sorrows of her life, although few would have suspected it. For five years she and Wylie lived together in equivocal harmony and loneliness. In 1915, when word came that Wylie's estranged wife had finally divorced him, the errant couple came home to marry.

They tried living in Georgia and in Maine, where the Hoyt family had spent the summers while Elinor was growing up at a place on Mt. Desert Island across from Bar Harbor, but neither place was right, although the latter was rewarding for Elinor in one sense. She rescued a tarnished silver pencil lying in a corner of a deserted room and polished it tenderly till the silver shone again and the slim stem felt smooth between her fingers. It seemed to her a sign that she must try to write poetry once more. It gave her the impetus to try to put into words the ecstasy and the agony she had experienced during the past five years, the bitter irony of life, and the joy she found in exquisite objects such as the silver pencil. She kept it on her desk as a symbol and source of inspiration from then on. After Maine the couple, finally married, went to Washington, where Wylie thought he might resume his practice. But Elinor discovered that even a born Hoyt was not welcome in the staid society of old Washingtonians who had not forgotten nor forgiven the scandal and sorrow she had caused. In their eyes she was responsible for Hichborn's suicide, and under such a cloud she could not return to her former position. She tried to rise above their slurs and snubs. As she wrote,

> Now why should I, who walk alone,
> Who am ironical and proud,
> Turn when a woman casts a stone
> At a beggar in a shroud?

For all her bravado, the growing poet, no longer a Hoyt, but Elinor Wylie, a name kept defiantly and used professionally till the end of her life, could not stand the silent censure of the Washingtonians. In 1919 she and Horace moved to New York. They lived in Westchester, where they had a lovely home, but life there was almost as stifling to her as in Washington. Her brother Henry and Bill Benét, both of whom had married in 1912, were by then sharing a place in the Tenth Street studios in New York City. Henry, who had served in the war from 1917 till the end, had taken up a career as painter and poet on his return. This evidently had not pleased his wife, Alice, who left him in 1919, taking their two children, Constance and Henry, with her.

Benét's wife, Teresa, a sister of the famous novelist Kathleen Norris, died in 1919, two years after the birth of their third child. Bill lived at the Press Club for a time after her death, then moved into the Tenth Street studio early in 1920. It seemed a fine arrangement all around. Elinor and the brother who had shared her early love for Shelley and poetry-making had become friends again after her long exile; and Bill, who had formed the Bennay Literary Agency, was helping both of them place their poems. In return, Henry did an etching of Bill as a Spanish grandee, reflecting Benét's Spanish ancestry.

In spite of their harmonious life-style, Henry was moody, going through alternating manic-depressive periods much like Elinor's. He was at "the crest of a creative wave," as Bill put it, dividing his energies between poetry and art. His ideas for future enterprises fired Bill with enthusiasm during their first months together—indeed they helped Benét to recover from the bereavement over Teresa's death. But during the summer of 1920 the depressive side of Henry took over. His dark moods became chronic, and in July he had a mental breakdown and entered a sanitorium for a few weeks. By August, however, he was well enough to attend the Bar Harbor wedding—a second ceremony—of his brother Morton to Tallulah Bankhead's sister, Eugenia. Elinor and Horace Wylie and the Hoyts from Washington were all there, and Connie, who had married a German baron, came from Europe with her two children. It was the last time the Hoyt family was all together.

One week later, on August 25, Elinor Wylie's sonnet "August" was published in the *New Republic,* and Henry received word that his poem "The Spell" had been accepted by *The Bookman*. It was a day that should have held bright prospects for the future but it was a day marked instead by deep despair and tragedy—Elinor's brother took his life by turning on the gas jet in the Tenth Street studio. Bill Benét found him lying on the floor dead when he came home in the evening. The studio was filled with gas fumes, but everything was in place and neat— Henry had put his papers in order before taking this fatal step he had evidently planned. When Elinor received word from Bill she was struck mute. Just as she had begun to regain the feeling of spiritual kinship she had known with her brother in childhood and adolescence, he had put himself outside the realm of the living. The loss seemed doubly great. But it would be three years before she could express her poignant grief in poetry, in the volume she called *Black Armour*, her second. For the moment she could make no statement, but when Bill arranged an exhibit of Henry's work at the Folsome Galleries in January 1921, she confided to him that she was too deeply affected by Henry's suicide to face his paintings. She met Benét outside the gallery, and Bill confessed that he felt the same way—although he had set up the memorial, he was about to leave without going in. He was alarmed by Elinor's pallor and she was trembling, he later recorded in his autobiographical narrative written in blank verse. He took her arm and led her to a nearby speakeasy. Over martinis she confided in a whisper, "I'm coming to New York. . . . I'm going to live alone."

She had discovered that marriage to the man with whom she had eloped was vastly different from being his "enchanting companion." At this early date in 1921 they had decided to separate as the first step toward divorce, though Elinor chose to keep his name since her first poems were published under it—the name was soon to become synonymous with glamor, striking beauty, brilliant wit, and fastidious, fashionable dress. For shortly after the memorial exhibit, Elinor Wylie, free for the first time in her life, came to live in New York City. Here her gifts, along with her vibrant personality and adventurous past, made her a heroine instead of an outcast.

Her instinct for elegance led her to a house that stood on the corner of University Place and Washington Square North—1 University Place, known among a select literary few as "the house with the beautiful staircase." On the first floor a large room with a high ceiling and an open fireplace was for rent. Off it was a small bedroom and a tiny kitchen. She took it at once and proceeded to furnish it in a style straight out of Edith Wharton and yet uniquely her own. She put period chairs around to match the grandeur of the former mansion, and set a large, elaborate silver mirror on the mantel, the frame overlaid with fine filigree that gave an immediate impression of quiet artistry and queenly wealth. Yet she had a limited budget and had discovered most of her objects in secondhand stores, except for a pale blue and white Wedgewood lamp, the one thing she had brought from the Hoyt household when she married Hichborn, which she had carried with her on her travels, cherishing it like a child. Old books graced the bookshelves, including an ancient copy of Shelley that she had bought at auction and the dog-eared copy she had read in her schooldays—that accompanied her wherever she went. Altogether the effect amazed the young men who came to take her to dinner shortly after she moved in.

On the floor above her lived one of the country's astute, upcoming critics of that time, Edmund Wilson. He had a sharp pen and an eye for beauty that was perhaps even sharper. He soon made himself known to Elinor and was one of those who clamored to take her out, as well as one who expressed amazement over the elegance of her ground-floor room. He described it in detail in the study of Elinor Wylie he published later in the twenties and again in his collection of critical writing, *The Shores of Light*. Soon he was taking her out, introducing her to his Round Table companions at the Algonquin Hotel, who welcomed her into their wise and witty circle at once. She became a regular, for Wilson, then on the editorial staff of *Vanity Fair*, suggested that she write for the magazine under a pseudonym, as his friend Edna Millay did, in order to pay the landlord. Elinor was grateful to "Bunny"—the nickname his familiars gave Wilson—and her life developed into a pattern of work and play suited to her psyche. She went at both with a will. "If you observe her tossing off a cocktail in the small hours with the Algonquins," wrote Elizabeth Sergeant, "you will think her perhaps just the latest celebrity." Always perfectly turned out, her lion-colored hair bobbed and shaped in a flawless Marcel wave, often wearing a silver dress, she personified the glamor of the twenties and was indeed a celebrity. In a 1977 radio

interview, Harold Clurman, theatrical producer-director, recalled that as a very young man he used to hang around the
lobby of the Algonquin hoping to catch a glimpse of "the beautiful poet, Elinor Wylie," as she passed through the lobby.
Often escorted by more than one man, "her harsh, unflurried,
unembittered laughter," as Wilson called it, rang out on her
way to the Round Table in the back room. And if there were
times when she looked like a harried woman who had known
tragedy, few ever saw her in any other light than the one she
described in a self-portrait early in her career:

> But you have a proud face
> Which the world cannot harm,
> You have turned pain to a grace
> And the scorn to a charm.
> You have taken the arrows and stings
> Which prick and bruise
> And fashioned them into wings
> For the heels of your shoes.
> What has it done, this world,
> With hard finger-tips,
> But sweetly chiseled and curled
> Your inscrutable lips.

As the last lines imply, her popularity was like a toy to her, a
gift she always had for playing. In another vein of self-
examination, she summed up her values and general attitude
toward life with vigor and eighteenth-century clarity:

> Now let no charitable hope
> Confuse my mind with images
> Of eagle and of antelope.
> I am in nature none of these.

The second stanza became famous:

> I was, being human, born alone;
> I am, being woman, hard beset;
> I live by squeezing from a stone
> The little nourishment I get.

And the third was almost as well known for its sharp thrust:

> In masks outrageous and austere
> The years go by in single file;
> But none has merited my fear,
> And none has quite escaped my smile.

If she played with the abandon of a cafe dancer, she worked with the intensity of a dedicated artist. She was living at last in the literary bohemia she had always dreamed of when in the caged society of her debutante years. On the top floor of the house at 1 University Place lived another poet, Winifred Welles, whose delicate and lovely verses had an almost uncanny psychological insight. And among the many who flocked to Elinor's ground-floor room was Bill Benét. He dissolved the Bennay Agency shortly after Henry's death and took a job as editor at the *Literary Review* (later *The Saturday Review of Literature*). He knew both Wilson and Winifred, and at one of their impromptu revelries in Elinor's elegant room he linked he names of Elinor Wylie and Winifred Welles "euphoniously in an idle rhyme like 'a ripple of bells.' " That was the way they sounded, he said.

Winifred, a native of Norwich Town, Connecticut, had published two books of poetry, *The Hesitant Heart* and *This Delicate Love*, and a delightful volume of verse for children, *Skipping Along Alone*, which was widely read by young and old alike. Winifred herself had a childlike charm. She lived quietly with her husband, Harold H. Shearer, on the top floor, but she was always ready to stop for a chat or a word of cheer if she and Elinor met as she was on her way to or from her office. She was one of the editors of *The Measure*, a magazine of verse founded by another poet, Genevieve Taggard. Through Winifred, several of Elinor Wylie's poems appeared in *The Measure*, and these gave her the impetus to keep sending out more till she had almost enough for a volume. The two poets occasionally compared notes. Elinor worked in a positive fever in whatever form she chose, and she chose to stay with the conventional rather than attempt the experimental. As evidenced in her personal appearance, precision was a passion with her. Depending on the content, she would write a ballad, an ode, a sonnet, or a finely wrought lyric, and like her silver, her poems were polished till they gleamed with perfection.

Winifred, on the other hand, confessed in a note to Benét that she "so seldom ended a poem on the spot where it began that she found her methods of piecing it together almost inexplicable." But her delicate poems had a certain strength. One of her favorites among her own poems was "The Heart of Light," which, she told Benét, described "a combination of lovely events" on Nantucket Island, where she spent her summers.

> Once, on a cliff, I saw perfection happen.
> The full, gold moon was balanced on the sea
> Just as the red sun rested on the moor.
> The summer evening ripened and fell open;
> And people walking through that fruit's rich core
> Were suddenly what they were meant to be,
> Quiet and happy, softly moving, lovely,
> With still, translucent faces and clear eyes,
> And all their heads and bodies brightly rimmed
> With delicate gold. So radiantly, so gravely,
> These people walked, so crowned, so golden-limbed,
> The cliff seemed like an edge of Paradise.*

Bill Benét of course was eager to see Elinor succeed. He was astonished and delighted at the decided skill of her technique and at the depth of her intellectual conclusions. He saw to it that some of her poems were published in the *Literary Review*, and she soon was accepted by the *Nation*, the *New Republic*, and *Poetry*. Benét found her even more fascinating now than as the girl he had known in Washington. And whereas before he had been too shy to speak, he now became one of her most ardent admirers, if not an outright suitor. Elinor put him off. She was enjoying her freedom and was too wrapped up in her writing—besides her poems, she had hurled herself headlong

* From *This Delicate Love* by Winifred Welles. Viking Press.

into creating a novel from the traumatic events of the past. At times she would shut herself up in her room, refusing to see anyone or to accept any invitations from the eager young men who wanted to take her out. Then she might decide to take a break in her unsparing labor and go out every night in the week. She was, however, more considerate of Bill Benét than of some of the others. He was a link to the lost brother she had loved, who had felt life too deeply to face its tragedy with an ironic smile and a show of bravado in some quip, as she did. The fact that Bill had been Henry's roommate made her feel closer to him than to any of the others, including Bunny Wilson—who had confessed that he was in love with Edna Millay, anyway.

In the fall of 1921, Elinor Wylie's first volume of poetry, *Nets to Catch the Wind,* was published by Harcourt, Brace. It was a signal event, not only in Elinor's life, but in the annals of poetry from the first quarter of the twentieth century. It is one of three books by women listed for 1921 in "A Short Calendar of Events in Poetry, 1900–1950" in *Poetry in Our Time* by Babette Deutsch. The reviews of this initial volume were unanimous in proclaiming that a finished artist had emerged, free of the usual fumbling one finds in a first volume. The poems sparkled with a brilliance that held in check a burning emotion, reflected a passion tempered by irony. Her metaphysical poems were compared to those of Blake and Emily Dickinson. Her descriptive poems had a tactile and auditory appeal. Nowhere was the last-mentioned more evident than in "Velvet Shoes," a masterpiece of sensory projection. One can almost feel the soft whiteness underfoot after a heavy snow, the hush of snow-silence, and see the whiteness over all:

> Let us walk in the white snow
>   In a soundless space;
> With footsteps quiet and slow,
>   At a tranquil pace,
> Under veils of white lace.

. . .

We shall walk through the still town
In a windless peace;
We shall step upon white down,
Upon silver fleece,
Upon softer than these.

We shall walk in velvet shoes:
Wherever we go
Silence will fall like the dews
On white silence below.
We shall walk in the snow.

One of the most perceptive and luminous reviews of the volume was written by Edna St. Vincent Millay, who was in Rome at the time it appeared, writing for various publications to pay for her trip abroad. She was so impressed with the poems that she not only wrote the review, published in the *New York Evening Post,* but also sent a letter of open admiration to the author of such magical poems as "The Fairy Goldsmith," "Bronze Trumpets and Sea Water," and "Velvet Shoes." It marked the beginning of a rare, responsive friendship between two brilliant, often brittle, yet passionate and compassionate spirits, who met in person as soon as Edna Millay returned to New York. As editor at *Vanity Fair,* Edmund Wilson felt it was a feather in his literary cap to introduce these two outstanding poets and personalities, both women of the hour in 1923. Edna Millay had just won the Pulitzer Prize for her latest volume, *The Harp-Weaver,* and for five sonnets published in *An American Miscellany,* the anthology edited by Amy Lowell and Louis Untermeyer. Elinor was expecting publication of her second volume, *Black Armour.* Both were beautiful in distinctive ways.

It was as if the two had always known each other. They became close friends at once, out of mutual admiration for each other's poetry, wit, and general attitude toward life—seizing the joy of the moment, facing tragedy with defiant gaiety, and acknowledging the universality of the spiritual in humankind.

There was only one subject that brought on violent verbal dis-agreement: the respective poetry and the relative suffering of Keats and Shelley, with Edna taking Keats' side, while Elinor championed "Mr. Shelley."

Elinor's devotion to Shelley was well known. It has been said that she cannot be understood without a knowledge of "her passionate cult for Shelley." Yet her poetry had little of Shelley's vagueness, and for all her devotion, she was never fooled into taking the archromantic nineteenth-century poet as her model. Edna Millay was equally zealous in spreading the word of Keats, and their lively sessions spent arguing over their respective idols became famous in poetry circles before long. The fact that they were in disagreement made no difference in their esteem for each other. Elinor and Edna argued, harried, laughed, and loved each other with literary and emotional fervor.

They compared notes on techniques and preferences in other poetry and people. Both of them had gone out with Bunny Wilson. Edna knew him as more of a lover or suitor than a friend—he had proposed to her and had not yet recovered from her refusal—while Elinor, on the other hand, regarded him as a kind friend and colleague. Both women were high-spirited, each expressing it in her own manner. Each was aware of the other's passion. The friendship did not diminish as these two came to know each other intimately. Though neither Edna Millar nor Elinor Wylie was physically strong, both gave the impression of having energy to burn, and it is true that they "burned the candle at both ends" more frequently than their frail constitutions could withstand. Edna had come back from Europe with serious intestinal problems, but only a few people knew of her illness, one of them Elinor Wylie. When Elinor suffered nervous exhaustion after finishing a sheaf of poems, it was Edna Millay who understood and tried to help her with silent sympathy.

Elinor spent the summers of 1922 and 1923 at the Mac-Dowell Colony in New Hampshire, where she actually worked very hard on her novel, turning out 1000 words a day, she reported to Bill. Her glamorous presence was enough to give rise to a series of anecdotes that made her a legendary figure whose ghost is still said to haunt the bedroom she slept in at the Eaves, a pre-Revolutionary farmhouse that housed the Colonists at night. It was later marked with a brass plate—"The Elinor Wylie Room." Judging from her letters to Bill Benét, Horace Wylie, and others, it is doubtful that her stays at the MacDowell Colony were eventful in such a way as to cause her to haunt the place. To her it was mostly a location for concentrated writing.

In 1923 both Elinor and Edna married. They married men who were stable, solicitous for the health of their wives, and understanding of a poet's need for privacy and periods of solitude, followed by a round of gatherings in congenial company or travel to a different scene of inspiration. Elinor, now that her career as a poet was established, and while she was in the midst of completing her first novel, finally acceded to the persistent wooing of Bill Benét. He was affectionate, dependable, and himself a literary figure of note. The name of William Rose Benét—in fact, of all the Benéts—his brother, Stephen Vincent, and his sister, Laura—would be an open sesame to publication doors.

Bill had been pelting her with ardent love letters. It is evident in correspondence acquired by the University of Virginia as recently as 1979 that Elinor reinforced his sentiments with her own tender, if ambivalent feelings. (Until these letters came to light, presumably through Bill's sister, Laura, it was thought that Elinor had not responded to his pleas, or that the letters had been burned.) In the midst of their plans, while decorators were working on the apartment they leased at 142 East Eighteenth Street and as Elinor was correcting proofs for her novel, tragedy struck the Hoyt family once more. Word came from Germany that Connie, the sister Elinor had once been close to, had committed suicide in some bizarre way after a broken love affair. Both Connie and her husband had condemned Elinor's action in eloping with Horace Wylie, yet Connie did not have the courage to defy convention when she fell in love. The whole affair was mysterious. Whatever emotion Elinor felt, the latest suicide did not prevent her from carrying out her wedding plans with Bill as soon as her divorce from Wylie was definite.

The marriage took place on October 5, 1923, at a friend's apartment on West Fifty-sixth Street. The families of both bride and groom stayed away. Elinor's mother was grieving over Connie's death, and the Benéts, particularly Bill's father, were leery about the success of the match. It was a quiet wedding but a delightful one. The best man was Franklin P. Adams (F.P.A.), and the maid of honor, Esther Root, both close friends of Edna Millay's. Edna had married Eugen Boissevain in July 1923 just before going into the hospital for a serious operation, and was only now recovering. Elinor's and Edna's friendship was, if anything, strengthened by their marriages. The two couples, with Arthur Davison Ficke—the poet who first and last held Edna's heart—and his second wife, Gladys, a painter, were often together in one or the other's place below Twenty-third Street. Elinor and Bill bought a house in New Canaan but kept an apartment in New York. It is fair to say that Elinor Wylie and Edna Millay were both fond of their husbands but not deeply in love. They were perhaps fonder of themselves and each other than of anyone else.

For Elinor this was a time of satisfaction. She grew more sure of her gift every day. One letter that gave her great confidence in the validity of her style came from Amy Lowell, who, since the end of the war had ceased her own defensive battle for Imagism, *vers libre,* or even the new poetry and now dwelt more on the freedom of the individual poet to express a thought or mood in the manner or mode best suited to it. She wrote, in part, "Were you to put any of these poems into cadenced verse they would lose at least half their value." Elinor answered her at once, beginning her note, "I must thank you with all my heart for your letter." Elinor did not object to Lowell's experiments as

many in the Poetry Society did, and she understood, more than
most, Amy's driving need for repeated recognition of her
poetry and her life pattern.

Among other comments that pleased her was that Elinor
Wylie had, like Athena, sprung in her "black armour" from the
head of a god. The reference was to her second volume, entitled
Black Armour, which displayed the same intellectual brilliance
as the first, this time tempered by a more discernible warmth.
In a review of *Nets to Catch the Wind,* Louis Untermeyer had
spoken of the "frigid ecstasy" Wylie's poems achieved. Although he did not find emotion absent from her lines, it seemed
"a passion frozen at its source." Elinor had been furious at the
implication that she was cold, and she voiced her objection
openly one day when she was scheduled to read at a hotel
luncheon together with two competent minor poets: Leonora
Speyer, who had just published *Canopic Jar,* and Jean Starr Untermeyer, who had just finished her second volume, *Dreams
Out of Darkness.* Elinor confronted Jean in the lobby of the
Biltmore with the accusation, "Your husband has reviewed my
book, and called me cold—Me, ME, who have lost two who
were dear to me!" Her voice rose. As usual, she looked the
picture of an exquisitely beautiful poet, but her almost un-
earthly beauty, like that of her beloved Shelley, was marred by a
high, shrill voice uttering close to a shriek of hysteria that was
especially characteristic of her when she was angry. Without
giving Jean a chance to reply, she then hurried away to send Bill
out in the rain to get a copy of her book, which she had forgotten. Jean, who had no understanding of Elinor Wylie's high-
strung nature or of the tragic events that had left deep scars of
psychic shock from which she never recovered, remarked in her
memoirs that, although she admired Wylie's poems, she could
not accept her "narcissism."

However, that narcissism was part of the "black armour"
that shielded Elinor Wylie from any more blows. And in her
new volume her sharpness was shown against a mellower mood
and a greater maturity. Here was the searing self-portrait and

the fanciful "Escape," with its indicative lead-in stanza: "When foxes eat the last gold grape,/And the last white antelope is killed,/I shall stop fighting and escape/Into a little house I'll build." In the "Puritan Sonnet" she proclaims: "Down to the Puritan marrow of my bones/There's something in this richness that I hate./I love the look, austere, immaculate,/Of landscapes drawn in pearly monotones." There were those that might think this a pose on her part; but it reflected the conflict between the material and the spiritual, between the finery she loved to wear and the sterner metaphysics of the mind that made her such a rare, indomitable person, adored by men, particularly by Benét. He congratulated himself on his good fortune in being married to such a gifted, beautiful creature and was ready to forgive her faults and petty foibles, her apparent narcissism and her nervous attacks.

When she felt she had to be by herself to work, she took herself off to England. Bill did not object, although some of his friends thought it showed lack of consideration for her husband. She was striving to complete her third volume and a second novel, but she still suffered public censure for her past life. The League of American Penwomen, which had invited Edna Millay to be the guest of honor at a gathering of writers, condemned Elinor for her personal life by withdrawing the invitation that she also had received. Millay's immediate reaction, although she had intended to accept the invitation, was to decline in a letter of withering scorn. She could not be the guest of honor, since the organization placed the circumstances of one's personal life above literary accomplishment. In that case she, too, was "eligible for their disesteem" and wished to be struck from their lists to share with Elinor Wylie a "brilliant exile from their fusty province." Her letter pointed up the loyalty and admiration she felt toward Wylie.

The poems in *Trivial Breath,* which Elinor was in process of compiling, are evidence of the creative genius that the League of Penwomen was rejecting for narrow-minded and irrelevant reasons. Many of the poems in this third volume were written

in England, where the ostracized poet went during 1927 to find
solace near the birth site of Shelley, on whom her third novel,
Orphan Angel, was based. She planned to see the publishing
house Heineman about a British edition, and she wanted to
study the manuscript writings of John Donne as source material
for her own metaphysical expression. Unexpectedly, she was
lionized by the literary and social aristocracy, who were far
more taken with her fantasy of Shelley than they had been by
poor Amy Lowell's painstakingly factual biography of Keats.
Instead of being assailed by critics for the liberties she took,
Elinor was praised by the London *Times* and the leading literary
reviewers for having captured the romantic personality of Shelley. Aldous Huxley, Cecil Beaton, the Sitwells, Llewellyn Powys
and his wife—to whom Edna Millay had sent a letter of
introduction—even Leonard and Virginia Woolf, who were not
pleased by her novel or the poet herself, sought her out, giving
her the attention due a celebrity. She was entertained at great
houses—Formosa, Wiltshire Manor, the Daye House, and
Rotherfield Greys, a fifteenth-century stone structure that was
the family seat of Henry de-Clifford Woodhouse and his wife,
Becky. It was at the last that Elinor became involved once again
with a married man. In what was more of an infatuation than an
affair, she fell madly in love with "Cliff" Woodhouse, making
no effort to keep it a secret from her English friends. But she
gave no hint of it to Bill in her letters, and with good reason: the
love, as such, was almost entirely on Elinor's part. Her friends
thought her completely mad, but she nevertheless arranged to
lease a house on the Woodhouses' land and the following summer returned to England.

One Sunday toward evening, as she was coming down the
ancient stone staircase to join the others for tea, she had a fainting spell and fell down the last seven steps. Though she picked
herself up at once, looking around to be sure no one saw her
fall, then making her way to the garden, she was in great pain.
She knew she had suffered serious injury but said nothing to
the others. When she got back to the apartment she was staying

in temporarily, she called a doctor, who found that she had fractured her spine. She was in bed a month during the hottest July England had known in years. She did not write Bill of the accident, since he was coming over at the end of July and she was sure she would be well by then. The Woodhouses could not help learning what had happened and were full of courteous remorse, but, to Clifford especially, her suffering was more of an awkward embarrassment than a cause for concern. Even Elinor's mother could not pay much attention to her just then—the specter of suicide had once again raised its head in the Hoyt family. Morton, who had been divorced from Eugenia Bank-head for the second time, threatened to kill himself if she would not marry him again and in July jumped off the steamship *Rochambeau* in midocean. Only by the quick action of the crew was he rescued from drowning. The story was played up in the papers, which emphasized the history of suicide in the Hoyt family. Few people knew of Elinor's accident. When news of it finally reached America, the papers capitalized on her past history and drew a connection with Morton's suicide attempt. Several reported that she had hurled herself down five flights of stairs. She was furious, and Bill was frantic.

He came hurrying over to England, where he learned the truth, including the fact that Elinor was in love with the man in whose house the accident had occurred. It was a bizarre situation, but Benét's devotion was such that he wanted the marriage to continue, if only on a companionate basis. Elinor was recovering, but the doctors warned her that she must rest a lot and stop drinking and smoking or be prepared for dire consequences. Elinor was well aware that she was taking chances—her blood pressure had been high for years—but she had begun to write a series of sonnets inspired by her latest love and could not stop herself from working at a high pitch. She was involved in a change in her poetry and in her love life, which demanded expression.

On her return she confided in Edna Millay. They were

alone, and Elinor, her eyes harrowed with anxiety, suddenly buried her face in her hands. It was so unlike her that Edna was startled, scarcely knowing what to do. She was torn between the desire to comfort her friend and the effort to keep from breaking down herself. She did not even stroke the other's bowed head, but maintained a sympathetic silence until Elinor's mood passed and she brought her body upright with a crisp remark about her momentary weakness. Later Edna wrote "Song for a Lute," expressing her deep anguish for the poet she revered, the friend whose life she feared for, "loving her utterly" as she did. Elinor was touched but silent. Edna was inclined to idolize those she loved, and Wylie accepted the worship, but she could not return it in full measure.

Trivial Breath appeared in 1928. A slim volume, it was indicative of the study Elinor Wylie had made of her own lines in relation to those of the metaphysicians like John Donne. In "Minotaur," she admonished herself: "Go study to disdain/The frail, the overfine/That tapers to a line/Knotted about the brain." The richly embroidered fabric of descriptive words that marked her first two volumes was being altered by a different weave, one of greater reverence for the spirit. In "Full Moon" she cried out,

> My bands of silk and miniver
> Momently grew heavier;
> The black gauze was beggarly thin;
> The ermine muffled mouth and chin;
> I could not suck the moonlight in.
>
> . . .
>
> There I walked, and there I raged;
> The spiritual savage caged
> Within my skeleton, raged afresh
> To feel, behind a carnal mesh,
> The clean bones crying in the flesh.

The critics agreed that her poetry burned with more of Shelley's fiery glow, but it also revealed a greater depth from spiritual truths discovered in John Donne. And the trend was to continue, culminating in a mysticism that was distinctly hers.

She went to England again in 1928. When she returned the doctors warned her once more that she had to change her habits—the consequences could be fatal. But she would not heed the warnings. Even when she had a slight stroke that left a facial paralysis for a time, she would not give in. She played as hard as she worked. There was one weekend of high revelry when the noted columnist F.P.A. was married to Esther "Tess" Root, the two who had stood up for the Benéts. Elinor and Bill Benét attended with Edna Millay and her husband and Arthur Ficke and his wife. They consumed "gallons of champagne," and afterwards the three couples spent Saturday night and Sunday at the Benét house in New Canaan, where they continued to celebrate. No one seeing Elinor that weekend, unless aware of her condition, would have believed that she had not long to live.

After another short trip to England, Elinor came back in late fall to prepare her fourth volume of poems for the press. She had been working intensely, had just completed a new "Birthday Sonnet" full of portent, and had also finished preparing her new book, significantly entitled *Angels and Earthly Creatures* (taken from John Donne). On Sunday, December 16, she and Bill were spending a quiet day for a change. Late in the afternoon, she was reading in her novel, *Jennifer Lorn*. Near dusk she closed the book with a bang, saying in her decisive way, "Yes, *Jennifer* is better than *The Venetian Glass Nephew!*" (her second novel, written in 1925), and she decided to start supper. Only a few minutes later, Bill heard her calling from the kitchen. When he rushed to her, he found her fainting. She wanted a glass of water, and as he gave it to her, she murmured, "Is that all it is?" He carried her to the bedroom, where she lingered only a short while before she died. For Bill, Edna Millay, Bunny Wilson, and those who had been close to her, it was as if a beautiful light had suddenly gone out of the world.

Shortly before she'd returned from England, Bill had walked
past the house at 1 University Place, which was empty, waiting
to be razed—it had been sold and was soon to be replaced by a
tall apartment building. He had written a poem, "Inscription
for a Mirror in a Deserted Dwelling," as a reflection of Elinor
and the life in that house during the days she lived there. She
and everyone who saw it, especially Winifred Welles and Wilson, had appreciated the poem, which immortalized the silver-
framed mantel mirror: "For you around the glass I trace/This
secret writing, that will burn/Like witch-fire should her shade
return/To haunt you with that wistful face." Now, a short time
later, he wrote a memorial poem—in truth, a tribute to her as
she lived in his memory. It was a brief poem, written out of
grief, called "Sagacity." It began,

> We knew so much; when her beautiful eyes could lighten,
> Her beautiful laughter follow our phrase;
> Or the gaze go hard with pain, the lips tighten,
> On the bitterer days.

A sigh of sorrow followed:

> Oh, ours was all knowing then, all generous displaying.
> Such wisdom we had to show!
> And now there is merely silence, silence, silence saying
> All we did not know.

Edna Millay heard the sad news the night after Elinor's
death. When she could bring herself to write to "Dearest Bill,"
she spoke of their "beautiful, brilliant adorable one," and bade
him remember how delightful Elinor was—so "gay and splendid about tragic things, so comically serious about silly ones."
Her later sonnet to Elinor opened in ecstatic exclamation: "Oh,
she was beautiful in every part!"

Angels and Earthly Creatures was published posthumously
in 1929. Hailed by the critics as Elinor Wylie's finest work, it

combined all her gifts: the keen, cutting comment, the balanced, synchronized syllables, and the subjective love for fine objects—filigreed silver, frail, delicately colored porcelains, and "pearly monotones." But in this final volume they are raised to heights above earthly concerns. Here the personal mysticism revealed in *Trivial Breath* reached its peak. In lyrics like, "Oh, Virtuous Light," "Hymn to Earth," and "This Corruptible," the poet is both visionary and philosophic. The last, a three-way discourse by the Mind, the Heart, and the Soul on the subject of the Body's dissolution, displays both compassion and insight; it is memorable for stanzas in which the Spirit speaks endearingly to the Body:

> O lodging for the night!
> O house of my delight!
> O lovely hovel builded for my pleasure!
> Dear tenement of clay
> Endure another day
> As coffin sweetly fitted to my measure

The Body alone "shall escape/In some enchanting shape . . ." The others are captive to the purpose they serve. The wise Spirit concludes in tender but chilling truth:

> " 'Tis you who are the ghost,
> Disintegrated, lost;
> The burden shed; the dead who need not bear it;
> O grain of God in power,
> Endure another hour!
> It is but for an hour," said the spirit.

A sonnet sequence, "One Person," portrays a tragic passion with a spontaneity close to abandonment; the reader may guess whether or not it is the poet's story. Her stern, prophetic "Birthday Sonnet," written as it was the day before she died, might be called Epitaph for a Penitent—it is almost a plea for death and absolution. "Take home thy prodigal child, O Lord of Hosts!" it opens, and the sestet implores,

Instruct her strictly to preserve Thy gift
And alter not its grain in atom's sort;
Angels may wed her to their ultimate hurt
And men embrace a specter in a shift
So that no drop of the pure spirit fall
Into the dust: defend Thy prodigal.

Her stature as a peer figure in the forefront of modern
American women poets needs no defense.

6

H.D.

OF all those who called themselves Imagists, the American-born "H.D." was the most consistent, and simon-pure in her poetry. Her life story is strange, neurotic, even bizarre; but her work has the serenity of the classical scholar, and she remained true to the Imagist principles longer than any of the early proponents of the movement. Harriet Monroe deemed her "at once the most civilized and the wildest of poets." Her birthplace was Bethlehem, Pennsylvania; her birth date, September 10, 1884. She was the daughter of Charles L. Doolittle, professor of mathematics and astronomy at Lehigh University, and his second wife, Helen Eugenia Doolittle née Wolle.

"Church Street was our street," H.D. once wrote, "the Church was our Church. It was founded by Count Zinzendorf who named our town Bethlehem." As a small child, she would explain, "But Jesus was not born *here*." Other children laughed at her seriousness, her naiveté. But in her mind there was always a spiritual link between her birthplace and the little town of Bethlehem that gave rise to the "Christian myth" of immaculate conception, as Freud later referred to it in one of his talks with H.D. The "H" stood for Hilda, a name that, combined with Doolittle, was enough to make any poet use her initials as a pen name.

When she was nine years old, the family moved to Philadelphia, where her father was director of Flower Astronomical Observatory at the University of Pennsylvania. Hilda went to the Friends Central School and to Bryn Mawr College. She had to leave college in her sophomore year because of illness, but one meaningful and enduring benefit of those years was her instant friendship with Marianne Moore, who was one of her classmates. Both wrote for the undergraduate publication, but Marianne was elected to the board, while Hilda was hardly known to campus editors before she had to leave.

Forced to stop her schooling, Hilda concentrated on writing. Her first published pieces were short stories for children in a Sunday school paper, but she turned out poems for her own gratification, some of them translations from the Greek, which she occasionally showed to a former young student of her father's—one Ezra Pound—who made no secret of the fact that he wrote poetry. She had known him before she went to Bryn Mawr.

After classes ended, Ezra often came out to the observatory in nearby Upper Darby, where the family lived. The rolling, lightly wooded countryside was ideal for long leisurely walks spent spouting poetry to a beautiful girl who listened to him and confided to him her own talent. So enchanted was Ezra Pound with Professor Doolittle's youngest child that he brought his friend William Carlos "Bill" Williams out to meet her. Williams was then a young medical student at Penn, living in the same dormitory as Pound. He also secretly wrote poetry, a fact he entrusted to "Ez," after the latter had regaled him with dramatic renditions of his own early efforts. Bill was not as enchanted by Hilda's beauty, which he found bizarre, though real enough as far as her facial features were concerned. But she was so tall and angular, flat-chested, hipless, and careless in her dress—loose-fitting long skirts and droopy blouses were her favorite clothes. She seemed indifferent to everything except matters of the mind and spirit. Yet she was friendly in a detached kind of way, and, although Williams thought Ezra had "exaggerated her beauty ridiculously," he too was fascinated by Hilda Doolittle and by the household.

Hilda's father, whom she resembled, a tall gaunt old man whose steel-gray eyes seemed fixed on the stars, was remote as the moon or the stars themselves from the hubbub around him as he presided at the head of the table during meals. He was noted for his precise measurements of the earth's oscillation on its axis and indeed focussed his full attention on the study. Hilda's mother, much younger than Dr. Doolittle and an intelligent, understanding woman talented in painting and music, knew by certain signs when her husband was ready to talk. At such a moment she "would silence everyone with a look," and then he would expound on whatever subject was on his mind, staring above the heads of those around him until his say was done. The young people at the table would wait decorously to make sure that was the end, then continue their chatter, as if he had not spoken. But he didn't seem to care or even notice.

Hilda, though she was like her father intellectually as well as physically, never bothered to pay deference to him as a scholar—or to anyone else, for that matter. Her very indifference, expressed by a shrug of her shoulders and a gently mocking smile, was part of her attraction for college students like Ezra and his friend Bill. They certainly did not make the trek by trolley out to the observatory just to look through a telescope, judging from Williams' account.

Hilda was fond of them both, but in love with neither. She was enthralled by Ezra's enthusiasm and inventive ideas for poetry, but she was not as enamored of him as he was of her—or claimed he was. She was amused by his theatricality, his dramatic protests of love, and by his undisguised jealousy of Bill when the latter began to appear at the observatory alone and asked her to go out with him. On one occasion, after they had attended a Mask and Wig tryout and dance at the university, he spent the night at their house, for which he got dark angry looks from Ezra, Williams reported to Hilda. Both of them, Bill especially, did their best to convince Ezra they were not in love. "For God's sake," Bill told him bluntly. "I'm not in love with Hilda, nor she with me. She's your girl and I know it. Don't be an ass!" Williams thought her a sort of wild creature, with her disregard for convention, her breathless way of speaking, and sudden bursts of laughter. Also, when it came to serious talk about literature, she was "a good guy," by whom he was both irritated and entertained. For her part, when she thought about Bill Williams at all, she considered him a rough diamond.

One April day when he showed up by himself she asked him if he wanted to go for a walk. So they started across the fields, ignoring the cloudy skies of spring. Williams spotted some deep blue flowers growing in a gully and wondered aloud what they could be.

"Grape hyacinths," Hilda said absently. She went on to tell him she was studying Greek—at Ezra's suggestion—to aid her in poetry writing. She had also heard that he, Bill, was writing poetry, too. He felt betrayed and angry—he should have known Ezra couldn't keep a secret. He didn't want to talk about his efforts because to his mind he hadn't produced anything to speak of. So he kept silent. Hilda, trying to encourage him, admitted that she had been attempting to write poetry for years, adding, by way of atonement, "Some are translations." But it was no help. They wandered silently along through deep grasses, "popping" fences, some of barbed wire. The back of Hilda's skirt was dragging, but if it caught and went up as she jumped down she didn't care. Edmondson, one of their friends, told Bill after a group walk once that "a fellow can't help but look sometimes!"

The clouds grew threatening, and Bill suggested that they turn back, but he might as well have been addressing the air.

Hilda only wanted to know if he had to have his desk neat and orderly when he started writing, if he prepared his materials or simply sat down and wrote. He told her he liked things neat, which was another laugh. Hardly hearing him, she told him it was a great help to her before writing to dip the nib of her pen in the ink bottle and splash a few blots on her blouse—it gave her "a feeling of freedom and indifference toward the mere means of writing." Bill saw that she was serious, so he agreed it was fine—if one liked it.

His words were nearly smothered by thunderclaps—there was going to be a downpour "damned soon," but Hilda made no move to leave the open pasture where the wind was lashing their faces and head for shelter under a tree as Bill would have. She probably knew, as he apparently did not, that trees serve as a ground for lightning, to be avoided during a storm unless one wishes to be electrocuted. She sat down in the grass at the edge of a slope and spread wide her arms. "Come, beautiful rain," she cried, turning her face up toward the sky. "Beautiful rain, welcome!"

Bill was not inclined to join in her ecstatic mood, but he sat down right behind her. "And let me tell you it rained, plenty," he wrote long afterward. "It didn't improve her beauty or my opinion of her—but I had to admire her if that's what she wanted." There was no doubt about it. For all her seriousness, Hilda was a creature of impulse, moved to recklessness by the elements. A year or so later, in June of 1906, a group that included her and Ezra and Bill received an invitation from Bob Lamberton, a friend who had played tackle on the varsity football team at Penn. They were to spend the day at Point Pleasant, New Jersey, where his family owned a summer place. When Hilda arrived, most of the party were there already and had gone for a swim. She quickly climbed into her clumsy bathing clothes and went to the beach to join them. She was hailed with shouts of welcome from her friends, most of whom were lolling on the sand. There had been a storm, and heavy, overpowering breakers were pounding in. Hilda, entranced at the sight, hardly waved back at the others. They saw her walk right out to meet the huge, oncoming breakers without waiting for the proper moment. She probably wasn't used to ocean bathing; she didn't know what was happening. The first wave knocked her down, and before she could rise, the second had rolled her into the treacherous undertow. If Lamberton had not been there and powerful enough to rescue her from the strong pull of the sea, it might have been the end. She was unconscious when they dragged her out. They resuscitated her and carried her up to the house to rest.

When Bill Williams, who arrived late since he was just starting his internship and couldn't leave the hospital, asked "Where's Hilda?" they regaled him with an account of the accident. By then she had begun to feel better, and after Bill examined her to make sure no serious damage was done, she joined the party again. A second storm broke an hour or so afterward. They all crowded into the pavilion with a variety of bathers from the beach. Hailstones as big as half dollars rained down, and a second narrow escape occurred, especially for Williams. He was standing with a billiard cue in his hand, "butt end on the floor," when a bolt of lightning hit the building, splintering the flagpole on the roof above their heads. Bill saw the streak go by him and out the door, and an electric shock like a slap shook the back of his neck, the wrist of the hand holding the cue, and the ankle on that side. A fat lady standing in front of him fell flat on her back. No doubt some people shrieked, but his own reaction was to laugh—a sense of catastrophe averted, as he said—and with it came relief. It had happened in a split second, and was over almost before it occurred—or before they knew it had, with the crash of the flagpole telling them that they had all had a narrow escape.

Like most summer showers, the storm passed, and the sun came out for the second time that day. After it had set, they all went canoeing on the river and sang songs that proved to be farewells. They never met as a group again, for the following year none of them were at the university. The party had been a graduation celebration, and most of Hilda's intimates went off to follow their calling. Ezra went to teach at a small college in Indiana, and Bill set up practice as a pediatrician in Rutherford, New Jersey, a profession he followed for forty-two years and which became an integral part of his creative output in poetry and prose. It would be years before Hilda saw him again, but she kept in close contact with Ezra and sometimes went to see his mother at Wyncotte, a suburb of Philadelphia. During his college years, the group had had an occasional party there, at times standing around the upright piano and singing loudly but not well to Mrs. Pound's playing. After the group broke up, Marianne Moore became a mainstay for Hilda in literary matters.

The Doolittles did not harass their younger daughter into completing her college education when she recovered her health. They did encourage her to go on with her writing. In 1911, she went to Europe for the summer—or so she planned when she left. As it turned out, she never came back except for a visit. Ezra Pound had gone to London in 1909, and had there quickly made a reputation for himself among the avant-garde literary lights. At a poetry meeting to which he invited Hilda toward the end of her stay, she was so captivated by his and T. E. Hulme's ideas that she was soon drawn into their "movement," based on ancient biblical and classical sources, as well as the modern French symbolism. Just as she had been fascinated by Greek and the poetry of Sappho, she was excited by Ezra's enthusiastic presentation of Imagisme, as he called it. She joined forces with the group, which included Richard Aldington, who altered her life.

Aldington was then a young poet, earnest, scholarly, kind, and attractive. Hilda Doolittle was to him young, extremely earnest, even other-worldly and beautiful. She had the classic beauty of a Helen, he thought, except that her aquiline features were delicate, her coloring blonde. With her deepset gray eyes and tall, reedy figure, she looked, and was, every inch a poet. High strung, hypersensitive, easily excited, she spoke in brief, explosive, rare sentences; her high-pitched vibrant voice, tinged with nervous tension, revealed the ardor beneath her classic appearance. When she discovered that Aldington had more than a passing interest in Greek poetry, the bond between them as Imagists was strengthened. With him she began translating the Greek poets, a project that influenced her poetry in subject matter and style, leaving an indelible stamp on her work.

As the two pored over their translations, in addition to their own creative efforts, they drew closer together, and, as might be expected, fell in love. Pound, although about the same age as they, looked on the romance with paternal approval since his crush on Hilda was over. He was their mentor, the self-appointed leader of the group. As such he took a personal interest in the lives of his followers. He was especially pleased with Hilda's progress as a poet, and, with her consent, sent several of her poems to Harriet Monroe for possible publication in *Poetry*. It was at that point that the Bethlehem-born poet decided to use her initials, adding, for Ezra's benefit, the word *Imagiste,* which lent an air of mystery and served as a testimonial for the kind of poetry he was promoting at the moment. To her vast surprise, Harriet Monroe accepted the poems and published them in 1913. It was cause for celebration. At Aldington's ardent insistence, they had an engagement party, the two young poets announcing their intention to marry very soon.

They were a radiant young couple when Amy Lowell arrived on the scene, in particular full of enthusiasm for the poems of H.D., with which she had identified her own early efforts. Happy to learn that those initials stood for a poet of her own sex and an American, Amy adopted a maternal attitude toward H.D., which she extended to Richard Aldington as well. Both of them looked to her for support against the dictates of Pound, who tended to take the making or revision of a poem into his own hands and expected the poet whose work it was to accept the results without question. Amy, as eager and willing to learn as she was in 1913, did not hesitate to ask the whys and wherefores of Pound's corrections or to express a doubt if she felt like it. And she was formidable enough in appearance to command his attention. If either H.D. or Aldington suspected that Amy Lowell's self-assurance was a false front to disguise her inner insecurities, they did not show it, and both of them were grateful for her protective, hearty approval of their ideas and her open admiration of their talents. They were married soon after her return to the United States, and the voluminous correspondence they kept up with her, together and separately, began that fall. In the Houghton Library at Harvard there are over a hundred letters from H.D. and Aldington, fifty-seven from H.D. alone, in the Lowell files.

Together with her husband, H.D. began translating Greek poets in earnest, with the idea of publishing a volume. Both wrote on their own, poetry and prose, managing to eke out a bare living that had to be bolstered occasionally by a check from H.D.'s parents, who, though far from wealthy, were in sympathy with their daughter's hopes of becoming a recognized poet. When Amy, now with Ada, came to London the following summer, she called the Aldingtons before she got in touch with Ezra Pound. They regaled her with the latest news and complaints against the erratic leader, who was devoting more time to a new group, the Vorticists, than to the Imagists, they said. Amy invited them to come to the Berkeley Hotel where she was staying, and they would plan a strategy. She wanted them to meet Ada anyway.

H.D. and Richard went right over. Both loved Ada, as most people did, accepting her at once as Amy's mate and a member of the Imagist circle. Amy's plan was to try to unite the forces of the newly found group with theirs, which would increase the strength of both. H.D. doubted that Pound would cooperate, but he gladly introduced Amy to the Vorticist leaders, inviting her and Ada to join them at one of their dinner meetings in the

Dieudonne, a French restaurant in London's Soho. The Vorticists wanted to take in all the arts in their revolt against convention and gave little time to poets in their discussions. Amy was
not able to get very far with her proposal, but she reciprocated
Pound's invitation by giving a dinner at the same place to mark
the publication of *Des Imagistes,* the anthology Pound had succeeded in bringing out. Hardly more than a chapbook, it was
still an achievement to get into print as a collective voice. H.D.,
as well as Amy—they were the only women represented—felt
the importance of the event.

Ezra Pound, however, seemed bent on minimizing, even
ridiculing the significance of the movement. A complimentary
copy of the slim volume was at everyone's place as a souvenir of
the occasion from the hostess. H.D., like the rest, checked her
own poems first for errors and then examined the others. Besides herself and Richard, there were poems by James Joyce;
Ford Madox Hueffer—later "Ford"; F. S. Flint; John Gould
Fletcher; Amy Lowell; and of course a number by the poet-
editor himself, Ezra Pound. Fletcher started handing his copy
around for everyone to sign, and with that they were all busy
autographing each other's books, congratulating Amy for the
idea of a celebration dinner with furnished copies of the book.
But when, over coffee and liqueurs, she attempted to get down
to a serious discussion of Imagisme, Pound saw to it that she
did not assume any leadership while he was around. He rebuf-
fed her efforts with ill-bred jocularity. In answer to her question
about a precise formula for Imagisme, which she thought might
be prepared for the next issue, Pound left the table and came
back in a few minutes wearing an ancient tin tub on his head in
caricature of a helmet of some knight-errant. He produced
hilarious laughter, in which Amy joined, but hers was a harsh,
hurt laugh.

H.D. alone did not laugh at all. To her, poetry was a sacred,
if difficult, all-consuming art form, whatever rules one followed
(or broke) in creating one's own poems. She was angry at
Pound, indignant at his obvious denigration of Amy. True, if it

had not been for Ezra's energetic efforts and successful promo-
tion there would have been no anthology to celebrate—they
were all obligated to him—but H.D. objected to his exploitation
of that sense of obligation to extend and maintain his power
over them. An early feminist, whether she declared it or not,
she resented the power men took for granted over women as a
right of their sex. As much as she looked to others for advice
and material support, H.D. had an independent spirit that was
to see her through many trials.

When she had to choose between Amy Lowell and Ezra
Pound as the future spokesman for Imagisme, H.D. did not
hesitate to support her sister-poet, nor did her husband. Both
the Aldingtons were genuinely fond of Amy. They enjoyed her
company, the excitement she engendered with her flamboyant
life-style, her cigar-smoking, the "vivacious intelligence," as
Richard called it, of the running conversation she skillfully kept
going at her dinner parties. They were both enthusiastic about
her idea for a cooperative volume of the group's poetry as the
next venture. Each poet, in Amy's outline of the project, was to
make selections individually, and a committee would pass on
them. The equal profit-sharing was most appealing: Aldington
had taken a job as editor of the *Egoist,* a little magazine that paid
a minimal salary, and the pittance they both earned from writing poetry or an occasional book review was even less.

After Amy went back to Brookline the Aldingtons wrote to
her nearly every week, asking advice, complaining about how
difficult Pound was being. Amy had sent him a prospectus of
her plan for the cooperative venture while she was still in England. He sent a reply to her at the Berkeley, saying that although
he might sanction such a volume, he would insist that he—
Pound—have no part in selecting the contents. He couldn't see
"being saddled with a dam'd contentious, probably incompe-
tent committee," and so on. If they wanted to form a separate
group, he thought it might be done "amicably," yet he himself
was not exactly amicable in attitude. His real grievance was that
the whole project would deprive him of selecting and promot-

ing the work of stray poets, and for all his talk, he would not relinquish his hold on the group. H.D., who was on the committee, found him trying in the extreme. He was involved with the Vorticists, yet he still wanted to be the titular head of the Imagists. He objected to the anglicized version of the name, for example, and generally made life miserable for H.D. with his meddling.

As the war in Europe accelerated, more and more British troops were sent to France, and Richard Aldington joined the forces some time in 1915. Their marriage was beginning to falter—early in 1915, Hilda had given birth to a stillborn child, which somehow caused a rift between them. H.D. took over his editorship of the *Egoist,* and she took advantage of the opportunity to publish poems by the friends whose poetry she felt should be recognized. One of the first was a lyric by Marianne Moore. Pound was so impressed with the caliber of Miss Moore's work that he asked H.D. for several of her poems. He wanted to send them to Harriet Monroe for publication in *Poetry.* Four were accepted, and H.D. was delighted. She felt that as editor of the *Egoist* she had launched a new star and a close friend on a significant career. She soon became known as one of the leaders among the Imagist poets, a designation she considered no more than her due, though at the same time an honor. In her letters to Amy Lowell, as much as she complained about the meagerness of her own output and the slow process by which she arrived at a completed poem, she felt free to give advice on policy matters. When the question of changing the title of the second anthology came up, she quickly suggested *The Six,* counting herself among the six important innovative figures.

At around this time she met the woman who was to loom large in her letters from 1915 on, to become an integral part of her life and life-style. This was Winifred Ellerman, better known as "Bryher," the pen name she took from one of the Scilly Isles off the coast of Cornwall, where she had often spent her holidays from school. Eight years younger than H.D., she was the daughter of Sir John Ellerman, a wealthy shipping magnate, and his wife, Hannah, who was completely domi- nated by both her husband and daughter. Bryher was brilliant, dark-haired, with a Dutch bang covering her forehead, and penetrating blue eyes peering from beneath. She was short and delicately built—the "perfect foil for H.D.," as Jean Starr Un- termeyer wrote. The English writer was reserved, but never shy, as Jean mistakenly supposed. She had been taken abroad a good deal as a child, on frequent trips to Switzerland, France, Italy, and Egypt. She was an innocent-looking sophisticate who knew what she wanted. Usually she got it.

She had been forced to give up her study of archeology by the war, and she began to write book reviews and literary arti- cles. One of her editors was Clement Shorter of *Sphere*, who, in opposition to Lytton Strachey's sarcastically destructive esti- mate of Amy Lowell's *Six French Poets*, had written a highly favorable review of the book. This sent Bryher to the bookstore for a copy, which she read with great interest and admiration. It led her to the Imagist movement and H.D., who accepted some of Bryher's reviews for the *Egoist*. Bryher helped to keep the little magazine going during the stringent days of the war, wheedling the money out of Sir John Ellerman, who, though a hard man of finance, was inclined to be indulgent toward his daughter. The original backer of the magazine, Harriet Weaver, a spinster of some means interested in promoting contemporary literature—who might be called the English counterpart of Har- riet Monroe—was unwilling to risk more of her small capital at this time.

It was a time of tension, of high emotional feeling over the brutality of the war and the mounting mortality rate among British troops. H.D., continunig the translations of Greek poetry, transported herself away from the dreariness of the London scene to the archipelago where ancient Greece lay warm and gold in the sunlight. Her own poems reflected the sea light of that classical landscape. With words carefully, sparingly chosen, she painstakingly drew pictures of a long forgotten landscape over which the spirit of Hellenic heroes hovered. Hers was an intense, controlled passion, as for example in "Orion Dead," where, in the final passage, Artemis, wild with grief, speaks these eloquent, short lines:

> I break a staff.
> I break the tough branch.
> I know no light in the woods.
> I have lost pace with the winds.

In purely descriptive poems her choice of vowels and consonants to suggest color tones is unerring. Note these lines in "Sea Gods," where the poet, promising to bring gifts to their altar, names as one the hyacinth-violet, "Sweet, bare, chill to the touch—/and violets whiter than the in-rush/of your own white surf." It may have been this description that caused the critic Emerson to remark of H.D.'s poetry, "We read with our ears." Yet she struggled over each word, line, and stanza, taking a long time to complete a poem. Writing to Amy on little square sheets of the *Egoist* stationery, she marvelled at the prolific productivity of the Imagist leader in America. "I wish I had one-tenth of your output." she wrote enviously. "Mine seems to be the most tenuous shoot of this Imagist Tree of Life."

As the months passed and the war continued, the sense of urgency increased. One never knew who would be called up next. The late summer of 1917 H.D. spent at Corfe Castle, Dorset, "waiting for near friends to be summoned to France. . . . in touch with a very delightful group of artists and soldiers and soldier-artists, that very soon after was scattered, through wartime tragedy of one sort and another," as she wrote long afterwards to William Rose Benét. It is likely that one of the soldier-artists who suffered a tragic fate in the war was attracted to H.D. and she to him. Apparently she and Richard Aldington had separated, though they remained friends. In "The Islands," a poem composed at Corfe Castle, H.D., under the guise of Helen of Troy, names and describes with exquisite economy of words the islands of Greece and more than once makes revealing query-statements such as "What can love of land give to me/that

you have not? . . ." and "What has love of land given to you/
that I have not?" and, "What are the islands to me/if you are
lost. . . ." Such lines could easily apply to a lover leaving for
the battlefield anywhere, anytime.

Conjecture aside, H.D. discovered she was pregnant. Soon
everyone in the Imagist group, Aldington included, knew that
H.D. was going to have a child, judging from the letters in the
Lowell file. D. H. Lawrence wrote to Amy late in March that
H.D. had pneumonia—everyone was afraid she would lose the
baby or that she would die before giving birth. It was very rare
that both mother and child survived in cases of pneumonia
during pregnancy—one or the other almost always died. But a
second letter brought the news that the baby, a girl, was born
safely, and both mother and daughter were well. Many years
later, H.D. wrote in notes that she made during her analysis
with Freud in Vienna in 1933, "My daughter was born the last
day of March with *daffodils that come before the swallow dares* out
of *The Winter's Tale.* . . ." And she called the baby Perdita, the
name of Queen Hermione's daughter in *A Winter's Tale.* When
Aldington returned to London, he also wrote Amy that H.D.
had had her baby, remarking that it was a fine little addition to
the Imagist circle. But however casually he appeared to accept
the situation, he was not willing to be father to another man's
child. A few years after the war, he and H.D. were divorced.

Bryher, who dubbed the baby "the Lump," probably because of the way the lean H.D. had looked when she was pregnant, insisted that they all go to live with Bryher's parents in
their Audley Street townhouse for a time. H.D., distraught and
still weak, let herself be persuaded to live with the Ellermans in
the "stuffy old museum," as Bryher called their mansion. The
two writers had vague plans for a small publishing business.
Bryher was working on a paper about Amy Lowell, which she
planned to publish in pamphlet form. H.D. was in favor of the
project and suggested that they bring out a volume of Marianne
Moore's poetry next.

Sir John and Lady Ellerman were kind to H.D. and seemed

to enjoy having her and the baby there along with their daughter. Some time in 1919, H.D., whose father had died the year before from shock at hearing that his son by his first marriage * had been killed in the war, received word that her mother, who was now living in California, wanted her daughter to come there with the baby. Bryher said she had always longed to see the United States, particularly the West. She was anxious to meet Amy Lowell, too. So they trundled the baby, just out of the cradle, along on an ocean voyage. Amy and Ada were at the New York docks to meet them when their ship landed.

Amy gave a small dinner party for them in her hotel suite. The Untermeyers were the only other guests, so it was an intimate party. H.D. had been one of the first poets chosen by Louis for the *American Miscellany* series of anthologies that he and Amy had conceived and compiled when the Imagist series ended. He and Jean had wanted to meet the Bethlehem-born poet, whom they considered to be in the top rank of the Imagists. Amy was eager to hear the latest literary gossip from abroad and plied them with questions. They told her that Aldington had decided to write novels and that Pound had taken over the editorship of the *Egoist* until it folded, after which he went to Europe. However, H.D. and Bryher had little more to tell her, since they had left the London scene, so Amy proceeded to give them advice on travel in America.

From California, where they stayed nearly six months, H.D. wrote to Amy, "Mother has been wonderful about the whole thing." The visit was prolonged because Bryher wanted to gather material for a book, which she eventually published under the title *West*. They stopped in New York again on the way back to England, and H.D. looked up friends in Greenwich Village, one of whom was Marianne Moore, who was living on St. Luke's Place with her mother.

At a party on February 13, they met Robert McAlmon, a poet-writer and publisher, with Wiliam Carlos Williams, of a

---

* H.D.'s half-brother, Eric, one of her childhood heroes. He had become a scientist like their father.

little magazine, *Contact*. He was one of the postwar rebels of the American literary world—outspoken, handsome and quick to accept a challenge. He and Bryher matched wits and admired each other's intellectuality. They were married the next day— Saint Valentine's—after what amounted to a proposition on Bryher's part. McAlmon wanted to go to Europe, particularly Paris. Bryher's own love for travel was hampered by the fact that her parents, particularly her father, who laid down the law, had ruled that a single girl ought not travel alone. Amy, who was in New York with Ada to do some research on Keats at the Morgan Library and to deliver a lecture on Whitman at the Brooklyn Academy, had H.D. and "the blushing pair," along with William Carlos Williams, up for dinner in her Belmont suite. There she gave them her blessing "with a quaking heart." Later the marriage was featured in the news as an international romance between a millionaire's daughter and a penniless poet, but Amy may have realized that it was rather a marriage of convenience, on Bryher's part at least. They would both be free to travel, and, as she was quick to point out, Robert could serve as a father figure for H.D.'s child.

Bryher had definite ideas about education and had offered to take over the upbringing of H.D.'s little girl. According to McAlmon's diary, he was not aware of the true situation until after he and Bryher had been married some months. As for H.D., still frail in health and uncertain about the future, she wanted most of all to write poetry, to get on with her career. She was temporizing because she did not know what else to do. In spite of all Bryher's eccentricities and her domineering ways, she was a loyal friend who believed in H.D.'s genius as a poet. Hilda returned the loyalty by staying with Bryher through all the emotional and maniacal conflicts that arose between Bryher and her family.

After spending a few months in London, the trio set up a residence in Montreux, Switzerland, using the allowance Sir John gave his daughter. It was a strange ménage: H.D. and her little girl, Perdita—Bryher more often than not called the child "the Lump," especially when she was "naughty"—Bryher, and McAlmon, who was soon to leave for Paris. There he would become a member of the literary avant-garde from both London and New York that gathered in the city of lights all during the twenties. Sometimes H.D. and Bryher joined him there; at other times, with the little girl, they stayed with Bryher's parents. The four, whether in Montreux or London, lived "all in a heap together," as H.D.'s daughter said long afterwards.* McAlmon wrote to Bill—William Carlos—Williams in 1921 from Paris, "The marriage is legal only, unromantic, and strictly an agreement. . . ." He was bitter about it. Although he had accepted the proposition in the first place, he had not realized how complex the situation was, especially with respect to Bryher's conflict with her family.

H.D. and McAlmon felt sorry for each other when Bryher was in one of her tyrannical, tormenting moods, especially when they were in London, where they collided with family fracases as well. McAlmon, as he noted in his diary, could always slip away to the nearest pub, but H.D. was saddled by her arrangement with Bryher for the upbringing of her child as well as constrained by her attachment to Bryher. Robert saw her as a high-strung, overwrought creature, "ready for the straitjacket," whom Bryher, merely by bringing up some unhappy incident during the war years, could bring to tears of frustration and sorrow. Though this might be true, H.D. knew from experience that Bryher would relent, that their tyrant was emotionally immature. It was a fact she did not fully realize until she worked with Freud, but she knew it intuitively at once, and she felt sorry for Robert because he was so bewildered in the beginning. She tried to introduce him to people she thought might be more congenial to him than Bryher's highly intellectual friends, among whom were Clement Shorter and the philosopher Havelock Ellis, fusty old men to the free-thinking, daring McAlmon. It was largely through H.D.'s efforts that Harriet

---

* In answer to a question from this biographer, February 1978.

Weaver, publisher of the Egoist Press, brought out a volume of McAlmon's poetry, *Explorations.*

There were many reasons for H.D.'s attachment to Bryher, not the least of which was her love of travel and ancient civilizations. After they left the United States in 1920, Bryher suggested they make a voyage to Greek islands: Rhodes, Samos, Naxos, "rising like a rock," as she had written. It seemed a miracle to H.D. that she should actually be in those myth-filled islands that had occupied so large a place in her thoughts and poetry. Corfu especially called forth her psychic powers, evoking a mystic light-vision, soul-shaking in its intensity.

In 1923 the two made a trip to Karnak in Egypt, a journey that was to stay with her, planting the seed for poems that grew and branched and came into full flower nearly twenty years later. They were in Egypt at a fortuitous time—the moment of the excavation of Tutankhamen's tomb. They saw the temple of Amen-Ra; they marvelled at the ancient shrines open to the sky. Bryher's knowledge of archeology enriched the experience of these priceless, historic treasures. The pilgrimage was an exciting, unforgettable adventure she would never have known if it had not been for Bryher.

H.D.'s greatest objection to the life they led was that she could not write enough poetry for a volume. Here and there a poem of hers appeared in magazines, and Amy had included her work in the *American Miscellany* anthologies she and Louis Untermeyer compiled after the Imagist anthology series ended. But it was almost a decade before H.D.'s first book of poems, *Red Roses for Bronze,* was published in 1931. She received enough attention to encourage her in her career. By then Robert McAlmon had asked for and received a divorce from Bryher (in 1927) and returned to the United States to live. But H.D. had no desire to reside in her native land. She and Bryher continued their pattern of life, dividing their time between London and Montreux—when they were not traveling to see some ruins that Bryher wanted to investigate—with frequent stopovers in Paris. Eventually they were invited to an evening at Gertrude Stein's salon, where they met some of the literary lights of the late twenties, among them Thornton Wilder. He was one of the few people to perceive Bryher's iron dominance beneath the veil of her reserve. After one meeting with her, he said, "Bryher is Napoleonic; she walks like him, she talks like him, she probably feels like him."

Whether or not H.D. began to feel that her friend was indeed a dictator and that she needed help if she was to remain with Bryher, sometime in the early thirties the poet sought out Sigmund Freud and began a series of sessions with him. It proved to be one of the most rewarding experiences of her life, as her book, *Tribute to Freud,* clearly shows. Published shortly after his death in 1939, the work, revealing much of H.D.'s inner life and struggle, is brimming with adulation. It brought her a good deal of applause, but there were also those who thought her tribute a mere overflow of maudlin emotion. One of her American colleagues, Louise Bogan, writing a comment of this sort to Edmund Wilson much later, concluded, "It's such a poor book, really." It proved a poor judgment on Bogan's part, since *Tribute to Freud* has withstood the test of time—the book was successfully reissued in 1975, going into several printings.

However, Bogan expressed much praise for the volume of H.D.'s poetry that was published a few years later, toward the end of World War II. This may well have been due in large measure to the deeper insights gained through H.D.'s work with Freud as well as to the valor and durability shown by the British nation during "the Blitz." She and Bryher were in London all through that traumatic and apocalyptic period of the air raids. She found inspiration in the fact that London was encircled by a ring of fire almost every night, and still wended its way through the rubble and fallen bodies to daily duties in the morning. Somehow, though many were semi-destroyed, the walls remained intact in an amazing number of cases. The bombings that at first brought a feeling of utter desolation became paradoxically a source of inspiration such as H.D. had not known for years. She created a series of poems of short, energetic stanzas—some of three lines each, but most only two. These were spare, unevenly rhymed imagist lines, with a strong, profound spiritual content invoking both Egyptian and Christian deities.

H.D. described desolate scenes viewed as she and Bryher walked through the streets of London in the daylight, heartsick at the sight of destruction—"An incident here and there/and rails gone (for guns)/from your (and my) old town square." These lines open the first of a trilogy of volumes she was to write. Yet, strangely, the scene reminded her of Egypt: "there, as here, ruin opens the tomb, the temple; . . . ruin everywhere, yet as the fallen roof/leaves the sealed room/open to the air,"/

> so, through our desolation,
> thoughts stir, inspiration stalks us
> through gloom:
> unaware, Spirit announces the Presence;
>
>   . . .
>
> trembling at a known street-corner,
> we know not nor are known;
> the Pythian pronounces—we pass on
>
> to another cellar, to another sliced wall
> where poor utensils show
> like rare objects in a museum;

The miracle of survival makes even poor utensils cherished museum pieces. She goes on to examine all things that struggle to survive, from sea shells and serpents to people—writers and their books. She denounces the burning of books as "the most perverse gesture/and the meanest/of man's mean nature." Then she observes with irony, "Yet they still cry for books—folio, manuscript, old parchment/will do for cartridge cases"; and she reflectively observes, "irony is bitter truth/wrapped up in a little joke. . . ." But the scribes, like the scribes of Pharaoh, will endure.

The first volume, entitled *The Walls Do Not Fall*, was published in 1944 and was dedicated to Bryher. Below her friend's name, in italics, were the revealing place-names and dates: "for Karnak, 1923/from London, 1943."

The page proofs sent to her by Oxford University Press carried a publisher's statement which began, "H.D. was at one time well known to all lovers of verse as one of the earliest 'Imagists.' " Frowning, she drew a firm black line through "was at one time," and above it wrote in large letters "IS." She had no compunctions about being an early Imagist; she was indeed proud of the fact. In going over the proof sheets, H.D. played a small game, marking certain passages with the initials of those to whom they seemed best suited. For herself she selected "We are voyagers, discoverers/of the not known." The passage is found in the last section of the book, the forty-third, which begins, "Still the walls do not fall,/I do not know why"; and it ends, "possibly we will reach haven,/heaven." This she marked with the initials O.S., for Osbert Sitwell lines in the same section. He was an old friend of Bryher's and often dropped in for tea. He had liked the poems to be included in *The Walls* so much that he had recommended the book to Sir Humphrey Milford of Oxford University Press for publication. When the volume came out, he wrote a very good review of it for the *Observer*. H.D. liked the review so much, especially the end comment, "we want—we need—more," so "be-dazzled" her that she sat right down, and during the last two weeks of May 1944, wrote another series, also of forty-three sections, which she dedicated to Sir Osbert, quoting the lines she had initialled for him.

She wrote the first of the new series sitting on the top of a bus "brushing through flowering chestnut trees on the way to Putney." She had bought a ticket to get out and enjoy the particularly bountiful spring that year—"never, never/was a season more beautiful." The beauty of the season was enhanced by the contrast with the devastation all around. Surely the seven unnamed angels who serve at the throne of God were protecting them.

Mysticism pervades the poems, and even a sense of number attaches to the book. The fact that all three volumes of the trilogy contain forty-three poems each, the digits adding up to seven, is a subtle indication linking the three volumes together. Half-way through the May series, in poems nineteen and twenty, the spirit Uriel appears in the former, giving a sign of resurrection in the fragrant blossoming trees of the city squares; and in the latter Our Lady Universal reveals a miracle in a half-burnt green and white may-tree—they "crossed the charred portico and passed through a doorless frame, like a ghost, entered the house through a wall," then "saw the tree flowering." The poem ends eloquently, "it was an ordinary tree/in an old garden-square." As Babette Deutsch points out in her comments in *Poetry in Our Time*, "The ordinariness is part of the miracle." The other part is that it was a charred,

> . . . half-burnt out apple-tree
> blossoming; this is the flowering of the rood,
> this is the flowering of the wood
> where Annael, we pause to give
> thanks that we rise again from death and live.

These lines, invoking Zadkiel, were repeated in a kind of codicil to this second book and in turn gave rise to the third book of the trilogy, *The Flowering of the Rod*, which was dedicated to Norman Holmes Pearson, with the last line repeated once more below his name. This final volume of the trilogy leaves war and destruction behind, rising to ecstatic heights of love and resurrection:

> now having given all, let us leave all;
> above all, let us leave pity
> and mount higher
> to love—resurrection.

The three volumes were first published separately in 1944, 1945, and 1946, then as a trilogy. They were well received from the start. In her praise of *The Walls*, Louise Bogan said that the work "shows tenser feeling, writing of more energy, and thought of a larger sweep than has been usual in [H.D.'s] poetry for many years." The trilogy represented a rebirth of the creative life of H.D. She went on to produce her long narrative poem, *Helen in Egypt*, her own version of love between Helen and Achilles, placing the story in a different setting from the traditional Troy. So persuasive is her poetry that the transport of the legend is utterly believable. Once again, the theme is love and resurrection, along with the mysteries of Egyptian hermetism. The work, not published until the year of her death, 1961, occupied most of her later years. There can be little doubt that she regarded it her most significant contribution to poetic literature. The reviews acclaimed it for both content and form. "The poem is as easy to read as breathing," the *Nation* declared, "it could be danced, it could be sung, the clarity of image is so perfect. . . . Tremendous suggestiveness and magnetic force radiate from the scenes invoked and their symbolic details. . . . H.D.'s verse has the balance, the amplitude and the clean outlines of a Greek temple." The work might be called the summation of her career as poet. She had devoted her time to it with the concentration and peace of mind gained from her association with Freud.

H.D.'s daughter, Perdita, by now grown up, from the time of the war, lived independently in her own apartment. Bryher, some years after her divorce from McAlmon, married a Scotsman, Kenneth MacPherson, with whom she was more compatible than she ever had been with Robert. She helped MacPherson, an authority on cinema, establish *Closeup*, the finest magazine devoted to silent films. In her own writing, like H.D. she turned to the past. She created a new kind of historical novel, was cited for its poetic style and evocation of the mood of ancient Rome. She had an eye trained for beauty and a "passion for moral beauty," in one critic's words. Bryher, surrounded by wealth all her life, had chosen to write not about the generals and heroes of Roman history, but about the common soldier and the common citizen. She and H.D. remained close friends and rejoiced in each other's successes. Bryher maintained the residence in Switzerland, where H.D. lived most of the time, occasionally visiting her daughter in London. Perhaps because she was too much married to her muse, H.D. never married again.

Like Amy Lowell, H.D. realized that the term *Imagism* could not accurately be applied to her poetry after a few years. "I don't know that labels matter very much," she said. "One writes the kind of poetry one likes. Other people put labels on it. Imagism was something that was important for poets learning their craft early in this century." After learning the craft, she felt it was a matter of finding the poet's true direction. Unlike Amy, H.D. adhered to her direction when she found it. She retained the best (for her purposes) of the Imagist precepts and discarded the ones that did not provide the guidelines she needed. Perhaps this accounts for the fact that she is still identified by the term. H.D. died at the age of seventy-five in 1961. In 1978, at its January 26 meeting, the Poetry Society of America held a panel discussion entitled "Homage to H.D., Neglected Imagist Poet."

In 1979, a new printing of the expanded 1975 edition of *Tribute to Freud* appeared. It was snapped up immediately by a new generation of H.D. followers. The section "Advent," containing the notes H.D. wrote during her analysis with Freud, reveals the surprising impression that D. H. Lawrence made on her psyche, and the friction caused by his frantic opposition to her sanguine views on analysis before she had had treatment with anyone. Also published in 1979 was *Hilda's Book,* the story of the early courtship and later stormy relationship between Ezra Pound and H.D. Both Lawrence and Pound had opposed analysis. Ironically, during the period she was in treatment with Freud, both pervaded her dreams, which she discussed with Freud.

H.D., hardly neglected, is regaining her place as an important early modernist among poets.

7

MARIANNE MOORE

UNDOUBTEDLY the unique figure among modern American women poets who began writing in the first quarter of the twentieth century is Marianne Moore. Another native of St. Louis, like several of her contemporaries, she was born, according to her own testimony, just ten months before T. S. Eliot—on November 15, 1887—and only four years after Sara Teasdale, two of her native colleagues. But she stands alone, as if she had been born in an era of her own. Whether this impression of her creative output is due to the singularity of her upbringing and her chosen way of life, or is simply the result of having possessed an alert, inventive mind, or, as is most likely, a combination of both factors, remains for the reader to decide.

Marianne Moore was "Irish by descent, possibly Scotch, but purely Celtic," which may account for the leprechaun quality of her language, her observations, and quick retorts. When she was four months old, her father, an inventor whose latest device, a smokeless furnace, had proved a dismal failure, suffered a nervous breakdown and went home to live with his parents in Portsmouth, Ohio. He apparently never regained his

177

health, for he never returned. Marianne was brought up in the home of her grandfather, a Presbyterian minister in Kirkwood, Missouri, a suburb of St. Louis, where she lived with her mother and older brother, John, until her grandfather died in 1894. The little girl of seven and a half then went with her mother and brother to live in Carlisle, Pennsylvania. She was a wiry little girl with fiery red hair and sharp blue eyes, a fast learner in primary school, and a voracious reader at the preparatory Metzger Institute in Carlisle. She entered Bryn Mawr College in 1906, at the age of nineteen, and in her freshman year became friends with Hilda Doolittle, who was to be an important influence in her career as poet, whether she acknowledged it or not. At that time Marianne had no real "literary plans," as she said, but she was interested in the undergrad magazine. She and Hilda both submitted manuscripts that were accepted, and to Marianne's surprise, in her sophomore year the editors elected her to the board. She stayed on and wrote for the alumnae magazine, *The Lantern.* Her major, however, was biology, so that much of her time at Bryn Mawr was spent in the bio lab, which she found "exhilarating." She even considered studying medicine, but her friend Hilda urged her to continue writing poetry. Hilda was very serious about becoming a poet and felt that Marianne, who was so talented, was dissipating her marked ability for turning a phrase—her succinct, apt descriptions of rare plants and animals were a direct result of her biology courses—and for unexpected rhymes and intriguing titles.

But young Marianne Moore possessed a mind that was stimulated by all things that aroused her admiration or curiosity. At one point she thought of being a painter. She went so far with that idea that, at her graduation from Bryn Mawr in 1909, when Mrs. Otis Skinner asked her what she would like to be, she answered without hesitation, "A painter." Perhaps it was only the mood of the moment, but the lady, looking at Marianne's red hair wrapped in a coronet braid around her head, her sharp blue eyes, and her bony, thin body wrapped in a sheer flowered dress, said, "I'm not surprised." The young graduate Mrs. Skinner was appraising certainly looked every inch an artist—and later was, but in another field. In 1909 she had no idea it was to be poetry.

After receiving her A.B. degree, Marianne Moore took her mother's practical advice and spent a year studying stenography, "typewriting" (her word), and commercial law at Carlisle Commercial College, from which she graduated in 1910. She and Hilda Doolittle were still experimenting with poetry, writing and reading each other's efforts, discovering through Ezra Pound, who was a friend of Hilda's, the work of the literary groups that gathered at Sylvia Beach's Bookshop in Paris, and in London at Harold Munro's Bookshop or in the dingy teahouses of Soho. Ezra, who had run away from America to "escape the iamb" as well as an undeserved accusation of creating a scandal at Wabash College, had published two small books of poetry, one in Venice and one in London in 1909. The latter, *Personae*, had won him considerable notice among various groups of poets in England. He worked at luring Hilda to London with his reports by mail of new trends in poetry. The excitement he felt was contagious.

In the summer of 1911, Marianne Moore, with her mother and Hilda Doolittle, decided to spend the summer in Europe. As long as her mother lived, Marianne seldom went anywhere without her. She rarely made any move or even released a poem for publication without asking the advice of both her mother and brother. From all accounts, theirs was an unusually harmonious family relationship, devoid of onerous dependence, but replete with a remarkable interdependence rarely characteristic of family ties.

In Paris, the travellers stayed at a small pension on the Left Bank. It was "the hottest summer ever known," Marianne felt as they walked along to 12 rue de l'Odéon to see Sylvia Beach's bookshop, with its sign "Shakespeare & Co." over the lintel. They went in and browsed a little, but Marianne did not introduce herself or say she was a writer. She felt it would be presumptuous on her part—she felt satisfied simply at having seen the bookshop she had been hearing about. They went to every museum in Paris except two, and those she never saw, for she never returned to Paris. In London they visited the literary landmarks. Hilda elected to stay in London when the summer was over, even though she had not been able to get in touch with Ezra Pound, who was out of the city. Marianne did not have any idea then that her friend would never come back to live in her native land and only once make an extended visit, after she had become well known as the Imagist poet, H.D. Hilda's parting words to Marianne were, "Keep writing poetry."

Marianne and her mother returned to America around the first of September. Soon afterwards an offer of a job teaching "commercial subjects" at the United States Indian School in Carlisle proved too appealing to turn down—the Moores needed the income. The offer seemed fortuitous to Marianne. She taught at the school more than four years. One of her students was the half-Indian Jim Thorpe, the legendary football hero who may have initiated her interest in athletics, which itself was to become legendary. During those years, she continued writing poetry, urged on by Hilda, who, with Ezra Pound, had founded the group called Les Imagistes. Her friend had also joined the staff of a magazine called the *Egoist*, and in 1915 Marianne's first poem was published in the May issue. T. S. Eliot, in his introduction to Moore's *Selected Poems*, commented that she had "no immediate derivations," except possibly in an early poem, "The Talisman," which reflected "a slight influence of H.D., certainly of H.D. rather than anyone." This, like most of her early poems, presents no difficulties to the reader:

> Under a splintered mast,
> torn from the ship and cast
>   near her hull,

a stumbling shepherd found,
embedded in the ground,
    a sea-gull

of lapis lazuli,
a scarab of the sea
    with wings spread—

curling its coral feet,
parting its beak to greet
    men long dead.

Later in the same year, *Poetry* magazine published four poems, which had been enthusiastically accepted by Harriet Monroe, who had been the first to publish H.D.'s work in America, and who had heard of Marianne through Hilda. Coming so close together, the publication of her poems on both sides of the Atlantic seemed simultaneous to the twenty-eight-year-old teacher at the Indian school, whose career as a poet was launched, whether she intended it to be or not. She was always of two minds about the art, as her cadenced statement, "Poetry," plainly shows: "I, too, dislike it: there are things that are important beyond all this fiddle. Reading it, however, with a perfect contempt for it, one discovers in it, after all, a place for the genuine." Poets, she felt, must present "imaginary gardens with real toads in them."

The following year, 1916, Marianne and her mother left their home in Carlisle and moved to Chatham, New Jersey, to keep house for John. Her brother had been attending theological seminary and was now an ordained Presbyterian minister assigned to a church in Chatham. They lived there only two years, for John joined the navy after the United States entered World War I, to become chaplain of the battleship *Rhode Island*, stationed when in port at the Brooklyn Navy Yard. Marianne and her mother took a small apartment on St. Luke's Place in New York's Greenwich Village, a pleasant "little quiet part of New York." Marianne enjoyed seeing the tops of the masts on the Hudson River from their door and walking down to the wharf to look at the craft on the water. She was employed briefly as a secretary in a girl's private school and as a tutor for a few of the pupils, suitable employment for an unmarried woman. At thirty-one, she was considered a spinster. Living in the Village marked the beginning of her friendship with poets striving to win recognition, particularly with contributors to Alfred Kreymborg's magazine *Others*, who included William Carlos Williams, Wallace Stevens, Kenneth Burke, Conrad Aiken, and Edna Millay.

Kreymborg was very "hospitable" to her, she wrote to Ezra Pound in 1919. Pound had sent a request for some biographical data, as he intended to do a feature article about her and another beginning poet for *Poetry*, and he wondered if her contemporaries might use some of her poems in an English publication. Her reply was that they were welcome to anything they had come upon first. She wrote also that she did not resent unfriendly criticism, much less "that which was friendly." However, she informed him, she had not been offering her work lately, since she had been refused by the *Atlantic* and was dissatisfied with some lines of hers that had appeared in Margaret Anderson's *Little Review*. She finished loftily, "I am less and less desirous of being published." But in the next sentence she spoke of the cooperation she found among the New York poets in "getting things launched" and that she was glad to have him keep the two poems he had for publication in his quarterly. Also she promised she would send him something new as soon as she had it. This hardly sounds like a poet who is "less and less desirous of being published."

In 1960 Miss Moore boasted that she'd sent one poem out thirty-five times before it was accepted, so she obviously soon recovered from her reticence to appear in print. Indeed, she kept a "wee book," systematically entering a notation of every poem sent out, when it was returned, or, if accepted, how much she received for a poem. She began appearing again when *The*

Dial, a "little magazine of high quality" supported by Scofield Thayer and Dr. J. S. Watson, was "reestablished in 1920." Kreymborg, too, was as good as his word and published several of her poems in *Others.* The group of poet-contributors to the magazine often gathered in the Village apartment he and his wife, Gertrude Lord, one of the loveliest persons Marianne ever met, occupied for several years. Kreymborg, who called himself a troubadour—he used the word as the title of his autobiography—would sometimes strum on his mandolute, a musical instrument of his own invention, as a very soft background, in accompaniment to his ballads.

Early in 1920, H.D. and Bryher came for a visit on their way back from California. They had stopped briefly on the way out, but now they had more time, so a number of parties were given for the pair. Marianne and her mother entertained for them, inviting the Kreymborgs so that H.D. could meet the editor of *Others,* who had been so "hospitable" to Marianne's work. Privately Marianne confessed that he probably considered her work a "novelty" that would add to the appeal of the magazine as an experimental publication. Kreymborg, who took pride in sponsoring new poets, was eager to meet H.D., since she was the best known of the Imagists and he was one of those who admired the movement. Marianne said bluntly that she wondered why in the world anyone would adopt the term—wasn't imagery the basis of all poetry anyway? There was a good deal of discussion, much of it heated, on the merits and demerits of any movement in connection with poetry. H.D. and Bryher defended Amy Lowell's tireless and largely triumphant efforts to spread the "new poetry"—she had made Imagism practically a household word in America—but Marianne would have none of such tactics. At the parties, or when the three young women were by themselves, they thrashed out their artistic differences of opinion with a fierce joyful fervor and wit.

It was like Marianne Moore not to ask any questions about H.D.'s private affairs and to accept Bryher as a good friend to her former college classmate. Yet when Bryher offered Marianne and her mother $5,000 to come to England for an extended stay, Moore turned it down at once. She wanted to be under no obligation to wealthy patrons, even those who were themselves involved in the arts. She attended the various parties for the visitors, including the one which ended with the engagement of Bryher and Robert McAlmon, and she was one of the few people who witnessed the harum-scarum wedding ceremony that took place the next day.

That whirlwind, madcap marriage must have set her to thinking about the subject, for soon after the newlyweds left for London in February 1921, with H.D. and her daughter, Marianne began writing a long, important poem, entitled simply and starkly "Marriage." Offhand, one might think it odd for a spinster who had had no experience with wedlock to take up this theme for a discursive poem. But a poet whose powers of observation and sensibilities were as keen as Miss Moore's could not help being aware of the discrepancies between the original concept of marriage and the actuality in the twentieth century. Whether or not she meant it to be, the poem was revealing of her disapproval of the hasty marriage between Bryher and McAlmon and the blatant headlines in the papers the following day.

The lines in "Marriage" also evidenced Marianne's lifelong habit of reading and retaining heterogenous bits of knowledge gained from the wide scope of her interests, which she then fused by her "hybrid method of composition," as she called it, into a harmonious whole of her own creation. "Marriage" contains no less than thirty references to and quotations (direct and indirect) from a broad variety of sources, including Francis Bacon and Shakespeare and ranging further from *Scientific American* and the *New Republic* to the Bible, Ezra Pound, and the inscription on the statue of Daniel Webster in Central Park, New York City. The poem definitely reveals Marianne Moore's own feeling toward marriage—the first seventeen lines indicate her intention whether she otherwise ever admitted it or not:

This institution,
perhaps one should say enterprise
out of respect for which
one says one need not change one's mind
about a thing one has believed in,
requiring public promises
of one's intention
to fulfil a private obligation:
I wonder what Adam and Eve
think of it by this time,
this firegilt steel
alive with goldenness;
how bright it shows—
"of circular traditions and impostures,
committing many spoils,"
requiring all one's criminal ingenuity
to avoid!

One cannot help wondering if Marianne Moore indeed used her "criminal ingenuity" to avoid marriage. The passage quoted above shows strong skepticism, and the poem continues, "Psychology which explains everything/explains nothing,/and we are still in doubt." The next passage extols "Eve: beautiful woman" with her individual powers, wishing at times to be alone, and refers to marriage as "this amalgamation which can never be more/than an interesting impossibility. . . ." Then follows a long section on Adam, who "has beauty also." But it is notable that the poet puts him in second place and that his flaws far outweigh his perfections. In Adam she finds "something feline, something colubrine" (quoting Philip Littell). He is a "crouching mythological monster" (her own phrase) who "experiences a solemn joy in seeing that he has become an idol" (from Anatole France). "He stumbles over marriage, 'a very trivial object indeed' " (a partial quote from Godwin's "Marriage is a law . . . and the worst of all laws. . . ."). Adam commends love "as a fine art, as an experiment,/a duty or as merely recreation./One must not call him ruffian/nor friction a calamity—the fight to be affectionate"—a telling phrase. The poem contrasts the views of men toward marriage with those of women, delineating the sharp differences by a series of observations from each. "He says . . . 'The fact of woman is "not the sound of the flute/but very poison." ' She says, 'Men are monopolists/of "stars, garters, buttons/and other shining baubles"—/unfit to be the guardians of another person's happiness.' "(This last from the 1921 Founder's Day address given by Ms. M. Carey Thomas, a thorough feminist, at Mt. Holyoke College, the year of composition of the poem, definitely begun in 1921 though not completed until two years later.) "He says, 'These mummies/must be handled carefully—/. . . turn to the letter M/and you will find/that "a wife is a coffin" ' " (the last a direct quote from Ezra Pound). The poet herself comments, ". . . he loves himself so much,/he can permit himself/no rival in that love./She loves herself so much,/she cannot see herself enough. . . ." Farther on she asserts, "Everything to do with love is mystery;/it is more than a day's work/to investigate this science." (The last is from the Tilney translation of the *Fables* of La Fontaine, an indication of the keen interest in the famous French fables that led to Moore's own translation of them in the early 1950s.) The poem ends in subtle satire, citing "the statesmanship/of an archaic Daniel Webster," and quoting the inscription on his statue: "Liberty and union/now and forever," then subliminally, without mentioning marriage, suggesting in the closing lines the standard, stodgy wedding photo: "the Book on the writing-table;/the hand in the breast-pocket." The entire poem, though difficult to follow, is a brilliant collage of quotations and observations, which, for all its patchwork, is a unique work of poetic art.

There was good reason for Marianne Moore to be skeptical of marriage. Her father had never resumed the responsibility of his family, and her mother apparently never made any effort to help him regain his mental strength. Since Marianne always consulted her mother, Mrs. Moore must have approved the feelings expressed in "Marriage." H.D.'s experience was a further warning to Marianne against any attempt to enter into marital alliance with a man. In 1921, she was thirty-four years old and, so far as one can tell from the record, there were no suitors among her many friends, half of whom were male. Not that she brooded about the matter: she had her say in this long poem, but she had too many intellectual interests to sigh over sexual love or the lack of it. Emotion was a controlled force to be expressed in her poetry. Her passion was for words, ideas, curious phenomena.

She was still tutoring as well as writing, and, being an omnivorous reader, she haunted the Hudson Park branch of the public library, which was right opposite their house. She usually stopped to chat with the librarian, Miss Leonard, so she soon became known as an ardent lover of books. One day while she was away from home, Miss Leonard came to see her. The librarian asked Mrs. Moore if she thought Marianne would care to be on the staff of the library, since she was so fond of books and liked to talk about them to people. The poet's mother said no, she thought not—Marianne would probably feel if she joined the staff she would have no time to read. When Marianne came home, she was appalled at her parent's turndown of the offer. "Why, certainly I'll tell her that would be ideal!" she exclaimed. However, in accepting the job, she decided that she would not work more than half a day. "If I had worked all day and maybe evenings or overtime, like the mechanics," she said long afterwards, "why, it would *not* have been ideal!"

She began at once and found that her post as Miss Leonard's assistant was a tremendous help to her writing. Staff members were also assigned books to review. Though she received no pay for this, it gave her a chance to "diagnose," and she "revelled" in that. It brought out "the worst-best" in her. She read novel after novel and became adept at criticizing them, recognizing the variations in prose style and plot structure. But she often wondered why the library didn't honor her with an art book, or one about science or history. It was always fiction, "silent movie fiction," as she said. Yet she did not complain about the selections assigned her, and in the end the training thus received was partially responsible for T. S. Eliot's comment, "She seems to have saturated her mind in the perfections of prose, in its precision rather than its purple; and to have found her rhythm, her poetry, her appreciation of the individual word, for herself."

Eliot's remarks were contained in the introduction he wrote in 1935 for a volume of Moore's entitled *Selected Poems,* but they were based on his reaction to her very first volume, published, to her own immense surprise, in this eventful year of 1921. Late in the year she had word from H.D. that she and Bryher had just brought out a volume of Moore's work via the Egoist Press. It was entitled simply *Poems.* Her first book published without her knowledge—incredible! Marianne was filled with mixed feelings. She was overwhelmed and "intensely grateful" to her friends, but at the same time she was piqued, almost annoyed at not having been consulted. In her eyes, book publication was premature at this point. And when the author's copy of her slim first volume arrived, she thought "the format was choicer than the content."

Nevertheless, *Poems* drew a great deal of attention in reviews from major critics, among them Eliot, who admired Moore's poetry from the beginning. The book launched her career as a professional, whether she liked it or not. The worst aspect to her was that it made her feel, in her words, "conspicuous"; and she claimed that "desultory, occasional magazine publication" seemed to her "plenty conspicuous." But *Poems* was a *fait accompli,* and she had to accept the consequences of her kind friends' generous if rash decision to publish her poetry without her permission. The results were not long in coming. More of her poems began to appear in the *Dial,* and in 1923 "Marriage" was published separately as a chapbook, *Mannikin #3,* in the series sponsored by Monroe Wheeler. The long poem caused much literary discussion of both its content and form, particularly of its maze of indirect and direct quotations. Some held that Marianne Moore approached plagiarism, but her tart reply was that her extensive use of quotes was due to her honesty and not stealing. If she felt that a writer had said something "ideally," she would calmly take it, but give the person credit.

She served as Miss Leonard's assistant at the Hudson Park branch library until 1925, always writing poems in her spare time, many of which were published in the *Dial*. In 1924, at the instigation of the magazine's editors, the Dial Press published a volume entitled *Observations*, which was actually a reprint of the London poems and some of those written since then. The book received the Dial Award for 1924, the first of many awards to come to Marianne Moore. The editors of the *Dial* asked her to join the editorial staff. Since Miss Leonard was retiring from the library, Marianne decided it was time for her to leave and move on to a job closer to her own talents.

Her association with the magazine had begun nearly ten years before. Initially she had sent them a couple of her poems, which they returned. Then Lola Ridge, the frail little poet with the big heart and big ideas for labor reform, had given a party in her rambling basement apartment on East Ninth Street in the Village. The liberal labor writer John Reed was there, just before he went to Russia, also Marsden Hartley, who was "confident with the brush," plus numerous poets and a few editors, among them Scofield Thayer. Much to Marianne's disgust, the poets were induced to read something they had written. When she finished reading the one she finally chose, Thayer said to her, "Would you send that to us at the *Dial?*"

Marianne had retorted, "I did send it!" and Thayer, undaunted, shot back, "Well, send it again." That was how it had begun. A few years later, after Marianne had become a regular contributor, Thayer said to her one time, "I'd like you to meet my partner, Sibley Watson." The poet invited the two to tea and was much impressed with Dr. Watson, whom she considered a rare man—deep, of few words—but what he said was "striking." On being asked to join the staff of the *Dial*, she had little hesitation about accepting, and within a year she assumed full editorship of the magazine, a post she held from 1926 to 1929. In those years it became known as a publication of incredible literary distinction—in one issue alone both Ezra Pound and George Saintsbury could be read. The feminine feminist editor became known for her keen judgment of manuscripts and her openness to the experimental. It was lack of fear that made the magazine so good, she felt. "We didn't care what other people said. We all liked what we were doing, and if we made mistakes, we were sorry but we laughed over them," she later recalled.

As Louise Bogan once wrote, the *Dial* made clear "the obvious division between American avant-garde and American conventional writing." But this was by no means a deliberate policy, Marianne hastened to point out. "Individuality was the great thing," she said. "Not conforming to anything." A piece must have "intensity." It was she who discovered Hart Crane and who, as editor, published an early version of "The Bridge." The idea of a poem about the Brooklyn Bridge struck her as "a grand theme," and though Crane later complained, unjustly, about some editorial changes made in his manuscript, he was delighted, not to say overcome with gratitude, at having his work accepted by Marianne Moore. The lady herself had by this time become a public personality. She was known for her wit, her integrity, her unusual vocabulary—and her hats. In summer she wore shiny straw sailor hats or very wide-brimmed black straw hats—to keep her fair skin from becoming a mass of freckles. In winter everyone could spot Marianne Moore in a crowd of writers by her black soft felt tricornes, the three-cornered colonial-style hats for ladies that suited her so well she stuck to them even after they had gone out of style.

With the July 1929 issue, the last number of the *Dial* appeared, and Marianne Moore, with her mother, moved to Brooklyn to be closer to her brother, John, who had continued as chaplain of the *Rhode Island* and was now permanently assigned to the Brooklyn Navy Yard. The Cumberland Street apartment, just off Myrtle Avenue, on a pleasant tree-lined street near the Presbyterian church that the Moores attended regularly was to be Marianne's home over three decades. After they moved to Brooklyn she "stayed put," as she said, except for a trip to England and four journeys to different parts of America. The first was a cruise through the Panama Canal up the west coast to San Francisco, and then by rail to Seattle. Three other trips to the west took Mrs. and Miss Moore to Los Angeles, San Francisco, and British Columbia. And for years every summer, during the pre-artist colony days at Monhegan Island, the Moores vacationed there, reaching the island by a seamy sailboat called *The Effort*. It regularly got becalmed, often causing them to arrive at a mooring out from the fishers' beach at low tide near midnight. Then they would hobble over stones and slimy objects by lantern-light, their luggage bumping along behind on a wheelbarrow. But it would all prove worthwhile the next morning when they looked out of their gabled attic room in a fisherman's cottage, onto a pile of split birch wood and an expanse of sea "rising from a jagged line of fir-tops." How they loved those views!

One of their favored lookouts was a ledge of rocks where they often paused to take in the vast sweep of the sea. They were watching the surf after a storm there one day when a man suddenly placed himself between them and the magnificent view of the foaming waves below. The nerve of him! the poet felt. But her mother said, "Don't be annoyed. It is human nature to stand in the middle of a thing." Her observation went into a poem entitled "A Grave," concerning the solemn aspect of the sea's fathomless depth. Though Mrs. Moore's remark was included verbatim, it was not set within quotations marks, nor was the source given except indirectly in a postscript to the 1935 volume *Selected Poems*. That was published by Macmillan (by Faber and Faber in London) and was a book Marianne also considered premature when it was first proposed in 1925. She thought the same as late as 1935. The postscript reads:

> Dedications imply giving, and we do not care to make a gift of what is insufficient; but in my immediate family there is one "who thinks in a particular way"; and I should like to add that where there is an effect of thought or pith in these pages, the thinking and often the actual phrases are hers.

"A Grave" was chosen by E. E. Cummings above any of his own as his favorite poem; it was the only one he would suggest when asked for his contribution to the *Auto-Anthology* edited by William Rose Benét. On being queried, Marianne gave her consent to have it represent her acceptable work, even if it was not a favorite. She commented, ". . . it has a significance strongly apart from the literal origin." The first five lines illustrate her point:

> Man looking into the sea,
> taking the view from those who have as much right to it as
>   you have to it yourself,
> it is human nature to stand in the middle of a thing
> but you cannot stand in the middle of this:
> the sea has nothing to give but a well excavated grave.

The theme is extended in a line farther on—"the sea is a collector, quick to return a rapacious look"—and throughout the poem to the end. Her mother evidently approved Marianne's treatment of her casual remark about human nature, or the poem would not have been printed.

Marianne once asked her mother about a certain poem— "How did you ever permit me to let this be printed?" Mrs. Moore's unhesitating answer was, "You didn't ask my advice." The procedure was not compulsive on Marianne's part, nor demanding on her mother's. Both were objective, adult, strongminded women. When Marianne wrote "A Face," she had first conceived an idea about "the adder and the child with a bowl of porridge," and her mother said frankly, "Well it won't do." Marianne said, "All right, but I have to produce something!" (Cyril Connolly had requested a poem for *Horizon*.) So she wrote "A Face," one of the few poems she ever set down that gave her no trouble, and one that is among her most comprehensible. Her mother, reading it, said emphatically, "I like it."

Earlier the poet had tortured herself over "The Buffalo," one of her many poems about unusual animals. She felt it would probably outrage any number of people because it, as she said it, had a "kind of pleasing, jerky progress" that readers might consider queer or poor. Then she thought, "Well, if it seems bad my brother will tell me; and if it has any point, he'll detect it." So she read it to John, who told her, "with considerable gusto," smiling, "It takes my fancy." His words made her "happy as could be," for now she knew she could let the pattern of "The Buffalo" stand; it began:

> Black in blazonry means
> prudence; and niger, unpropitious. Might
> hematite—
> black incurved compact horns on a bison
> have significance? . . .

Many readers found it difficult to discern a definite pattern in Moore's poems, but, except for a conversation-piece like "Marriage," she wrote to Ezra Pound (in 1919), "Any verse that I have written has been an arrangement of stanzas, each stanza being an exact duplicate of every other stanza." This was early in her career, but in the 1935 *Selected Poems* there are many examples of the Moorean method. "The Fish" is a delight. It introduces another of her devices, that of using the title as part of the first line:

> THE FISH
>
> wade
> through black jade.
>   Of the crow-blue mussel-shells, one keeps
>   adjusting the ash-heaps;
>   opening and shutting itself like
>
> an
> injured fan.
>   The barnacles which encrust the side
>   of the wave, cannot hide
>   there for the submerged shafts of the
>
> sun
> split like spun
>   glass, . . .

The poem goes on, following an exact pattern, yet one that suits the subject and the thought, not produced as simply an intellectual exercise. T. S. Eliot, in his introduction to this volume—one of the features that made it a landmark in her career—commented on the emotional value of the simile of the mussel shell opening and shutting itself "like an injured fan." Only a mind of extreme sensitivity and alertness would conjure up such an image. He spoke, too, of her "amused and affectionate attention to animals—from the domestic cat . . . to the most exotic strangers from the tropics—monkeys, remote lizards (the plumet basilisk), snakes, mongooses, an octopus, sea unicorns and land unicorns, and perhaps the most unique—the jerboa." The last she introduced as "a small desert rat,/and not famous." If today school children in Evanston, Illinois, and elsewhere raise jerboas in cardboard boxes as a science experiment, it may well be that Marianne Moore's description of the little creature made him famous.

> . . . lives without water, has
> happiness. Abroad seeking food, or at home
> in its burrow, the Sahara field-mouse
> has a shining silver house
>
> of sand. O rest and
> joy, the boundless sand, the boundless sand,
> the stupendous sand-spout,
> no water, no palm-trees, no ivory bed,
> tiny cactus; but one would not be he
> who has nothing but plenty.

As Eliot pointed out, it would be hard to say exactly what the subject matter of "The Jerboa" is, but the above conclusion gives the careful reader a fair idea of the way Marianne Moore felt toward these agile little creatures whose active life was built on plenty of nothing. In any case, the poem, and the volume itself with Eliot's introduction, established Marianne Moore as a top-flight modern American poet.

In closing, Eliot wrote: "My conviction, for what it is worth, has remained unchanged for the last fourteen years [i.e., since 1921, when H.D. and Bryher published Moore's *Poems*]: that Miss Moore's poems form part of the small body of durable poetry written in our time; of that small body of writings, among what passes for poetry, in which an original sensibility and alert intelligence and deep feeling have been engaged in maintaining the life of the English language." Earlier, he had asserted that, although innovative, "Miss Moore's versification is anything but 'free.' Many of the poems are in exact and sometimes complicated formal patterns, and move with the elegance of a minuet." The last was a phrase that stuck.

Yet this poet of elegance had a tough, wiry fiber in her nature that came out not only in her work, but in her play. From this time on, she published a volume almost every year, winning many honors and awards—from the Helen Haire Levinson Prize and the Shelley Memorial Award to a Guggenheim fellowship and a joint grant from the American Academy of Arts and Letters and the National Institute of Arts and Letters. But her favorite recreation was to go to Ebbetts Field to watch the Brooklyn Dodgers play ball. A great lover of baseball, she was an ardent fan of the Dodgers. A virtual mascot of the team, she was almost as well-known as a Dodgers fan as a poet. And if it seemed a strange hobby for a poet of her sex whose hallmark was "the elegance of a minuet," to her it was a most natural interest. "I don't know how to account for a person who could be indifferent to the miracles of dexterity to be witnessed at the ballpark," she once wrote. She cited a baseball player's great backhand catch or the unconscious rhythm of the pitcher's windup. The Dodgers were her team, and she rarely missed a home game. Asked in 1960 if, after they had been lured to Los Angeles, she missed the Dodgers, she answered, "Very much," adding, "And I understand *they* miss *us*." She gave the little laugh, halfway between a chuckle and a covert snicker, that often escaped her after some tart or cogent comment.

Like her close friend and colleague Robert Frost, with

whom she early formed a mutual admiration society, she maintained her reputation as a baseball fan to the end and beyond. As recently as May 1976, the *Christian Science Monitor* carried a feature story, "A Look at Two Baseball-loving Poets," with photographs of the two facing each other. This was soon followed by an article from the pen of George Plimpton, also a friend of the ubiquitous Miss Moore, who recalled a series of events he attended with her. Although still a loyal fan of the Dodgers, she once consented to take in a Yankee game with him. He recorded her comments with considerable mirth and a touch of condescension. She took notice of the "interesting gesture" the pitcher made after each windup and toss—bringing his hand down to the crotch of his uniform and giving a slight heft between his legs. When someone in the party suggested mentioning it to him, she said, "Oh no, let's not mention it; that would take away the spontaneous innocence of it." Plimpton's conclusion was that she was more interested in the human side of the players than in baseball, implying that she knew little about the game itself; but it is a safe bet that Marianne Moore knew the rules as well as he, and could detect an error as well as an "interesting gesture."

In 1947 Marianne's mother died, leaving a terrible void in the life of the poet, who had valued and relied on her mother's judgment in many things besides poetry. But Marianne Moore was not one to wail or withdraw from the world because of her grief. That same year she was elected to the National Institute of Arts and Letters. She had literally hundreds of loyal friends who delighted in her company as well as her work, and she in turn was a loyal friend to all. But she chose not to enter into a permanent alliance with any one person. William Carlos Williams called her "a rafter holding up the superstructure of our uncompleted building" in the early days, but she scoffed at the idea. "I never was a rafter holding up anyone," she said, "the group comprising *Others* or others!" She referred to the little cluster of poets that, following the demise of *Others*, contributed to

Broom, the little magazine that was in some respects the best of the lot. It was run by Lola Ridge from her Ninth Street apartment and bore the stamp of Miss Ridge's social consciousness.

While Marianne Moore's "observations, experiments in rhythm, composition, and subject matter" as she defined her poems, were vastly different from Lola Ridge's, she always admired the latter's grit, integrity, and intensity. These last two were qualities she often cited, along with sincerity, as a yardstick of a poet's worth. Her friendships were formed on the basis of these qualities, sometimes through correspondence, and if her interest was drawn to a person, she became and remained a friend.

Only by a few outward signs did Marianne show how deeply she felt the loss of her mother. In 1951 her *Collected Poems,* published by Macmillan, bore the dedication "To Mary Warner Moore (1862–1947)." It was one of the few of her volumes that was dedicated to anyone, for she did not hold with the practice of dedicating a book to a specific person, group, cause, or idea. That alone indicates the significance of this simple gesture. Its very restraint revealed the love and reverence with which she regarded her mother, a person as individualistic as Marianne herself. Theirs had not been the usual parent-child relationship, but rather one of outwardly matter-of-fact companionability and mutual respect.

The volume itself proved worthy of the homage she paid her parent; *Collected Poems* received the Pulitzer Prize for poetry, the National Book Award, and the Bollingen Prize—triple recognition placing her in the top rank of American poets. She was invited to be a visiting lecturer at her alma mater, Bryn Mawr, in 1953, and the same year received the McCarey Thomas Award and the gold medal from the National Institute of Arts and Letters.

Yet, in spite of numerous honors, she felt she was not "producing," another typical Moorean term for the creative process. Whether it was because her mother was not around to say, "Well, it won't do" or "I like it"—her brother was not readily available—or whether she had reached a plateau of creativity and did not feel the urge to go on, she turned somewhat away from poetry. She began to translate the *Fables* of La Fontaine at the suggestion of a publisher who died soon after she began the project. She "struggled on for a time, but it didn't go well," so she turned to Macmillan, who had published several of her books. However, the translations editor there, though he pretended to show interest, tried to dissuade her from continuing the work at that time. "Put it away for a while—about ten years," he said. "It will hurt your own work; you won't be able to write your own poems." She tried to make him realize that that was one reason she had undertaken the translation. "I thought it would train me, assist me, give me incentive," she explained, but to no avail.

In telling the story, Marianne revealed this to be one of the few times in her career when she felt "most dejected." She tried to find out whether the problem was that the meanings were not sound or that the rhythms were off, but all the editor would say was that there were "conflicts." Just what they were she never knew, but when he finally returned the manuscript without even a covering note, the "ultimatum was devastating." Then, just as she was at her lowest point, Monroe Engle of Viking Press wrote asking if she would let Viking see her *Fables*, provided she did not have a commission for them. She was grateful to him for that letter, but said that in all honesty she couldn't offer something "when somebody else thinks it isn't fit to print." She would have to have the assistance of someone to stabilize her translation and guarantee that the measures were "sound." When Engle asked whom she would take, she named Harry Levin, because he "had written a shrewd review of Edna St. Vincent Millay's and George Dillon's translation of Baudelaire." Engle was not sure Levin would have time to do it because of a heavy teaching schedule, but the project proved a "refreshment" to Levin, who gladly took it on. Marianne's comment was, "It was a dubious refreshment, let me tell you; he is precise without being abusive, and did not resign."

The book proved very successful, although it was critically assailed by Helen Vendler in a *New Yorker* article of October 1978. She held that, despite many felicitous phrases, the work as a whole was "unsatisfying" as Moore poetry. She cited Howard Nemerov's early criticism that the poems were "very jittery as to the meter." The final complaint was that the translations could not even be claimed as examples of Moore's affinity with La Fontaine, since he was not a naturalist, and she was. His animals existed only as creatures of fable, whereas Marianne Moore's were real in the biological and visual sense, as well as the philosophical.

A few years later, Macmillan, having regretted its rejection of the *Fables,* approached Marianne with the idea of doing further translations from the French. She chose three of Charles Perrault's fairy tales: "Puss-in-Boots," "Sleeping Beauty," and "Cinderella," all of which she really adapted. The project enjoyed equal commercial success. In between she took on another assignment, which was completely unsolicited and probably could have occurred in no other country: she received a letter from the marketing executive of the Ford Motor Company seeking her help in naming a new car. They wanted to find a name as successful as Thunderbird had been. Since she was known for her poems depicting strange animals and birds—rare creatures like the jerboa, the pangolin (a Malaysian animal that characteristically rolls itself into a defensive ball, attaching its body-scales tightly together to minimize vulnerability to attack), the frigate pelican, and the plumet basilisk—they had thought of her at once.

The name, the letter said, should have "some visceral feeling of elegance, fleetness, advanced features and design. A name, in short, which flashes a dramatic, desirable picture in peoples' minds." It seemed a large request, but Marianne Moore assumed that they merely wanted her to "exposit the irresistibleness of the car." She accepted the assignment and went about it with her usual vigor. "I got deep in motors and turbines and recessed wheels," she said. Her correspondence was lively and should have inspired the market research department of Ford with any number of ideas. At one point she found the name Tinkoturbine, a rare mammal fish that propels itself by rapid whirring. On another track of investigation, she discovered the Silver Sword, an exotic wildflower, perhaps too lyrical and far removed from motorcars, but she offered it anyway. Then one day she received the executive's final reply to all her gleaming suggestions: "We have chosen a name out of the more than 6,000 odd candidates that we gathered. It has a certain ring to it. An air of gaiety and zest. At least, that's what we keep saying. Our name, Miss Moore, is—Edsel. I know you will share your sympathies with us."

Marianne was more amused than shocked, and the human tone of the executive's letter was of course endearing. In fact, she defended the entire proceeding—it had seemed to her "a very worthy pursuit." "I was more interested in the mechanics," she said. "And I enjoyed the assignment for all it was abortive." They sent a young demonstrator to call for her in a black Edsel to convey her to the auditorium when the new model was publicly presented. "There was nothing wrong with that Edsel," she contended. "I thought it was a very handsome car. It came out the wrong year."

Marianne Moore lived in Brooklyn until 1965, and she probably would have stayed there till the end, sticking to the rather dim, drab railroad flat she and her mother had occupied so many years, if the neighborhood had not become dangerous. Her friends were less and less willing to make the trip by subway and "el" across the bridge and out Myrtle Avenue to Cumberland Street. She herself found it risky to go out alone at night. Her front door opened onto a long narrow hall, dimly lit, lined with bookcases, the rooms leading off to the right. At the end of the hall was the living room, overlooking the street. Here piles of books stood everywhere. On the walls hung a number of dark, murky oil paintings, set off by one bright-colored canvas of a New Mexican scene, sent to Marianne by Mabel Dodge Luhan. Aside from the clutter of books and a stack of *National Geographics*, the room was orderly and neat, somehow homey, in spite of the heavy, dark, old-fashioned furniture that matched the 1910 oils on the wall.

Marianne never made a habit of staying out late. Even in the early days she had never attended the wild parties given by Hart Crane for the group she belonged to. In this connection M. M. had suggested that Crane "moderate" some of the scenes in his long poem, "The Bridge," which outraged him. Much later, though she complained of *his* complaints against her, she conceded that since she had never attended those parties, it was "lawless" of her to suggest changes. In the sixties the crime rate went up so alarmingly around Myrtle Avenue one never knew what might happen even in the daytime. So Marianne Moore, at age seventy-five, returned to her first New York neighborhood, the Village. She was welcomed back publicly by the *New Yorker* in a long interview and by her close friends individually: Elizabeth Bishop, who had previously written a delightful poem urging Miss Moore to "fly over from Brooklyn"; Babette Deutsch; May Swenson, who looked upon Marianne as her mentor; Louise Bogan; and Jean Garrigue; to name only a few who were concerned about her. Old friends like Bill (William Carlos) Williams and Robert Frost had died two years before, and W. H. Auden, who had lived on Montague Street in Brooklyn when he first came to America, now spent only half of each year in his apartment on St. Mark's Place in the East Village—in a few years he was to leave it forever for a place he thought would be more secure, a don's cottage at Oxford.

Auden was a staunch admirer of Marianne Moore's, though it had taken him a while to appreciate her. "When in 1935, I first tried to read Marianne Moore's poems, I simply could not make head nor tail of them," he wrote in a section entitled "Two Bestiaries—D. H. Lawrence and Marianne Moore," from *The Dyer's Hand*, a collection of essays published in 1962. "To begin with, I could not hear the verse. . . . Syllabic verse, like Miss Moore's, in which accents and feet are ignored and only the number of syllables count, is very difficult for an English ear to grasp." He had been acquainted with Robert Bridge's experiments in syllabic verse, but those were confined to a regular series of six- or twelve-syllable lines. "A typical poem by Miss Moore, on the other hand, is written in stanzas containing anything from one to twenty syllables; not infrequently a word is split up with one or more of its syllables at the end of a line and the rest at the beginning of the next, caesuras fall where they may, and as a rule, some of the lines rhyme and some are unrhymed. This for a long time, I found very difficult." Marianne herself said of her syllabic lines that she never planned a stanza. "Words cluster together like chromosomes, determining the procedure. I may influence an arrangement, or thin it, then try to have successive stanzas identical with the first." When working, she kept an array of different colored pencils at hand, and made her rhymes "conspicuous" by underlining with red, blue, yellow, or green—as many colors as she had rhymes—to differentiate. If phrases recurred in "too incoherent an architecture in print," she found that the "tune" did not sound right. She might begin all over, or she might put the poem away and not complete it for years. But she was thrifty. She salvaged anything that was promising and set it down in a small notebook.

Auden found not only her style difficult, but for a long time he found her process of thinking very hard to follow. Rimbaud seemed like child's play compared to some of her passages. But Auden liked the "tone of voice," so he persevered. Eventually he found her poems provided him a pleasure that few poets gave him. His key to appreciating her poems, an intuition he had from the start, was that Marianne Moore was "a pure Alice. She has all the Alice qualities, the distaste for noise and excess;

. . . the fastidiousness; the love of order and precision; the astringent, ironical sharpness." He felt that some of her best poems were, overtly at least, about animals, exotic animals for the most part, those that took her fancy; and he enjoyed her treatment of them—as either emblem, or "a moral paradigm." In particular he cited "The Pangolin."

Auden concluded with the tribute: "Miss Moore's poems are an example of a kind of art which is not as common as it should be; they delight, not only because they are intelligent, sensitive, and beautifully written, but also because they convince the reader that they have been written by someone who is personally good." He quoted her answer to the question of the relationship between art and morality (also quoted by Donald Hall): "The villains in Shakespeare are not illiterate, are they? But rectitude *has* a ring that is implicative, I would say. And with *no* integrity, a man is not likely to write the kind of book I read." She also said, "If the emotion is strong, the words are forthright and unambiguous. Someone asked Robert Frost if he was selective. He said, 'Call it passionate preference.' " That was her own feeling about words. She was fond of quoting Frost, with whom she had much in common, although their art was diametrically opposite in style—Frost frequently said he would "as soon play tennis with the net down" as write unmetered lines. And yet he was one of Marianne's early admirers and promoters.

Like Frost, Marianne Moore gave readings to some of her largest audiences during the last years of her life. Her asides between poems were filled with crackling humor. She never lost her sense of surprise at public approbation of her "experiments" in poetry. Once, when Mrs. August Belmont, along with Katharine Cornell, Ada Russell, and some of their Social Register friends, arranged a reading for Miss Moore, the poet remarked before she began her first selection, "I never dreamed I would be reading my work before such a distinguished group of society women." Again, when she was invited to participate in the first Bollingen Poetry Festival at Johns Hopkins University, and later, to read before thousands of people in Central Park during some holiday program, she was as astonished as she was pleased.

The last ten years of her life were almost as active and productive as the rest had been. In 1967, Viking Press, which had published several volumes of her poetry following the success of the translations of La Fontaine's *Fables*, brought out the *Complete Poems* of Marianne Moore, including her extensive and entertaining "Notes," which Auden called "sort of a joke with her" and an indication of her scrupulous literary honesty. He disapproved of footnotes and glossaries as a rule. "But when she does it—i.e. glosses—it really helps you to understand the poem," he said in 1970.

Neither poet could know then that they had not long to live, although Marianne was nearly twenty years older than Auden. She had begun to suffer from some intestinal disorder, but she was not one to dwell on death. She accepted its inevitability, but did not brood on the event. In all her poems there is scarcely a mention of death—the emphasis is rather on life. Her animals leap with joy at the mere fact of survival. Her dragons—her 1962 volume was entitled *O to be a Dragon*—are positively attractive in their appearance and demonic cleverness. Yet when her time came to go, she was a lamb rather than a dragon. One of her lines, "Even so deference; yes, deference may be my defense," comes to mind. She deferred to death in 1972, at the age of eighty-five, following a long, active life of mental and creative fulfillment.

Marianne Moore is still very much alive in her poetry and in the hearts of poets and readers who loved her. The article by Helen Vendler in the *New Yorker*, quoted above, was inclined to diminish the worth of Moore's contribution to modern American poetry from the time of the publication of *Observations* (1924). Even the 1935 *Selected Poems* is questioned, and "subsequent volumes show a falling off, in the judgment of many critics," according to Vendler, who claims the same is true of Moore's prose. Vendler cites overrevision, suppression, and omissions as the causes for the falling off of Moore's work. But those who knew her well have inveighed against this evaluation as a vicious and unjustified assault on Moore's consistent creativity and on the high level of her interpretation of life as she saw it, in her poems.

The Walter Hampden-Edwin Booth Theatre Collection and Library at The Players

8

EDNA ST. VINCENT MILLAY

COMPARED to Amy Lowell and Sara Teasdale, Edna St. Vincent Millay started life as a waif. Her earliest memories were of the constant quarrels between her parents—over her father's gambling, his mishandling of the family income, his meager salary as a high school teacher and small-town superintendent of schools—and of the moves from one Maine town to another, with the hope that each would provide a fresh beginning and a permanent home.

She was born in Rockland, Maine, on Washington's Birthday, February 22, 1892, the first child of Cora and Henry Tolman Millay. Both expected their first-born to be a boy. Cora was so confident she had already chosen a name. While pregnant, she had received word that her young brother, a sailer who had been seriously injured during a storm at sea, was recovering well under excellent care at a St. Vincent's Hospital. She was so grateful that she decided to name her son after St. Vincent, patron of the sick and protector of the wine-growers.

When the baby turned out to be a girl, Cora nevertheless included St. Vincent as a middle name, and in the family circle they called her Vincent. For her first name, they chose Edna,

derived from an old Norse word for poetry; in Greek and Hebrew the word means rejuvenation. A name fraught with more
appropriate symbolism would be hard to find, and it proved
prescient on her mother's part.

From the time she was a small child Vincent showed an
amazing awareness of life and a responsiveness to the moods
and problems of those around her. The most vivid of those early
memories was planted at the age of seven, when she watched
her father, suitcase in hand, stride away to the town railroad
depot. Her parents had quarreled again—this time her mother
had told her father not to come back, not unless he would "do
better." But seven-year-old Vincent sensed with the intuition of
a precocious child that her father would never come back. There
was an air of finality about the scene that sent a chill of loneliness through her veins.

It was a feeling never quite dispelled by warm, demonstrative affection from her mother and her two younger sisters,
Norma and Kathleen. Cora Millay tried to be both mother and
father to her girls, a difficult role in any case, and in her case the
financial struggle to support her children caused her to be away
much of the time. She was a woman who combined common
sense, a droll wit, and honest open affection with more than a
dash of musical talent and a touch of the poet. She had managed
to study voice and piano as a girl, and she gave her daughters
their first music lessons, along with imparting her own lively
appreciation of the arts.

If Cora Millay had a favorite, it was her first-born. During
the disruptive years of her marriage, she found both comfort
and diversion in fostering the growth of the seeds of grace in
the daughter she had presented with such a symbolic name.
Small Vincent, though hardly a saint, seemed to combine the
poetic with a pantheistic joy in being alive. At nearly five she
composed her first poem: three rhymed couplets on the theme
of "One Bird." It was a child's poem, the simplest of songs. But
the lines showed an observant eye, a sense of the rhythm so

necessary in a poet, and they brought praise from her mother, her primary source of inspiration.

Mrs. Millay obtained a divorce, despite the taboos of the time, and she remained cheerful and matter-of-fact. Nevertheless, there was bound to be a certain amount of upheaval as a result of the family breakup. Vincent, who had turned eight by the time the decree was granted, experienced bewilderment and a feeling of abandonment, which was to become outright skepticism toward the concept of enduring love between man and woman. The theme of the fleeting beauty of love was to run like a dissonant leitmotif through most of her work.

Soon after the separation, Cora packed up the family belongings and with her three little girls went to "live around with" her three sisters in three different towns. It was a jumpy sort of existence. In Rockport, one of the towns where the girls attended school, Vincent made, on her own, a giant leap in literary taste from Mother Goose to Shakespeare, which she read with amazing ease for an eight-year-old. The language of poetry seemed natural to her, and the Elizabethan lines enchanted her.

Cora had taken a training course in practical nursing and she finally decided to take up working as a nurse in the seacoast town of Camden, Maine. It was a delightful resort and shipbuilding center, set between the mountains and Penobscot Bay, its snug harbor dotted with fishing boats, shining yachts, and tall-masted schooners. In 1903, the little family moved into a house at 40 Chestnut Street, which remained their address all during the years in Camden.

Here the poet passed, in her words, "an extraordinarily happy childhood," though it was never a pampered one. She once quipped that they had "all of the luxuries, but sometimes few of the necessities." She, the oldest, had to shoulder the household duties when Mrs. Millay was away on a case.

Camden was a country village, shady and green in summer, starkly white in winter. The woods provided a special haven for a wild-flower seeker like Vincent. Small wonder that, with her gift for words in rhythmic pattern and her scholarliness—she excelled in Latin translations in high school, especially the love poems of Catullus—she should be inspired to write poetry of her surroundings.

Her first efforts were published in the high school paper and in that remarkable magazine, the *St. Nicholas,* which, from the 1890s until well into the 1920s, served to inspire more than one young genius who later became famous in American letters. The magazine awarded silver and gold badges to the writers of the best manuscripts submitted from among its young readers. Winning entries were printed in the back "League" section of the monthly issue. Urged on by her mother, Vincent sent in a number of poems signed "E. Vincent Millay" and had the thrill of seeing her poem "Forest Trees" in the October 1906 issue. The following year three more were accepted, one of which won the coveted gold badge. More important, it was reprinted later in *Current Literature* with the comment, "The poem that follows seems to us phenomenal. . . . Its author (whether boy or girl, we do not know) is but fourteen years of age." The future poet was already on her way to wide acclaim, although for several years she wavered between poetry and music as her career. Music was as much a passion with Vincent as poetry. However, the budding poet had had a number of poems published in the *St. Nicholas* by then, and when, in her senior year, she received the top award of five dollars for her poem "Friends," as well as a prize of ten dollars for her graduation poem at school, aptly titled "La Joie de Vivre," her decision veered definitely toward poetry. In her junior year, a third possibility for an artistic career had come to the fore—she showed a marked talent for both playwrighting and acting.

It was another year before she knew that the music of words would probably strike the decisive chord in her life, that no matter how many loves she might have, human or divine, poetry would always be her overpowering passion. After graduation, she was at a loss to know which way to turn. Although she had decided, with her mother's approval, to be a poet, she felt the need for further study; but there was no money for college.

Wild and beautiful as the scene around her was, Vincent Millay was filled with vague yearnings to extend the horizons of her life physically as well as artistically. She began to analyze her feelings in a long narrative, allegorical poem in iambic tetrameter, the meter of "The Rime of the Ancient Mariner." Like Coleridge, she used simple language to create an eloquent saga of mystical experience and spiritual truth. The poet depicted an imaginary supernatural experience based, she asserted some years later, on a similar vision that came to her during one of her predawn watches on the mountaintop. It was a poem of death and rebirth, through which the poet learns the miracle of life despite all human sin and suffering, human guilt, "every greed, every lust," every tragedy and sorrow. In its conclusion, she celebrated the joys of being alive once more, hailing the source of life in a celebrated couplet still quoted from present-day pulpits:

> God, I can push the grass apart
> And lay my finger on Thy heart.

The poem was begun while Vincent was eighteen; she was still working on it when she turned nineteen. She often consulted her mother, who was also writing verses in her spare time and sending them to New England papers. One day Mrs. Millay came across the announcement of a poetry anthology, *The Lyric Year*, to be published as soon as the hundred best poems written by American poets during the year had been selected. A first prize of five hundred dollars and a second and third of two hundred and fifty dollars each were offered for the top three among those chosen. Cora Millay lost no time in urging Vincent to submit the poem at once.

As the poet prepared the manuscript, she decided to give her work the French title "Renaissance," perhaps hoping to duplicate the success she had had with her prize-winning poem, "La Joie de Vivre." She included the latter and several others along with "Renaissance" and mailed the package with a high heart. But odds were staggeringly against her—over ten thousands poems had already piled up in the publisher's office, many by much more established poets than "E. Vincent Millay."

However, although it had a narrow escape from the waste-basket, when the first reader threw it there with a laugh, "Renaissance" came close to being the first prize winner. A letter addressed to "E. Vincent Millay, Esq," and inside, "Dear Sir," contained enthusiastic praise of her poem from Ferdinand Earle, editor and sponsor of the project as well as one of the judges who rescued it. He rashly said that according to his rating, the poem would probably win the first prize of $500. His only suggestion was that, since this was to be a volume of American poetry, she change the title to "Renascence."

Wildly elated, Vincent rejoiced with her mother and sisters, and ran to tell her friend and fellow-poet Abbie Huston Evans the news.* "Just think, Abbie, I'm going to be in that book!" she kept saying. It was evident that publication in a work of national importance came first, but the prize money meant plans for a college education. Unfortunately Earle had reckoned without the opinions of the other two judges when virtually promising the first prize to the author of "Renascence." Neither one agreed with him, nor could either be shaken in the belief that, although the poem was excellent, it was not of prize-winning caliber. "Renascence" placed fourth in the list of the hundred selected.

Vincent was crushed for a time, but with her Irish practical-

---

* Evans was well known locally. Years after Vincent was dead, she took part in the "Poets for Peace" program against the Vietnam war, held in New York City, reading her own recent poems. Evans' most recent volume appeared in 1979, when she related the above to this biographer. She was held in high esteem by Louise Bogan.

ity, she realized that it was a mark of recognition to finish among the top five. She began to look forward to publication. In the meantime, the poem received unexpected recognition privately. Her sister Norma invited Vincent to be her guest at the annual "Ball for the Waitresses," held by the Whitehall Inn, the principal resort hotel, to honor daughters of the local families who worked at the inn, as Norma did during the summer. Vincent was persuaded to perform with Norma some ballads she had composed, after which she was asked to recite verses she had written. She decided to try out "Renascence" in front of an audience. She recited her long poem gravely and simply in her musical, deeply dramatic voice, forgetting her listeners entirely. All were enthralled. One woman, Miss Caroline B. Dow, head of the National Training School of the YWCA in New York and a summer visitor in Camden, was so touched by the poem and its youthful author that she offered to help Vincent get a college education. She arranged interviews and made plans for Vincent to stay at the YWCA's training quarters in New York while taking preparatory courses at Barnard the following spring.

Vincent could hardly wait till February to leave. Before then, however, she was caught up in a literary controversy of such magnitude that erupted when the anthology *The Lyric Year* appeared in November 1912 that she was famous before she ever went to New York. Because of the judges' failure to award "Renascence" a prize, Vincent was at the vortex of a public and professional storm of protest, which was as remarkable as the early fate of the poem. The most memorable letter of those that poured in came from two professional contributors to the anthology, Arthur Davison Ficke and H. Witter Bynner. Both had reputations that had been established by steady publication in periodicals. Ficke had two volumes to his credit in print, and a third book was soon to appear.* Bynner was writing criticism as

* Three volumes of Bynner's work were reissued in June, 1978. His prose writings and letters appeared in the fall of '78, along with a complete bibliography.

well as poetry. The two had been roommates at Harvard a few years earlier. By Bynner's account, he had gone to spend the November holiday with Ficke, who had married and was practicing law in his home town, Davenport, Iowa. Arthur had just received a copy of *The Lyric Year*. On Thanksgiving day, Bynner was leafing through the book for the second time. Suddenly the title "Renascence" took his eye; after glancing at the first few lines, he read the entire poem aloud to Ficke. Both of them were carried away. As they wrote later to Earle, "It seems to both of us a real vision, such as Coleridge might have seen. . . ." They read the poem to Arthur's wife, and the three wrote a letter of appreciation to the author beginning, "This is Thanksgiving Day and we thank you. . . ." Vincent was deeply moved by their tribute, which, sent through the editor's office, arrived December 5. She answered at once: "You are three dear people. This is Thanksgiving Day, too, and I thank you." After "Very truly yours," she signed her full name. In their letter to Earle the men had doubted that a young girl could have written "Renascence." "It takes a brawny male of forty-five to do that," they exclaimed—another instance of the early attitude toward women poets.

The editor passed their remarks along to Vincent, who was quick to defend her sex. As proof, in her second letter she included a snapshot of herself, adding, "The 'brawny male' sends his picture: I *have* to laugh." So began the exchange among the three poets. Between Ficke and Millay there was an inner communion at once. He was to be her spiritual advisor long before he became her "beloved," but from the first she asserted her strong individuality in regard to her work.

By the time she began the term at Barnard in February 1913, Edna St. Vincent Millay's name was so well known in poetry circles that she received a number of invitations from notables, among them Louis Untermeyer, who had been the first to praise "Renascence" in a review of *The Lyric Year* in the Chicago *Post*. To both Untermeyers, Vincent, with her red-gold hair, delicate features, and dainty figure, her breathless way of greeting them, seemed the embodiment of a poet, though she felt more like a "scared little girl from Maine." Her host, with his beady eyes, hawk nose, and crooked grin, seemed to be leering at her. But his enthusiasm for poetry in general and "Renascence" in particular was so infectious that she lost her self-consciousness and was soon reciting recent verses other than the prize-losing poem that won her fame.

When Miss Jessie B. Rittenhouse, secretary of the Poetry Society of America, gave a party to introduce Edna Millay to some of the most illustrious members, however, Vincent was so overwhelmed by the number of celebrities that she could not shed her shyness long enough to recite her poetry. Among the guests were Mr. and Mrs. Edwin Markham, Mr. and Mrs. Louis Ledoux, Sara Teasdale, Anna Hempstead Branch,* Alfred Kreymborg, and, to her happy surprise, H. Witter Bynner. She had come to know Bynner well by correspondence, and now in his kind, courtly way, he made her feel as if he were an old friend who would look after her in the company of strangers. Soon she was calling him Hal, like any of his intimates, and felt enough at home with him to ask that he read "Renascence" aloud to the guests while she sat on the sofa listening intently.

After the Rittenhouse party, Vincent was caught up in a whirl of invitations from people in New York literary circles. She was determined not to miss anything and was away from the training school so much that Miss Dow must have wondered when her poet-prodigy had time to study, let alone do creative work. But Vincent wrote in her bare little room at the Y as she had at home, late at night or early in the morning before going to class. Less than a month after her courses at Barnard began she sent two new poems to the editor of *Forum* magazine, and on April 8, when Vincent opened a letter from the magazine, a check for twenty dollars fell out—her first actual sale. In May her college preparatory semester was over, and she

---

* Famous for her long narrative poem "Nimrod" and her settlement work at Christadora House on New York's Lower East Side, where she formed the Poets' Guild to familiarize the neighborhood young people with poetry of both past and present.

returned to Maine to bone up for her entrance exams at Vassar.

Unexpectedly, college life had countless drawbacks. The entire code of conduct seemed nonsense to her at twenty-one, the age of most seniors, and she rebelled by avoiding or ignoring rules and regulations. She cut classes to write poetry, often forgot mealtimes, and had an extra hour's sleep instead of going to chapel. Since smoking was banned on campus she had the pleasure of her cigarettes in the open air, sitting on the low wall of the cemetery across the road.

The fact that she turned in brilliant papers and showed an amazing aptitude for languages, especially Latin, besides contributing to the campus publication, only infuriated some teachers, who complained to the president about her high-handed ways. Henry Noble MacCracken, one of the most progressive college administrators of his time, reasoned with her, trying to show her that the college rules were necessary. He finally told her he would never expel her—"I know all about poets in college, and I don't want a banished Shelley on my doorstep!" And though Vincent was still defiant, retorting hotly, "On those terms, I think I can continue to live in this hell-hole!" she was in the midst of a dozen activities before the semester was over.

She gained a new awareness of social issues like the suffragist movement and women's rights in general, then coming to the fore in the changing world of the twentieth century. MacCracken came out publicly in support of the suffragists, and the college sponsored a series of lectures on the movement. One of the most stirring was delivered in the spring of Vincent's sophomore year by Inez Milholland, a glamorous, prominent alumna of 1909. Inez, called the "Amazon Beauty" of the suffragists, made an eloquent appeal for their cause, and the poet was moved to join in the fervor that swept over the college in favor of the franchise for women. Inez Milholland became one of her idols. Vincent paid tribute to her in the dedication of a sonnet long after the speaker's sudden tragic death in 1916, less than a year after the Vassar appearance. Another significant note sounded at the occasion of this lecture was the poet's first greeting from Eugen Boissevain, then married to Inez, though neither he nor Vincent had any inkling then that he was to become a major figure in her life.

An important influence at Vassar on Vincent's career was the theater. Play writing, acting, and play production were among the foremost activities on campus, and the poet was inspired to write several plays produced by the college.

At this time the noted English actress Edith Wynne Matthison came to Vassar in an advisory capacity when the college set up a theater workshop. Both Matthison and her husband, playwright Charles Rann Kennedy, who headed the Bennett School of Acting in Millbrook, New York, praised the poet's acting ability in the highest terms. Vincent was so elated that she decided to make the theater her second career. She idolized Matthison and often went to Millbrook, where she studied Edith's methods, listening closely to the reading of Shakespearean lines for which the actress was famous. This no doubt was responsible for Millay's own clear, cleancut diction when later on she read her poetry before large groups.

After her graduation, which took place in the wake of an academic storm, a "splendid row" that became legendary, Vincent spent a summer preparing her poems for publication in her first volume, to be brought out by Mitchell Kennerly, publisher of *The Lyric Year*. In the fall she invaded Greenwich Village. The Provincetown Players, which was founded on the Cape in the summer of 1915, but came to New York in the winter, and was now in the second successful season, artistically if not financially, let it be known that anybody could try out at the Provincetown, provided one was willing to work for practically nothing. Remuneration was to be in the form of dividends, depending on the future prosperity of the Players. The prospects of such were still remote, but the stage-struck poet was ready to risk it.

It was as if she had come in on cue. Floyd Dell, one of the "radical" thinkers and writers of the time, had issued a casting call for the lead role in his new play, *The Angel Intrudes*. The poet "looked the part to perfection," and "read Annabelle's lines so winningly that she was at once engaged at a salary of nothing at all," he recorded. When he discovered she was Edna Millay, the "author of that beautiful and astonishing poem, 'Renascence,' " he was overwhelmed by his good fortune. His rapturous praise for her poetry amused and pleased her. The opening night performance proved her acting ability. When it was further learned that the poet had plays to offer, she was voted a full-fledged member of the company.

On the strength of her prospects in the theater and her promised advance on book sales, which Kennerly subsequently failed to send, plus in anticipation of an occasional check for an accepted poem, Vincent summoned her sister Norma to join her. Floyd Dell had found an icy one-and-a-half rooms for them at 139 Waverly Place. He tried to persuade her to share his ramshackle apartment, for he had fallen madly in love with her, but she preferred to live with her sister. Indeed she had plans to bring her mother and sister Kathleen to New York as well. She was flattered by Dell's attention, but his ardor bored her.

Edna Millay was far more sophisticated than any of her suitors—as Edmund Wilson termed those who were serious about her and who usually called her Edna—ever suspected. She led Floyd Dell a merry chase, eluding him at every turn, yet managing to keep his friendship and adoration. She did listen seriously to the Socialist dialectic he poured into her ear; she admired his pacifism and his support of conscientious objectors. When he and others who founded the original *Masses* magazine had to stand trial for opposing U.S. entry into the war—among them were Max Eastman and Art Young, the famous cartoonist—Millay was among those who went down to court to give the defendants moral support in the fight for a free press.

However, she would not listen when Dell tried to convince her to enter psychoanalysis. He claimed analysis would help her to overcome her "sapphic tendencies," which she neither admitted nor denied. The more he insisted the more stubborn she became. Like Amy Lowell, she held that it would be harmful to her creative process to strip off all the layers until she saw the "dour" depths of her being. She finally told him there were doors in her mind he must not try to open. She crystallized her sentiments in the sonnet "Bluebeard," a stern poetic indictment of his meddling.

Still Dell persisted. He hoped to duplicate the success that Charles Ellis, the Provincetown artist, set designer, and actor, had in wooing Norma Millay—the two eventually married. Edna, however, remained tantalizingly out of Dell's reach. She epitomized the duality of her emotional make-up in "The Singing Woman from the Woods," demanding defiantly, "What should I be but a harlot and a nun?" This impish, rather weird and bitter ballad was taken literally by many readers and did much to engender the legend of Edna St. Vincent Millay as a libertine poet. It is true that from the time she played the role of Annabelle, her physical beauty seemed to blossom. Where before she had been appealing, she was now ravishing in the eyes of many men.

It was through Floyd Dell, however, that two men came into the poet's rapidly growing course of romantic adventures who were to be fixed stars in her love constellation, lasting forces in the future of both her everyday and creative life. One was Eugen Boissevain, who, since the death of Inez Milholland, had shared living arrangements with Max Eastman and was the mainstay of the latter's communal household in nearby Washington Place. The other man was her fellow poet Arthur Ficke.

Edna had long recognized Ficke's spiritual affinity through their correspondence, but now he entered her life with the blinding impact of physical beauty. She was surprised to learn from Dell, who was also from Davenport, that his old friend Ficke was in town—"showed up wearing a Sam Browne belt and puttees, a *Major*, carrying dispatches from Washington to General Pershing." Ficke had asked Floyd to introduce him to her. Edna was delighted, but she was not prepared for the tall, broad-shouldered, superlatively handsome man who came to the apartment at Waverly Place one evening in the early spring of 1918. For once in her life, Edna was dazzled by male physical perfection, combined, as she already knew, with a high order of intelligence and a gift for poetry. Before the evening was over, both had acknowledged the unspoken, profound feeling between them.

The hour of their love was brief. A night, a day, and part of another night was all they had together before Arthur sailed on his mission. During the days and weeks following his departure, there was a rapturous exchange of love sonnets such as probably never occurred before and has never been duplicated. Ficke's sonnets to Millay have been overlooked in the annals of poetry, but they are among his best. And the love sonnets of Edna Millay that were inspired by Arthur Ficke are among her most lyrical and spontaneous. To her line "After the feet of Beauty fly my own," he answered with the sonnet beginning, "For Beauty kissed your lips when they were young. . . ." And, in a sonnet Ficke deemed "almost flawless," she wrote, knowing they could not be together, "Into the golden vessel of great song/Let us pour all our passion; . . ."

Her love found expression not only in the sonnets, but in a general surge of creativity—short lyrics, odes, and verse plays flowed from Millay's fertile mind. She expanded her publication credits to *Poetry*, the *Dial*, and *Reedy's Mirror*. These magazines, however, paid so little that, after meeting W. Adolphe Roberts, editor of the popular *Ainsley's*, labelled a "trashy magazine" by Edmund Wilson, some of her poems appeared there. When Roberts asked if she had any fiction, she dashed off a short story, but decided to use a pseudonym, Nancy Boyd, for this and all fiction and prose pieces in the future. The name Edna St. Vincent Millay was to signify a poet only, and she never compromised her stand on this point. From mid-1918 until 1921 *Ainsley's* proved a steady source of income.

In June 1918 Edna found an apartment large enough to hold

the Millay family of four at 25 Charlton Street. This was the most celebrated Millay residence in the Village. With the family reunited, the poet set herself a schedule that would have worn down a much less fragile physique than hers. For the next two or three years, her output of work, in addition to acting, the direction of her own plays, and a gay night life, was staggering. She "burned her candle at both ends," evidently under an emotional strain after her encounter with Arthur Ficke. Although she edified her actions in the defiant "candle quatrain" that was to make her reputation as a wit and the voice of "flaming youth" in the twenties, she must have undermined her health during this period. Armed with several packs of cigarettes, she would lock herself in her room, where she wrote "with the same inspired precision that a sculptor chips marble," to quote Wilson, trying to achieve a perfect poem. Or, if she was writing a story for *Ainsley's,* she would pound the typewriter for hours. She claimed flamboyantly that her double burning candle gave "a lovely light," but it was rather a glare of bravado.

Edmund Wilson, whom she met in 1920 shortly after production of her most successful verse play, *Aria Da Capo* (which opened at the Provincetown in December 1919 and was published in *Reedy's Mirror* in March 1920), became one of her most serious suitors after he heard her read her poems at a party at Hardwicke Nevins'.* Wilson's friend, poet John Beale Bishop, had come to the party with him, and before long the two were among Edna's most devoted escorts, taking her out together or separately as often as she consented to see them. Both were on the staff of *Vanity Fair,* and Wilson wooed her by way of the magazine. He pointed out to Frank Crowninshield, the editor-in-chief, that the work of Edna St. Vincent Millay was far above the level of a magazine like *Ainsley's,* which was publishing almost all of her prose at that time plus an occasional poem. Crowninshield was quick to act on Wilson's hint. He, like others in the literary world, had been impressed with a group of

---

* Nephew of Ethelburt Nevins, the famous composer.

twenty sonnets by Millay published in *Reedy's Mirror* in April 1920, which greatly increased her reputation as a literary figure. The group included some of the sonnets inspired by Arthur, as well as those provoked by Floyd Dell and other suitors. They revealed a mastery of the form and a fresh handling of it at a time when the modernists were trying to erase the word *sonnet* from the poetic lexicon. The remarkable aspect of the sonnets in the *Mirror* is that they are modern in language and feeling as well as flawless in form. Gone were the classic *thee* and *thou*; in their place was the present-day *you*. Like Robert Frost, she employed "language common to all"; the style was twentieth-century.

Emotionally, the fourteen-line poems presented a modern woman who was at times almost masculine in her attitude toward love. It is the woman who takes the initiative in ending a love affair—"I shall forget you presently, my dear/So make the most of this, your little day"; and, "faithless am I except to love's self alone." Here was the "new" woman, free in her attitude toward love, yet "stern in her soul's chastity." Her loyalty was to her first love, poetry, written as she saw fit to create, singing out unconventional ideas in traditional forms. As Floyd Dell said, "She learned the molds first, into which she later poured her emotions while hot." Even the most avant-garde literary critics were outspoken in their admiration of these sonnets, and Edmund Wilson was one who never changed his mind about their merit or in according Edna Millay high status as a poet.

Soon after they met, she became, through Wilson, a regular contributor to *Vanity Fair*. It also gave the two young editors much more opportunity to be with her. For a time the three—Wilson, Bishop, and Millay—discussed poetry and exchanged and quoted their respective efforts at all hours and places. Edna once read them a sonnet she had just completed on a Fifth Avenue bus while on the way to the Claremont for dinner. One night, very late, after they had consumed a bottle of bootleg gin while talking about poetry, they all wrote self-portraits. Edna's was a clever, self-perceptive piece, ending with a delightful description of her body and based on a single word image, "unexclamatory." Bishop's self-sketch was published in *Vanity Fair*. The magazine wanted to print Edna Millay's as well. She had no objection, but Norma considered the portrait lewd and convinced Edna that it should not appear. But it was finally printed in 1952 in the Millay *Collected Letters*.

Often in the early weeks of that spring of 1920, the three were together. Wilson recorded their erotic adventures graphically in his journal, including instances of Millay's "schoolmarm-ish side," when she, objecting to certain practices, refused to comply. Frank Crowninshield complained about having his two assistants distracted by love for the magazine's shining new contributor. Many of the Nancy Boyd "distressing dialogues" appeared in *Vanity Fair*, and the poetry of Edna Millay as well. For the fall of 1920 Crowninshield planned a full-page feature on the poet to include four of her lyrics, four sonnets, and a photograph.

Edna herself was fond of both Wilson and Bishop, but not in love with either. And neither of them could know that she was longing for Arthur Ficke, who, instead of coming to New York as he had promised, had decided to take his family and accompany Witter Bynner on a trip to China. She kept hoping that he and Hal would soon come home from the Orient—she missed them sorely. She was worried, too, about the publication of her second volume. She had read proofs of her book early in April. Entitled *Second April*, it was to come out before the end of the month. Suddenly it was June and she still had no word from Kennerly—no author's copy, no advance money.

Just as Edna was wondering how she would get through the summer, Susan Glaspell and "Jig" Cook, respectively playwright and director, as well as founders of the Provincetown Players, offered the poet and her family a cottage they had in Truro on Cape Cod for the summer. The place was no more than a shack, but to the poet, happy to be near the sea again, it was a "dear little house." She began to write almost at once.

The Millays brought along a wheezy old Victrola of Allan Mac-Dougall's, along with his one recording, Beethoven's Fifth Symphony, which she played over and over at night until she could whistle it by heart as she ran barefoot along the beach looking for shells. Here was the genesis of one of her best-known and most accomplished sonnets, "On Hearing a Symphony by Beethoven." And here it was that Edmund "Bunny" Wilson proposed marriage to Edna St. Vincent Millay.

Edna was in a quandary on the question of marriage. Years before, when she began corresponding with Ficke and Bynner, she told them she would wait for them. And she must have sensed from Arthur's letters that, although he took his family on the trip with Hal, his marriage was faltering. Yet she could not tell if Arthur, aside from the sonnets he kept writing to or about her, still cherished their brief encounter as she did. She kept looking for a letter from China while she was in Truro, but when one came, it turned out to be from Hal, and she wondered if he might not be a more stable marriage choice. She still hoped to hear from Arthur. She put off Wilson.

Back in New York in September, she located a "lovely big room" for herself at 77 West Twelfth Street, near Fifth Avenue. Much as she doted on her family, she now wished to live by herself so there would be little distraction from her work.

The poet furnished her apartment so that it looked "as Chinese as China" she wrote to Hal Bynner—it was her only means of following him and Arthur to the Orient. The fall passed and still no word came of their return. On October 29, 1920, suddenly she decided to write to Arthur, declaring that she loved him, "too," and always would, just as she did the moment she first saw him. This began a series of tender, touching letters from Edna Millay to Arthur Ficke. In this one, in a few eloquent paragraphs, she set down her emotions, just as both had done in their sonnets. In one prophetic sentence she stated simply that they "would never escape from each other." She closed with a quiet vow that he would never be lost to her in any way and signed herself simply "Vincent."

For all that, Edna did not seclude herself. According to Wilson, who continued to court her, she was "besieged by suitors," who flocked to her door. One of the callers, and a lasting admirer, was Llewelyn Powys, the scholarly English essayist and critic. He arranged a meeting and was struck by her "sharply-cornered, witch-green eyes" and her daintiness, "compared only with the daintiness of Queen Anne's lace." He did detect "an April shadow of vanity in her look," but beneath it "the divine spirit of poetry." The friendship formed that day was lifelong. Edna, with her Irish impudence, dubbed him "Lulu," which seemed to tickle his own sense of the incongruous. He saw that beneath her sophistication there would always "remain a barefoot poet, doomed yet redeemed, under the shadow of Eternity." He epitomized his feelings by dedicating his book, *The Verdict of Bridlegoose,* "To Edna St. Vincent Millay, A Leprechaun Among Poets."

They saw each other frequently that fall of 1920, which must have been a blessing, for she was worried, ill, and depressed much of the time. Foremost of her anxieties was the failure of Kennerly to bring out her volume, *Second April,* and his silence on the subject. Before Kennerly went "into hiding," he had agreed to publish the light verse Millay had been writing separately. It was to be issued under the title *Figs from Thistles,* right after *Second April.* But his delinquency made her feel that both volumes might be gone aglimmer, so she decided to have *Figs* published as a chapbook immediately by Frank Shay, owner of a Village bookshop. Perhaps she thought it would prod Kennerly into action and that separate publication as a chapbook would do no harm to her reputation as a serious poet. However, she reckoned without the tremendous response of the public to the poems in the little paper volume, which appeared in November, finally entitled *A Few Figs from Thistles.*

A disillusioned postwar generation identified at once with the defiant spirit of "First Fig," the soon to be famous and much quoted—or misquoted—"candle quatrain." Those four lines, beginning with the calm statement "My candle burns at both ends,/It will not last the night," but gleefully assuring foes and friends that it "gives a lovely light," catapulted Edna St. Vincent Millay into an enormous popularity as "the poet laureate of the twenties." It was a dubious honor and one she never completely lived down. She was also hailed as "the spokesman for the new woman" and "the voice of rebellious, 'flaming' youth." The second "Fig," taunting tradition in a neatly worded couplet—"Safe upon the solid rock: the ugly houses stand/ Come and see my shining palace built upon the sand!"—was almost as widely quoted as the first by a generation kicking up its heels in revolt against Victorianism. And she flaunted the independence of women in love in such poems as "Thursday," in which the poet asserts, "And if I loved you Wednesday . . . I do not love you Thursday"; "Daphne"; "The Penitent"; and "To the Not Impossible Him." These poems brought Edna Millay the undying admiration and loyalty of the "new woman," but she was not entirely pleased to be ranked their spokesman.

The five sonnets in this small volume included, in Wilson's judgment, two of her best to date: "Love, though you riddle me with darts" and "Oh, think not I am faithful to a vow!/Faithless am I save to love's self alone." The latter, expressing a dominant Millay theme, became a kind of credo among young neophytes of feminism. Whatever the shadings of merit in the poetry, however, *A Few Figs . . .* was widely read and quoted. It was also often parodied. The poet was rather dismayed by its popularity, not to mention the notoriety the volume brought her over the next ten years. Her decision to publish light verse separately had seemed wise, but it was one of her undeniable mistakes. The volume created an image of Edna St. Vincent Millay that was not easily dispelled and that was only a fragmentary view of her essentially serious art.

That December Edna's apartment was so chilly she could not stay up long enough to type her current Nancy Boyd piece, which she was now doing regularly for *Vanity Fair*. Bunny Wilson brought her his electric heater and found her looking so forlorn and miserable, bundled up in a bathrobe under the covers, that he suggested she have a complete change—perhaps join the general exodus of American literary lights who were all leaving for Europe. The notion appealed to her, and so "it was decided she should go abroad," according to Wilson. Crownin-shield arranged for her to go as a foreign correspondent for *Vanity Fair*—she was to send in two articles a month, which made it possible for her to be paid on an allowance basis.

After hectic preparations for her journey, in the midst of which Kathleen's marriage took place, and a hasty trip to see her mother, who was again living in New England, Millay sailed for Europe on January 4, 1921. She wrote to assure her mother that the travel plans "had nothing to do with any love affair, past or present." She was going as "a free woman, a business woman, and because she wanted to travel," she said. Bold words, from a sorely aching heart. She received a genial welcome from the French editor of *Vanity Fair,* and she enjoyed the sights along the Seine, the Louvre, and the Tuilleries. She also had the company of compatriots at the cafés—poet brothers Stephen and William Rose Benét, Edgar Lee Masters, and com-poser Deems Taylor. There was in addition Allan MacDougall, who was on hand editing a column like F.P.A.'s "Conning Tower" for the Paris edition of the *Chicago Tribune*. All of these people should have made her feel at home. However, the ele-ment uppermost in Millay's letters from abroad is one of homesickness and nostalgia, alternating with heartsick longing, pleading for word from Arthur Ficke.

She soon met members of the famous circle that came to be known as the "lost generation," but she had no interest in joining them. F. Scott and Zelda Fitzgerald, foremost of the luminaries, made slight impression on her. In fact, as she later told Wilson, Fitzgerald was always self-consciously wise-cracking about his art. He made her think of a stupid old woman with whom someone has left a diamond: proud of the jewel, showing it off to everybody, to the surprise of all who see it because of her inept remarks about it.

The most notable event of her stay in Paris was perhaps the

dinner she had with Brancusi, the gifted sculptor then coming into prominence. He, on meeting her, broke his strict rule of solitude and invited her to his studio. Her description of his atelier—high, white, and spare—in which he lived like a monk, of the dinner he cooked on a stove he had built of stone, and of their congenial chatter in different French dialects, was one of the few communications devoid of an indication that she was pining for home, her family, or her beloved Arthur.

Ironically, just at this time *Second April* finally appeared on the stands in the United States. To Millay, far away in France, preoccupied with emotional problems and involved in new work, its publication was an anticlimax. But it was hailed with shouts of praise by critics at home. Harriet Monroe, writing in *Poetry*, was the first to "sound a fanfare and blow trumpets" for the lyrical volume. Here was the serious poet once more, with verses like "The Blue Flag in the Bog," strangely meditative and metaphysical. The series entitled "Memorial to D.C." (classmate Dorothy Coleman who died in the flu epidemic, 1918), which with "Wild Swans," a brooding cry of eternal longing and loneliness, closes the volume, were especially welcome to readers who found the *Fig* poems too flippant for a poet of Millay's stature. However, the earlier publication of the latter led to an error by critics and some biographers, which was to regard the poems in *Second April* as "more mature" rather than a return to the serious mood of "Renascence." They reacted as if the new poems were written after *Figs*, when in fact most of those in *Second April* were composed during the same period or earlier. The keen quips of Millay's light verse are only indications of the duality that enabled her to be a gay companion, ready for a drink, a dance, a duel of wits, or a momentary romance, while at the same time writing serious poems in varying moods.

It was natural that, as a result of the nearly neurotic nostalgia flooding her letters with waves of homesickness, the work that broke Millay's fallow period should be a fanciful ballad celebrating her mother's jaunty defiance of adversity. Cora Millay's courage, her debonair endurance of the practical nurse's demanding schedule, her constant self-sacrifice, and above all her mysterious ability to provide "most of the luxuries of life," including music lessons and pretty clothes, formed the threads of a half-fable, half-fairy tale, "The Ballad of the Harp-Weaver." First published in 1922 as a chapbook, this brought the poet her most prominent award. Just as Melville used the clumsy, hand-made "grego" in *White Jacket* and the young sailor's old hunting jacket in *Redburn* to signify his own penury and forlornness of spirit, so Edna Millay created little jackets and breeches, woven by a dying widow on "the harp with the woman's head," fabricating "the clothes of a king's son," to denote the spiritual riches she had received from her mother.

At times the letters Edna sent her mother from abroad, brimming with filial love and affection, are almost embarrassing to read—one frequently quoted paragraph cites her mother as the *raison d'être* of the poet's whole career. Their closeness was in direct contrast to the equally devoted but far more reserved relationship between Marianne Moore and her mother. Both were apparently free from compulsion, though the Moore ties became entwined, extricable only by death, not as Millay's were to become loosened by marriage. Rarely in poetry's biographical history are there two such examples of mother-daughter involvement.

In spite of her output, her busy writing schedule, and her travels to England and back to the continent—she even undertook a strenuous tour through the wilds of Albania—Edna Millay continued to feel melancholy and lonely. She was still pining for word from Arthur Ficke. At her request, he had sent her a large photograph of himself, which she carried with her through Albania, but she longed to see *him*. She knew from correspondence with him and Hal Bynner that they had returned from the Orient and that the trip had not improved Arthur's marriage. He was still sending the poet in Europe love sonnets she had inspired, asking her opinion of them, and his letters expressed sentiments of love seared by conflict, so she never was sure what his feelings toward her really were. In October, before she left Albania, almost a year after her first declaration, she wrote him another ardent love letter, expanding the images in some of her sonnets to emphasize her deep feeling for him. Again she received no immediate response. It was a month before she had any word from him, and that a brief inquiry concerning the safety of a rare Japanese print he had loaned her. She was bitterly disappointed, depressed.

By then Edna was staying in a shabby hotel in Vienna, where she had gone because living was cheap and her funds were low. She was perplexed, to say the least, by the sudden change of mood in Arthur's letter. She was lonely and miserable in Vienna. A surprising, indirect marriage proposal from Bynner—received through Arthur, in another cryptic note— seemed at the moment the sole spar to cling to in a sea of uncertainty. On December 23 she sent a halting, quizzical letter of acceptance to Hal, alternating between fond recollections and bewilderment.

A recently published letter from Bynner to Millay * reveals that she must have been too anxious to wait for his answer, so she called him during the holidays at the Players Club, where he stayed in New York and where, she later learned, Arthur was visiting. Hal's letter contained a poem, "The Millay Fingers," half-satiric and sensuous—two stanzas in rhymed free verse written in his keen *Spectra* ** style. Below it, in his scrawled backhand, was a note to "Beloved Edna," which began, "Your call, with its breath of you, stirs through my days." Instead of going back to China, he said, he would come to Europe in the spring and they would "talk deep." He ventured that marriage for either of them "would be jelly," adding, "Uncannily I feel the beckon to be rather for Arthur than for Hal," his oblique way of telling her that he knew Arthur came first in her affections.

---

* *Letters* of Witter Bynner, 1978. Edited by James Kraft. Farrar, Straus & Giroux, New York.
** See the chapter on Amy Lowell; the hoax Bynner and Ficke played on Amy and her Imagism.

Ficke was evidently in a dilemma. He had fallen in love with a young painter, Gladys Brown, whom he had met in New York. Bynner, in a moment of high gallantry, had sent the proposal of marriage to Millay thinking to help her save face, but now he was having misgivings. Arthur, who was aware of Bynner's motives—and probably also knew of Bynner's homosexual leanings—sent a note warning her not to rush into marriage. His next contained a sizeable check to help her over her financial stress; it was followed by his confession of love for the young artist who had come into his life. Though Edna had suspected there must be someone, the news no doubt was a blow. Anyone less spirited would have fallen under it, but although she was momentarily shattered, Millay rallied heroically. She sent a document to Arthur that reached a high point in bravado and feminine strategy. It did not matter "with whom he fell in love, nor how often, nor how sweetly." It would in no way affect their relationship. Alternating between justification of her marriage to Hal and reaffirmation of her ardent vow to his closest friend, she again expressed her profound feeling. As both she and Arthur had said in their sonnets, they would love each other for all time. She commented objectively on some of the poetry he had recently sent her, and in return included a batch of her own, obviously written at this time, and published in her next volume (1922). Several contain lines that point directly to Arthur and her, as when she bids him to

> forget not. . . .
> How first you knew me in a book I wrote,
> How first you loved me for a written line:
> So are we bound till broken is the throat
> Of song. . . .

Arthur Ficke's sonnets and poems concerning Edna Millay and himself present a deeper conflict from the start and a definite ambivalence toward her. In the two-part poem entitled

"Go!" and "Stay," and in the description in "To a Girl Singer," he expresses both admiration and terror at the thought of her.

Whatever her other reactions, Edna gratefully accepted Arthur's check and fled to Budapest, where Dorothy Thompson and a group of writers were spending the winter. With them, she plunged into a round of parties to forget her heartbreak and keep from brooding over her coming marriage to Hal. Still upset by the whole situation, she felt as if "a bee was chasing her and she did not know which way to run." She wrote. Then suddenly a hilarious note came from Hal, letting her know he was more frightened of the future than she. It was followed by a long letter from Norma, describing their mother's deep disappointment at the postponement of a trip to Europe that Edna had promised her. In a flash the poet saw her problems resolved. Nothing, not even marriage, was as important as bringing her mother over to see Europe at her daughter's side. Luckily, Otto Liveright sent a check for five hundred dollars as an advance for a novel Millay had contracted to write, and she sent three hundred dollars of it to Mrs. Millay for passage on the next boat to Paris.

They spent six weeks having a "swell time" in Paris, taking in all the sights together, though the poet was ill much of the time from the food in Vienna and Albania. Often she had to stay in bed, but she didn't want Cora to miss anything, even the "rough parties," so she pushed herself when she should have been resting. In the midst of it all she received the startling news that Arthur and Gladys Brown were in Paris. They had eloped on a sudden impulse, Gladys said long afterward.

Arthur wanted the two women who were so important in his life to meet. He invited the Millays to have lunch with Gladys and him at the fashionable Prunier's restaurant. Whatever Edna Millay may have felt privately, she rose to the occasion with her usual overt enthusiasm. When Arthur introduced Gladys, she made a great fuss over the younger girl. "I just knew when I saw you across the room as we were coming in that you were Gladys Brown!" she exclaimed. "I said to myself, 'There's the girl who took my fellow away!' And then Arthur brought us over to you—and you look so pretty in your red hat and red dress, I just know why he fell in love with you." With that she flung her arms around Gladys and gave her a warm hug. By coming out with the truth she made light of it, and she was so disarming that Gladys was won over instantly, though not permanently. This account, with verbatim quotation, was given to this biographer by Gladys Ficke in 1968. Though she later resented Millay's high-handed ways, she could not help admiring her at first, enjoying the poet's scintillating moods of bright, almost feverish gaiety.

After weeks of sight-seeing by day and partying by night, the Millays decided to leave Paris for England and the quiet of the Dorset downs, where Edna had earlier visited Llewelyn Powys. She was seriously ill, in dire need of rest. Powys found rooms for them in the peaceful village of Shillingstone. There was a tiny hut in the fields there where the poet could rest all day by herself and write, if she felt up to it. A number of poems came out of these quiet weeks, notably the free flowing lyric "On First Having Heard the Skylark," published in *The Buck in the Snow* six years later.

The Millays went on to Ireland and the south of France, where, as before, Edna overtapped her strength. In December she wrote Arthur that she could hardly "drag around." In his manner, he announced that he and Gladys were to be married as soon as he got his divorce; Edna responded that the news was "marvelous," but in the next paragraph she only repeated that she would love him till the day she died. And in her own way, she did. Certainly her early prophecy, that they "would never escape from each other," came true, whether by accident or design.

The close of 1922, although a low point in the physical and emotional life of Edna St. Vincent Millay, marked a high point in her career. "The Ballad of the Harp-Weaver" was printed by

Frank Shay in much the same format he had used for *A Few Figs* and was dedicated to the poet's mother. An expanded edition of the latter appeared. And eight of her sonnets were published in the *American Miscellany of Poetry,* the anthology compiled by Amy Lowell and Louis Untermeyer. In recognition of her artistry in these works Millay was awarded the Pulitzer Prize, the first in the field of poetry to be won by a woman. It was a source of great satisfaction to Millay that "lady poets" were being recognized at last, a principle that meant almost as much to her as the fact that she was the one whose poetry had broken down this particular barrier against her sex.

Books were dedicated to her in 1922—Floyd Dell's published version of *Sweet and Twenty* in a volume of his one-act plays; a long section in an expanded edition of Arthur Ficke's *Sonnets of a Portrait Painter,* entitled "Epitaph for the Poet V (A Hymn to Intellectual Beauty), to Edna St. Vincent Millay." Composed of seventeen sonnets, the latter included most of those Arthur had previously sent to her.

Following the announcement of her award, Edna was invited to make public appearances, and the Liverights were clamoring for her to finish her novel. But her illness prevented her from enjoying this acclaim as she should have. She was too worn out to work on her novel, which she finally abandoned. She huddled in her apartment on Waverly Place and saw few friends. Her mother had gone back to Maine on their return from Europe, and Norma had married Charles Ellis, so now both the poet's sisters had households of their own.

Occasionally Edna went out with her erstwhile suitor Bunny Wilson, and it was through him that the one gleaming event of the dreary winter occurred—her meeting with Elinor Wylie, whose first volume, *Nets to Catch the Wind,* Millay had reviewed while she was in Rome. It was a proud feather in Wilson's literary cap to introduce, as the trusted friend of both, these two accomplished poets and reigning beauties of the twenties. Elinor, with her cameolike, aristocratic face framed by her marcelled hair, with her tall, slim figure, was always perfectly groomed, in keeping with the imagery of her poems. Her incisive irony, and "harsh, unflurried unembittered laughter," in Wilson's words, were a match for Edna Millay's warm, flashing wit and ravishing, red-haired, incandescent charm and impeccable appearance. An immediate and lasting kinship linked these two strong-minded poetic spirits, a feeling that was to become one of the remarkable friendships between poets of the same sex. Their lively sessions arguing over the relative suffering of Keats and Shelley, with Edna taking the side of "Mr. Keats" while Elinor championed "Mr. Shelley," became famous in poetry circles before long. They fought and harried and laughed and loved each other with literary and human fervor.

By spring Edna could barely concentrate on preparing a new volume of poetry, which was to be brought out by Harper, her publisher from this time on. Harper had also agreed to bring out new editions of the three volumes Kennerly had earlier published—he had gone bankrupt and was out of business. However, it was an effort to select and compile the poems she wanted to include. Tess Root, the friend with whom she was sharing an apartment, had been visiting people at Mt. Airy near Croton—Doris Stevens and Dudley Field Malone, an ardent advocate of women's rights—and she persuaded Edna to accompany her one weekend in April.

Arthur and Gladys were there also, and in the evening various friends from the literary community that had sprung up around Croton dropped in. Among them were Floyd Dell and the wife he had finally found for himself, who lived nearby, and Eugen Boissevain, appearing like a benevolent giant or genie for the third time in the poet's life. He was alone. He and Max Eastman had bought a small house on Mount Airy, in the neighborhood, but Max was in Russia. By himself, Eugen may have been more susceptible to Edna Millay's electric allure. In spite of her illness, she had never sparkled more brilliantly, perhaps because she was always inspired by Arthur's "divine absurdities," as she called them in a poem. Ficke's gift for devising games or literary diversions was well known, and his inventive mind produced the vehicle that brought Edna and Eugen together.

Arthur proposed that they put on an impromptu takeoff on a Broadway hit, but reversing the situation. In their drama, an innocent couple from the city is invited to spend a weekend in the country; they unwittingly walk into a clutch of evil country folk who avidly try to bring about their downfall. Edna and Eugen were cast as the innocent pair, and in the course of the action, to their own vast surprise, fell in love right before everyone's eyes! Before she quite realized what had happened, Edna Millay found herself loved and cared for by a man whose love she returned.

Eugene Jan Boissevain had a bonhomie about him. A combination of the successful businessman and a sensitive, artistic spirit, he was of Dutch-Irish descent. His mother's father had been provost of Trinity College in Dublin, and his father was publisher of Holland's principal newspaper. His Dutch ancestors had been shipowners, dealing in East Indies trade. He had come to America as a young man and established a prosperous import firm in downtown Manhattan dealing in coffee, sugar, and copra from Java. He was a well-known *bon vivant* who frankly and openly believed in free love. He had had some analytic treatment with Jung, and was able to view the world with an amiability that won him many friends. As Max Eastman said, Eugen had "the daring to enjoy life."

He now hoped to enjoy it with "Aidna," as he called her, or "Vincie." He saw how ill she was beneath the "high, bright gaiety," and persuaded her to stay in the country and rest, driving into town with him twice a week for diagnostic tests. On July 18, 1923, they were married at Croton-on-Hudson. Arthur Ficke and Gladys Brown were present at the ceremony. In the afternoon they all drove into New York, where Edna entered the hospital for major surgery.

The operation was successful, but it left the poet so weak she could do nothing but rest at Mount Airy. When the proofs of the new book came from Harper, Arthur had to correct them for her. She knew his eagle eye would pick up any errors. From this time on, Arthur Ficke worked with Edna Millay on almost all her published volumes, and he kept a journal—now in Yale University's Beinecke Library—with notes on the preparation of each. He discovered that she passed the time during convalescence memorizing the poetry of those whose work she admired. She knew more of his sonnets by heart than he himself could recite.

The Harp-Weaver and Other Poems came out in November to wide reviews and praise, not only for the title poem, but for its lyricism in general. This was the first of Millay's volumes to yield financial returns as well as fame. With her royalties, plus the enormous fee she had been offered for a lecture tour she was to make after the first of the year, she began paying off debts—her own and the family debts in Camden. She took a fierce pride in the fact that every cent had been made by her writing; she did not want people to think it was her "rich husband" who paid her debts. Her spirit of independence, which Eugen understood from his previous marriage to feminist Inez Milholland, asserted itself in spite of the poet's willingness to have him take care of her. When she was invited to compose and deliver the dedicatory sonnet honoring three suffragist leaders—Susan B. Anthony, Lucretia Mott, and Elizabeth Cady Stanton—at the unveiling of a commemorative statue, she made the trip to Washington, D.C., although she was still not strong. As she read the lines ending "Take up the song; forget the epitaph," she felt deeply gratified at being able to contribute to the cause of women's rights. She dedicated the sonnet to Inez when she included it for publication in *The Buck in the Snow*. The fact that Inez had been one of her college idols was a further bond between Eugen and herself.

The duality of Edna Millay's nature—the conflict between masculine and feminine impulses—seemed always present in her relationships. It may be what caused her "neurotic ill-

nesses," as Wilson termed them. It was probably the basis of
the irritant in their friendship. It was that element, also, which
contributed to Arthur Ficke's doubts and concern, and which
had scared off Hal Bynner on the eve of their marriage. *The
Harp-Weaver* contained all the sonnets she had written in connection with Arthur and the strange triangular situation result-
ing from Hal Bynner's proposal that had now been resolved into
"two right angles," as she said, through Gladys and Eugen.
Any man less understanding, affable, and outgoing than Eugen
Boissevain would have been either lost and discouraged or annoyed. He was admirably suited to be the husband of a mercu-
rial, complex, and gifted poet like Millay.

Eugen was twelve years older than she and, besides his love,
offered her the kind of protection she had never received from
her father—not only loving care, but an adulation like that of a
doting male parent. Her mother had given her encouragement
and inspiration from the beginning, but not the adoration that
Eugen now lavished upon Edna. Within a few years, he gave up
his import business and devoted his whole life to Edna's career.
This may or may not have been a wise move on his part, but it
was an indication of his outlook on life as well as of his attachment to her. Moreover, there were no strings of possession or
possessiveness attached to his devotion. A believer in free love,
he combined the virtues of a lover and companion with those of
a dedicated husband, almost to the point of ubiquity when she
was ill.

Eugen watched over Edna like a nursemaid until she recovered from the operation, and so it was always whenever she
was ill. He found a house for them in New York when she
returned from Washington. Located at 75½ Bedford Street,
right around the corner from the Cherry Lane Theater, it is one
of New York's early three-story brick dwellings—since designated for preservation by the city's landmarks commission—
only nine and one-half feet wide by thirty feet deep. It soon
became famous as "Edna Millay's, the narrowest house in the

Village." They were scarcely settled before the poet had to leave for Pittsburgh and points west on her first reading tour, which proved a huge success despite her fears.

As soon as she got back from that, she and Eugen sailed on a world cruise for the belated honeymoon Eugen had promised her.

The Fickes, following their marriage in Edna and Eugen's Bedford Street house—a hectic affair which the poet herself arranged with her usual flurry—had moved into a studio apartment she found for them around the corner at 42 Commerce Street, above the Cherry Lane Theater, overlooking the Boissevains' courtyard. The four were together a great deal in rapport unusual even among close friends.

Millay's career continued to burgeon. *The Harp-Weaver* went into many printings, and her audience grew with the readings. She received a signal honor in 1925, when Deems Taylor, who had been commissioned by the Metropolitan Opera to compose the first American opera to be produced by that eminent company, asked her to write the libretto. He felt it should be in blank verse, and he preferred her to other American poets. She was pleased but approached the project with some trepidation, in spite of her background in music and the theater. Eugen, who was "utterly delighted" that "Aidna" had received the offer, believed that all she needed was a proper place to work. This meant the quiet and seclusion of the country. They both agreed that "the narrowest house in New York" was too cramped, no matter how quaint. But the Mount Airy home was now occupied by Max Eastman, who had returned from the Soviet Union, bringing his Russian bride, Eliena. Since Eugen had always wanted a country place with some land, he and Edna started looking around. They found a sprawling fruit and berry farm near Austerlitz, New York, just across the Massachusetts border. The house and outbuildings needed much repair, and the seven hundred acres of orchards and berry patches drastic pruning.

They often went to the country for weekends with Arthur and Gladys or visited Elinor Wylie and Bill Benét, who had a home in New Canaan. In May, Tess Root, whom Edna had introduced to F.P.A., was married to the famed columnist in a lovely outdoor ceremony at the country home of friends near Greenwich, Connecticut. Afterward, Edna and Eugen drove to New Canaan with Arthur and Gladys and Elinor and Bill. The six notable personalities spent "Saturday night and all of Sunday together" in both intellectual and social harmony, pierced only by sharp repartee on literary subjects.

None of the six at the weekend party, except possibly Benét, was physically fit. Yet all of them burned with the highly intelligent, emotional fervor of the artist. They reveled in the recklessness of the era and scorned prudent health care as they scorned Prohibition. They had all consumed "rafts of caviar and oceans of champagne" at Tess and F.P.A.'s wedding and were not inclined to drop the mood of celebration. They acted and spoke as they felt, on impulse and inspiration.

In June Edna received word that on the fifteenth she was to be awarded an honorary Doctor of Letters degree from Tufts College, another milestone for her. She and Eugen decided they would move into their new country home right after the presentation, no matter how little progress had been made on remodelling the house. By June 22, 1925, they were there, "in one of the loveliest places in the world," Edna wrote her mother. Surrounded by the forested rims of neighboring mountains, the property was covered with wildflowers, particularly steeplebush, a wild spirea whose tall, pink spires dominated the fields and meadows. Edna combined the flower name and the site of the estate to form "Steepletop." Arthur Ficke, following her lead when he and Gladys bought a home in nearby Hillsdale, called his place Hardhack, another common name for the same wildflower. Though it took longer than they expected to remodel the house and reclaim the farmland, Steepletop was the home base for Edna Millay and her husband for the next twenty-five years—the rest of their lives.

For the first months it was no haven, however. The poet found sanctuary from the constant din of the renovation in a shanty she had fixed up as a study, off in the fields. Here, with only a table, a chair, and a "pot-bellied stove" to "roast her back" in winter, she started work on the opera libretto. She had chosen an old legend from the Anglo-Saxon chronicles of tenth-century England, similar to *Tristan and Isolde*. She finally entitled it *The King's Henchman*. Although an opera libretto placed certain limitations on her, she succeeded in making her characters move by their emotions to the music of poetry, particularly in the love scene of the second act, which Edmund Wilson, in his laudatory review, called "one of the high points of her poetry."

Her achievement was remarkable, since she wrote the libretto with little knowledge of the composer's score. She and Deems Taylor had only four conferences in the year and a half they spent creating the opera. Most of their exchange was by mail. And she was working under various handicaps. In addition to the hubbub of the household, she could not get rid of a constant headache, which was accompanied by dancing spots in front of her eyes. She and Eugen left the farm only to consult doctors, but the specialists were as baffled as the patient, for they could find nothing wrong with her eyes. She was worried, too, about the health of her two most cherished friends, Arthur Ficke and Elinor Wylie. The condition of both was alarming.

Her own peculiar problem persisted all winter. As she worked in her little shanty, she occasionally looked out at the snow-covered fields, only to see them "through a dotted veil," as she wrote Frank Adams. It was strange, in view of her new life—the peaceful surroundings, and especially her success as a poet. The libretto composition was also going well. In the midst of all she was trying to do, including a preface to a book of poems by her old friend Abbie Huston Evans, she would have to stop and consult another specialist. Among the many who offered gratuitous advice was the psychoanalyst Merrill Moore (a friend of poets who wrote over a thousand love sonnets himself), who cornered her at a cocktail party and suggested that she might subconsciously have an "occasional erotic impulse" toward someone of her own sex, causing inner conflict and tension. Edna's typical reaction was to exclaim, "Oh, you mean I'm homosexual! Of course I am, and heterosexual, too: but what's that got to do with my headache?" Her retort put an end to any possible cure of her headache through psychiatric treatment. She would not countenance the idea that her spotted vision and persistent headache, which lasted well over a year, was in any way due to her complex emotional life.

The Fickes, who had gone to Santa Fe, New Mexico, for Arthur's health, invited Edna and Eugen to visit them—entirely at the formers' expense.* Arthur thought Edna's condition might clear up in the high altitude, and he would help her prepare her libretto for the publishers. He was overjoyed to see them arrive in mid-October, Edna radiant with relief at the thought of having a good time with close friends instead of consulting a doctor. Hal Bynner, who had settled in Santa Fe in 1922, was on hand much of the time. By December 6, the manuscript for *The King's Henchman* was mailed to Harper. Now Edna could relax completely and enjoy the Southwest.

She and Eugen left New Mexico in time to be at Steepletop for Christmas, and early in January rehearsals began for *The King's Henchman*—February 17 had been set as the premiere. Opening night was a gala event. A spectacular audience filled the hall to capacity, and judging by the ovation the opera received, followed by cries for the composer and librettist, Edna Millay might understandably consider herself a famous woman. She appeared onstage with Deems Taylor to acknowledge the applause in a brief expression of gratitude: "I thank you—I love you all," she said, bowing. Taylor, also bowing, seconded her

---

* As related by Gladys Ficke in an interview with this biographer in 1968.

words gallantly with equal simplicity. "That's just what I was going to say," he told the audience.

Henchman received excellent reviews from the music critics, and was given five performances following the premiere, playing to capacity audiences. The production was taken on a highly successful road tour, and it did much to sweep away the barriers against American opera and opera sung in English. The published version appeared less than a month afterward and within three months was in its nineteenth printing. It was dedicated to Eugen Jan Boissevain, but, as might be expected, the dedication gave no indication of his relationship to Edna St. Vincent Millay. Like Ruth Hale, a feminist writer and friend of hers who was married to Heywood Broun, Millay adhered to the prime precept of the Lucy Stone League all her life. The League was founded by feminist Lucy Stone, who refused to take her husband's name, and convinced many women to adopt the same stand, forming an active League, still in existence.

The year 1927, which began so auspiciously, ushered in a portentous period of her life, one that involved an increasing social consciousness, sense of justice, and a greater concern for human welfare and world affairs as well as the arts.

Ever since her return from Europe Millay had been involved to some extent with the movement to save the anarchists Sacco and Vanzetti from the electric chair, a fate to which they had been consigned by an unrelenting jury and judge on insufficient evidence in 1920. In the seven years since, many committees had been formed to petition a new trial, but all appeals had been denied by Judge Thayer of Massachusetts, who cited a state law allowing the judge who tried a case initially to refuse appeals for retrial. A committee of literary figures had joined the movement midway in the struggle, and Edna Millay and her sister Kathleen, along with Robert Benchley, Dorothy Parker, John Dos Passos, Maxwell Anderson, John Howard Lawson, Arthur Ficke, and Witter Bynner, to name a few, sent letters and signed petitions on the prisoners' behalf, but to no avail.

The date of execution was set for August 23, 1927. In a forerunner of today's protest marches, Edna joined the parade organized by the defense committee in Boston to plead for a stay of execution. She and Dorothy Parker, along with the male leaders of the literary contingent, were arrested and held on bail till Eugen came to their rescue. But Millay would not rest until she had seen the governor privately. She wrote him a passionate plea for mercy, which was delivered by messenger an hour after her interview. But all efforts failed, and she was among the silent crowd standing in a deathwatch directly in the shadow of the Old North Church. Toward midnight prayers were said, and Edna read the first of five poems she was to compose in commiseration for the condemned prisoners, "Justice Denied in Massachusetts." Half an hour later, Sacco and Vanzetti died in the electric chair.

Edna was determined to do "anything to keep people from going to sleep on the subject." As usual, she was overzealous in her efforts. Back at Steepletop, she took precious time from her poetry writing, which was at fever pitch just then, to finish an article for *Outlook*, a current events magazine, because she felt it important to keep people aroused. Entitled "Fear," the piece had the passion of dramatic poetry and was almost biblical in tone. Without mentioning Sacco or Vanzetti or any statistics of the trial, she wrote a heated jeremiad in moving and poetic prose in the hope of awakening in American people an awareness of the enormous miscarriage of justice that had taken place, that could take place again if they did not change the laws and rid their lives of the real criminals—greed and blind prejudice.

The article, published November 9, 1927, brought invective and denunciation down on its author. She was called a Communist, an advocate of anarchy, and a "parlor pink" for her efforts to insure a measure of justice for the future. The one bit of mail that gave her pleasure and comfort was a note from Bynner, full of praise for the writing, and admiration for her courage.

Disillusioned temporarily, she still continued to compose poems relating to the case, writing in company with many other writers who felt as she did—novelists, playwrights, and other poets. It may well be that the literature they produced aided in bringing about legal reform.

From 1927 on, Edna and Eugen spent part of each winter in a warm climate and usually part of the spring or late fall on tour. As a rule, Eugen accompanied her, making the hotel arrangements, seeing to it that she was not disturbed by phone calls, reporters, or any intrusions that might prevent her from resting or writing between appearances. Sometimes his ardent care was resented by people who had scheduled the poet to read, especially when he whisked her away the moment she finished, as he did when she appeared at the Open Book, a shop in Pittsfield run by Robert Frost's daughters, Lesley and Marjorie. Scores of fans who had expected to meet Edna Millay or get her autograph in copies of her books were disappointed. Lesley was both annoyed and amazed. How could a feminist like Millay allow herself to be led off by her husband like a child? It was a riddle to those who had seen a militant Millay in action during the recent controversy but did not know her well enough to understand that Eugen's protective care filled a long-neglected need in her life. This was another paradox in her complex makeup. She was both feminist and feminine, militant and reticent, intellectual and emotional.

During the fall of 1927 and the winter of 1928, Edna wrote many of the poems that were to form her new book, *The Buck in the Snow*. The title was taken from a pensive lyric evoked by the sight of a dead buck she discovered one winter day, his "wild blood scalding the snow," shortly after she had seen him and his doe rise in "lovely long leaps" over the wall into the hemlock woods. The question of life and death—the imposing inevitability of death—alternately engrossed, terrified, or angered her. Written in a subdued tone, this was to be her most somber, brooding volume to date. There were only a few sonnets to be included, one of them the noted "Sonnet to Gath," cited by her friend Edmund Wilson as among her finest.

In preparing and proofing the volume, she had the help of Arthur Ficke, who returned with Gladys to the East to live in the house they bought near Steepletop, staying with Edna and Eugen till their place, Hardhack, was ready. Hal Bynner, who came east to see his mother in New Hampshire, visited at Steepletop and read Edna's new work as she and Arthur prepared it for the press. But he offered so little comment that she could not tell what he thought of it, though he did praise the title poem.

The Buck in the Snow was published in September 1928. It was not received by either critics or readers in America with the enthusiasm that had greeted her earlier volumes, probably because the gravity of the poems did not match her public image. To most readers Edna Millay was a more amorous personality. Those who looked for the bittersweet love lyrics typical of *Second April* and *The Harp-Weaver* were disappointed, and those who expected again to find the gay flippancy of *Figs* were disgruntled.*

But the most sweeping, condemnatory reaction came in a recently published letter from Hal Bynner to Arthur.** Written from Santa Fe on November 11, 1928, his words expressed his "sadness over Edna's book." In a "whisper" he confided, "It seems to me much worse in print than it did in manuscript. In fact except for the title poem, 'Hangman's Oak,' perhaps the Beethoven and certainly one or two of the sonnets . . . I should say the poems were negligible. From her they are a shock: thin substance and strained form. It is as curious a change, almost, as Lindsay's. Maybe it's the subtle curse of lecturing and reading." He thought maybe she should write prose a while, adding, "There was heartache in her 'Fear.' There is mainly

---

* Much later Wilson, in *The Shores of Light* (New York, Farrar, Straus & Giroux, 1952), lauded many of the poems in *Buck* for their lyrical quality and objectivity, including "Dawn," "The Bobolink," "The Cameo," and the telling "Portrait" of himself.

** See *Letters* of Witter Bynner (Farrar, Straus & Giroux, 1978).

headache in this volume. Poor little darling. It makes me love her all the more. She's done enough anyway." Mercifully, Edna never saw his letter. She was deeply disappointed in the reviews, but she would have been bitterly disillusioned if she had read his letter, especially the last part, in view of his previous treasured note praising her article. His paternal air, with its overtones of male condescension, would have both amused and angered her, particularly his indication that he felt her period of true literary output to be past. In 1928, though shaken by the Sacco-Vanzetti ordeal, she remained very much in control of her literary disciplines and was on the verge of making a signal contribution to literature.

She felt compensated, too, for the indifferent reviews in America by the splendid notices she received in England. The British press universally praised her new volume, placing *The Buck in the Snow* above any she had published so far. Whether reviews were discouraging or gratifying, however, they did not cause Millay to change her ways. She wrote as she felt and in the style she considered best for her. In the fall of 1928, she went on a long arduous reading tour, which began at the University of Chicago, where she was introduced by George Dillon, a young, handsome senior who had won several prizes for poetry and who was to be the inspiration for her next, most remarkable volume.

The tour ended in Brooklyn at the Academy of Music, after many stops. Edna had been worried about Elinor Wylie and thought to herself that as soon as this last "chore" was done, she would rush up to New Canaan to see her lovely friend. It was the evening of December 17 and she was backstage getting ready to go on when one of the staff people, without knowing of the close attachment between the two poets, casually mentioned that Elinor Wylie had just died. Edna was stunned. She learned the details of Elinor's death later, but at the moment she felt as if a crushing blow had hit at the vitals of her own life. She had no time to collect herself—she walked out on the stage and, instead of her own poetry, began to recite lines of Elinor Wylie that she had loved and learned by heart. It was a spontaneous gesture; she hardly knew what she was doing.

Edna's bereavement for Elinor Wylie did not find its full expression until ten years later. For the moment she wrote only a few heartbroken lines, beginning "When I think of you/I die too," included two and a half years later in the dedication of *Fatal Interview* to the departed poet but never printed elsewhere. She also wrote "1928," which later became part of the elegiac series of six poems she was to compose as a memorial to her dear witty, beautiful, and unique friend.

One of the poems dealing with life and death in *The Buck in the Snow* was the prescient lyric "Dirge Without Music." In it Millay speaks with subdued rage against death taking the lovely, intelligent people down into the dust. She was "not resigned," nor would she ever be, to the law of life and death. By way of showing her defiance, after the wave of grief for Elinor had subsided, Edna determined to pack every moment that she herself was still above the ground with the joy of living. Despite further sorrows and unexpected reverses, she expressed fully the hedonistic facet of her mystique.

Sometime during 1929 she entered into a love affair of tremendous impact, which inspired the first of her major sonnet sequences, one that was to restore her status as "the finest living lyric poet among women in America" and certainly its "best known," to quote William Rose Benét writing in 1933. For several years the identity of her lover remained a mystery, but it was surmised that it was George Dillon. At their meeting in Chicago, the rapport between the two had been electric in its intensity. Both must have known they would meet soon again.

Although he was only twenty-one at the time—fifteen years younger than Millay—George Dillon was already recognized as a distinguished scholar and gifted poet of great promise. After graduation, he became associate editor on Harriet Monroe's *Poetry,* and he was soon known as one of the most charming men in literary circles, a reputation he never lost. Just when he and Millay realized and fulfilled their love is difficult to place, but from Dillon's letters to his sister in Virginia, and from the testimony of contemporary poets who knew him well, the affair began shortly after her appearance at the university and ran its course in about a year. As with Arthur Ficke, Edna remained Dillon's friend and colleague long afterwards. In any case, *Fatal Interview*, her volume of fifty-two sonnets in celebration—or commemoration—of a recent love affair, dedicated to Elinor Wylie, was published by Harper in May 1931. It was hailed by the critics generally for the sustained quality of its passionate lines and its artistic maturity. Two decades after it was published, Edmund Wilson called it one of the great volumes of poetry of this century.

The sonnet sequence traces the course of a troubled and fervid love relationship from its inception through its heady Olympian consummation to its deep, sorrowful, poignant close. Millay took her title from the opening phrase of John Donne's sixteenth elegy in his celebrated series immortalizing a tragic love affair: "By our first strange and fatal interview. . . ." She began by questioning the worth of her objective, wondering why she should want to "forsake her spiritual wings to journey barefoot with a mortal joy." As the Celtic pagan in her wins out over the New England puritan, she grows rapturous over an irrational and as yet unreturned love. This phase culminates in an outburst of disarming generosity toward her lover, the desire to give all, openly and without guile.

With lilting lyricism Sonnet XI begins, "Not in a silver casket cool with pearls/Or rich with red corundum or with blue," and leads to a figure of speech as refreshing as a field of wildflowers in the morning. There is an eloquence that seems to epitomize the poet's entire philosophy. "Love in the open hand," the first phrase of the sestet, which she read with deliberate emphasis, almost too slowly some thought, in readings and recordings, reveals the core of Millay's concept of sexual joy. To picture the gift of love as "a brimming hatful of freshly gathered cowslips or a skirtful of shining apples" is to see love as the constant and timeless rejuvenator; then the ever-present child in the artist comes forward as Edna Millay in the often-quoted final couplet appears with overflowing arms, "calling out as children do, 'Look what I have! And these are all for you.' "

The next sonnet is an ecstatic expression of joyful sexual consummation, a powerful paean to the pleasures of sexual joy, which endow the lover with the gifts of the gods. The images are in direct contrast to those of the preceding sonnet; the woman in the poet has superseded the child. The other sonnets present their own varied richness. Readers thrilled to the idea in the twenty-sixth sonnet of "love like a burning city in the breast," one of Millay's most felicitous images. Perhaps the most celebrated of the fifty-two is the thirtieth, which begins, "Love is not all: it is not meat nor drink/Nor slumber nor a roof against the rain." Her recorded reading of these lines is almost chilling in intensity, and the sonnet is often cited in books, as in *Love, Sex and Identity,* used as a text in a course on "The Erotic Impulse" at New York City's Pace University.

The immediate effect of *Fatal Interview* on her public career was to increase her popularity, doubling the demands and the fees for her readings. Everyone was eager for a look at the poet who had written such an amazing book of love sonnets precisely at a time when the form was being actively denounced and repudiated by such as T. S. Eliot and Ezra Pound. Millay scorned Eliot's edicts and paid no heed to her detractors; she had more than enough admirers. People everywhere jammed lecture halls to hear her. She received offers for a series of radio broadcasts, which soon materialized in a network series of poetry readings by Edna St. Vincent Millay, an unheard-of sort of venture in radio entertainment. Magazines and newspapers clamored for interviews. And all the time controversy and rumor ran wild over the "names and dates" of the principals in *Fatal Interview.*

It so happened that Dillon's second volume, *The Flowering Stone*, appeared in 1931 also, winning the Pulitizer Prize for poetry. As he was the youngest recipient of that award to date, he was accorded much praise and publicity. His name was quickly linked with Edna Millay's, especially since she was one of the sponsors for the Guggenheim Fellowship he received in 1932. And by the time Millay's first biographer, Elizabeth Atkins, came forward in 1936 with the statement, on Eugen's testimony, that "a still-breathing married woman, name and dates given, has written a poem of extra-marital passion," some of Edna's colleagues assumed that the identity of the lover had been disclosed. One poet vowed that Atkins named George Dillon, though she at no time named anyone.

Edna let Eugen handle everything and took no part in publicity matters aside from the readings. When the book came out, she was deep in sorrow over the death of her mother, who had died suddenly of a heart attack in March 1931 while Edna was still mourning the loss of Elinor Wylie. Edna wrote memorial poems that caught the spirit of both these women who had meant so much to her. The fact that she dedicated *Fatal Interview* to Wylie, whose work she esteemed so highly, is indicative of the value she herself placed on the book. This volume and the sonnet sequence that followed it, "Epitaph for the Race of Man," ensured Edna Millay's literary reputation as a sonneteer of the first rank and a major American poet.

"Epitaph" had been brewing in the poet's brain for almost fifteen years. In 1920, when she was caught up in the antiwar fervor that produced *Aria Da Capo*, she began thinking of man's tendency toward self-destruction. She first cast the poem in the same form as "Renascence." Initially, the theme was evolutionary, tracing the story of man from the early stages through his rise and to his fall by his own undoing. The poem surprised her friend Wilson when she read parts of it to him one night in his apartment, giving him a new idea of her range. He had not suspected that she possessed a "tough intellectual side," as he termed it. She put the work aside for years but began to consider it again after she and Eugen moved to Steepletop. There they often studied the stars with Arthur and Gladys, or alone. As her knowledge of astronomy increased, her concept in this study of man expanded to take in his behavior in relation to the universe.

Viewing Earth as a microscopic planet in the cosmos, the sequence starts with the prediction that long before its core is cold, Earth will be utterly still, and man and his engines will be gone. From there the sonnets look backward in time to the age of dinosaurs, then proceed slowly forward "through fifty million years of jostling time," to man, "crawling out of ooze and climbing up the shore." Destined to stride across the sky like the sun, this strange, brilliant creature capable of laughter and "droll tears," of music and art and the invention of engines, is then mysteriously gone without a trace, and the silent Earth cannot tell the story of his demise. It is the poet who reveals the tragic reason for his eradication. Following him through the trials of the ages, the sonneteer tears away the veil of mystery to show him receiving destruction "at his brother's hand."

The last five sonnets in this sequence are a core of Millay's canon of antiwar poetry. The play on words is inadvertent but not inappropriate, for she waged a war of words against violence and destruction by the military until events in Europe leading up to World War II caused her to become an interventionist. The theme of man's inhumanity to man, of his cancerous greed, is sounded in eloquent, powerful passages, until, in the seventeenth sonnet, the reader, with a sense of horror, sees man "set in brass on the swart thumb of Doom." In the closing sonnet, she sings with melodic phrasing a heartbreaking lament for "most various Man, cut down to spring no more," and "all the clamor that was he, silenced, and all the riveted pride he wore." Then, with a masterful stroke, in answer to the wracking question, "What power has brought you low? whose the heavy blade?" the poem ends with the tender admonition, "Strive not to speak, poor scattered mouth; I know."

At the time "Epitaph" appeared, in the volume *Wine From These Grapes,* published in November 1934, it was usually lumped together with the rest of the social-problem poems in the book, like the acrid "Apostrophe to Man," a withering denunciation of war included in a 1973 anthology of antiwar poems. Readers who were dismayed by the opening line, "Detestable race, continue to expunge yourself, die out," and critics who cited the poem as evidence that the author of "Renascence," there a reaffirmer of the vitality of the human spirit, had become a pessimistic cynic. They apparently neglected to note the explanatory subtitle, "On reflecting that the world is ready to go to war again." The element that sets "Epitaph" apart from other poetry about social problems is its broad perspective and poetic excellence, which enables the work, while retaining its value as social commentary, to reach the realm of art. Yet the significance of "Epitaph" is rarely recognized. In fact, it is seldom mentioned by chroniclers or anthologists.

Most anthologies include, besides "Renascence" and "God's World," only the lighter verse and the easily understood love lyrics of Millay. They leave out many sonnets in the major sequences. Fortunately, a few eminent critics—like Edmund Wilson, Robert Hillyer, and Max Eastman—and a handful of discriminating admirers have been unafraid to place Edna Millay's mastery of the sonnet in its proper perspective. Although it is true that she has always been overplayed or underplayed, lauded beyond all bounds or dismissed as a youthful exponent of free love expressed in conventional forms, the sequence comprising "Epitaph" has been generally neglected in either case. But the timelessness of the theme, ironically, more applicable today than it was in 1934; the flawlessness of the technique; and the depth of feeling combine to make this eighteen-sonnet poem profound and enduring. For whatever reason, *Wine* was an immediate success and went into multiple printings.

The years from 1930 to 1936 represent the peak of Millay's

career professionally and financially, as well as creatively. Her popularity was at its height after 1931, and she could not help taking pride in the armload of fan mail, forwarded from the publishers, that Eugen brought back every day from his trip down the hill to the little post office at Austerlitz. It was a pride that became vanity as her reputation grew—Arthur Ficke later wrote that she was "the oddest mixture of genius and childish vanity" that he had ever known.

However, in spite of the fact that outwardly things were going well, in the early spring of 1935 Edna was still a prey to inner doubts and neurotic fears. Her plaintive mood may have been due to a letdown between books, but she soon became involved unexpectedly in an entirely new project. George Dillon, back from extended travels on a renewed Guggenheim award, wrote to ask if Edna would provide the introduction for his translations of Baudelaire. They had often discussed and argued about the French poet's *Les Fleurs du Mal* from a literary point of view. Edna consented at once to write the foreword. He sent a few translations for her to look over, and before she knew it, she was a full-fledged collaborator on Dillon's book. At first they worked separately, but George came to Steepletop for most of the month of August, translating the French "flowers of evil" together with Edna. He then accompanied Eugen and her to Ragged Island, a retreat in Casco Bay that the Boissevains had bought in 1932, for a week's rest.

It was a busy summer and would have been free from worry except that Arthur Ficke suddenly became ill again and was rushed to the hospital for an operation. He nearly lost his life through a surgical error, which extended the usual hospital stay. Even after he came home, it took many weeks till he recovered. He undertook to write of his traumatic experience in a long free verse poem, "Hospital." As always, Arthur read his latest work to "Vincie" and Eugen. Millay was deeply impressed with the fact that Arthur, in spite of his loyalty to the sonnet and his satire of the free verse cultists in *Spectra*, had

adopted the modernists' mode of expression. His reversal undoubtedly influenced her own change of style in her next book.

One cannot help feeling that she already had this next project in mind when she wrote the long introduction to the
Baudelaire book, which included her only discussion of the
creative process in poetry. An "incipient poem," she stated,
shows in shadowy outline that it may be "rhymed or unrhymed; it is trimeter, tetrameter and pentameter; it is free
verse, a sonnet, an epic, an ode, a five-act play." Her next
offering was to contain a sampling of most of these varieties,
and even before she finished the foreword or the final polishing
of her Baudelaire translations, she sent off a few experimental
poems, which her publishers printed in *Harper's Magazine*. She
was exhausted by the time the Baudelaire manuscript was ready
for the press, and took off for Florida, where she could do the
chores of proofreading and revision in a warm climate, rest a
little, and perhaps complete the verse drama she had begun.
Eventually everything was accomplished. *Flowers of Evil* was set
for publication on April 2, 1936. Her own manuscript, which
she called *Conversation at Midnight* and which she planned to
dedicate to Arthur, was completed in its first draft.

She and Eugen drove north again, planning several stops
along the way. The first was at Sanibel Island off the Florida
coast, where the poet hoped to find rare sea shells to add to her
collection, an interest she had kept up since the days in Camden.

When they arrived at the little hotel on Sanibel Island, it
was a full hour before sunset, and Edna was eager to start her
search along the shore. They had the luggage sent up to the
room; one suitcase held the manuscript for her new book. A
short time later, some impulse made her turn and look back up
the beach. To her horrified, unbelieving eyes, she saw the hotel
engulfed in flames! In what must have been a flash fire, the
building was burnt to the ground, and all their belongings,
including the manuscript, burned with it. They drove misera-

bly back to Steepletop, and finally got home, weary and be-draggled.

The poet went to work at once, trying to recall the lost lines of her experimental verse drama. It was an almost impossible task, since, as she explained in her foreword, she was acutely conscious that, except for the few poems published in the magazine, "no line of the book existed anywhere except in her memory." She wrote under constant strain, hardly aware of other events in her career. To add to her troubles, another accident occurred a few weeks after their return.

She and Eugen were driving home from a party one night. Edna was leaning against the car door. Suddenly it flew open as they took a sharp turn, and she was "hurled out into the pitch darkness." Her right arm was hurt, and several nerves were injured. For a time then, and again two years later, she had to wear a sling, and could not play the piano or use the typewriter, a serious handicap at a time that she was preparing a manuscript for her editor.

The strange mishap was almost symbolic of Edna Millay's ensuing career, which went downhill from this point on. The publication of the Baudelaire translations, which she insisted be entitled *Flowers of Evil*—the French poet's own title—instead of *Selected Poems of Charles Baudelaire*, as the publishers suggested, did little but confirm her relationship with George Dillon in the public eye. There were other sexual episodes in Edna Millay's life from time to time. These are recorded obliquely in the five poems of "Not So Far as the Forest"; more realistically in "Theme and Variations," a group of eight lyrics. In "Rendezvous" there is an account of a meeting in an Eighth Street apartment. But Millay was never specific as to a lover's identity. She later flatly refused her publisher's idea for a book concerning her "impulsions" with the classic retort, "Though I refuse your proposals, I welcome your advances."

Professionally, the translations and *Conversation at Midnight* did little to advance her financial situation. She was never as prosperous as she made it appear. More deleterious was the effect both these books had on her literary status. Academic recognition continued at this time and later. In 1937, New York University conferred on her the degree of Doctor of Humane Letters, the third such honor she received. Others were from Tufts and Russell Sage College. In 1940 she was elected to the American Academy of Arts and Letters. However, the reviews of *Conversation at Midnight*, published in 1937, brought the first signs of a serious decline in applause from critics and audiences alike. The verse drama, set in the drawing room of "a fine old house in Tenth Street," contained too much dialectic to make either good drama or poetry. It featured seven male dinner guests of different religions, professions, and political persuasions, in a late night conversation over brandy that revealed Millay's own growing concern for the direction of world events. The style was diffuse, and the work failed to sustain readers' interest with anything like the intensity of "Renascence," *Fatal Interview*, or "Epitaph for the Race of Man." Even passages of pure entertainment, like the rhymed speeches that parody Ogden Nash, sounded more like Nancy Boyd's "Distressing Dialogues" than the poetry of Edna Millay. That point was made by her friend Edmund Wilson, who reviewed the volume.

Wilson's article had overtones of sorrowful lament for the "old strong beat of English verse" in general. "Now Edna Millay," he said, "one of the sole surviving masters of English verse, seems to be going to pieces, too. . . . In *Conversation at Midnight*, you see metrics in full dissolution." His conclusion, however, was: "I don't complain of this state of affairs. I know that it is all in the cards. And *Conversation at Midnight* is, in any case, a highly entertaining interlude in Edna Millay's work. Miss Millay at her most relaxed is livelier than most of our poets at their brightest. Yet I miss her old imperial line." Edmund Wilson never deviated from his high opinion of Millay's "imperial line," or indeed of her work as a whole. Two years after her death he paid full tribute to "this great writer," as he called her.

And as late as 1970, two years before he died, Wilson wrote in a letter to this biographer, "I agree with you that Millay is scandalously underrated today."

It is undeniable that Millay's poetry had become unfashionable by the time she died. Unfortunately, she was not able to keep herself from writing poetry with a "message," to the detriment of her art. Through members of Eugen's family, who suffered under the heel of Hitler, she became acutely aware of the danger of that dictatorship as early as 1933. By 1938, the fall of Czechoslovakia and the terrible mounting turmoil in Spain, in addition to her discernment of the incipient "holocaust" in Germany, all evoked strong poems of anguish and despair, as indicated by the title poem of her next book, *Huntsman, What Quarry*, published in 1939. The metaphor of the lead lyric unmistakably refers to the human quarry being hunted down in Europe. Again, in the moving sonnet "Czecho-Slavakia," with its unorthodox rhyme scheme suggesting broken sobs, the poet says she would seek a balm in Gilead for the unhappy land but "the oils and herbs of mercy are so few;/Honour's for sale"; "the barking of a fox has bought us all." She employs the same hunting figure but in a different context.

Huntsman was artistically saved by many lyrics and sonnets unrelated to world problems. Beginning with "The Ballad of Chaldon Down," which opened the volume, there were half a dozen poems of fanciful turn, the product of Edna and Eugen's visits with the Powyses in Dorset. They must have cheered Edna's beloved friend Lulu, who had suffered from tuberculosis for years. He was in a Swiss sanitarium by the time the book came out, and he died on December 2, 1939, to Edna's profound grief. He had disapproved of the introduction to the Baudelaire translations, though he'd still consented to write a paragraph for the jacket. These poems, especially the melodic ballad, restored his faith in Millay's gift.

Edna included in *Huntsman* at last the six elegiac poems she had written to Elinor Wylie, beginning with the 1927 "Song for

a Lute" and ending with the beautiful lyric, "Over the Hollow
Land." (This was her third series of six-poem elegies, and all
three were to women.) Nor was sexual love neglected in this
volume. Part II opens with a sonnet addressed to "almighty
Sex." The poet admits that though her "lofty tower" was
"reared to Beauty, it was wrought from the human mortar of
honest bone, anguish, pride, and burning thought." As if in
postscript, she adds that "lust was there, and nights not spent
alone," emphasizing, with the restraint of quiet statement, the
most important factor in the towering emotion of sexual love. In
the third sonnet of Part II, she reaffirms her belief in the
genuineness of love, no matter how fleeting, and she utters,
with God as her judge, the cry of "holy, holy/Upon the name of
love, however brief."

Here also are poems describing the joy of marital companionship as the autumn of life nears, depicting a relationship
that obviously paralleled hers with Eugen. "Thanksgiving Dinner," a loosely woven lyric of great charm, discloses a hidden
"pride in her love" through the metaphor of the frost-bitten
"broken garden." The monologue "Menses," which has the
stage direction, *"He speaks, but to himself, being aware how it is
with her,"* is an objective portrait of herself and Eugen. The
vicious barbs she could deliver in sudden fits of antagonism,
and her own chronic moodiness and quixotic behavior is per-
ceived through the patient, understanding eyes of her husband.
The poem is obviously a tribute to his devotion and forbearance
and was perhaps written to atone for her increasingly fretful
and trying temper tantrums. The trenchant poem of self-
accusation that follows it, "The Plaid Dress," bears out this
theory. An intense personal conflict, the eighteen-line free
verse reveals petty sins and selfishness and the deep inner
guilts from which the poet evidently suffered.

Millay's neurotic state was aggravated by a prolonged re-
currence of the bursitis she'd had following the strange automobile accident. This second siege, brought on by strain in

trying to rid the lawn of plantain weed, was more severe; the constant pain was at times sheer agony. She could hardly lift her arm to eat, let alone type, or play the piano. She bore her arm in a sling again and tried to make the best of it, hoping the bursitis would run its course. However, when the pain had not subsided by the end of summer, Eugen insisted that she consult a doctor, and a long series of medical treatments ensued. She was in the hospital three times in one year for nerve surgery, and was in addition subjected to countless X-rays, infrared ray treatments, and medication, including morphine, that had hardly any effect. Eugen, who learned how to give her the injections, was almost ill himself with worry over her, and over his family in Europe and their diminished finances. His own income was abruptly cut off with Hitler's entry into Holland; the Boissevains, a prominent family, were stripped of their fortune and position. Though Eugen's parents were safe, one of his cousins was tortured by the Nazis, and others were in continual danger.

Ill as she was, Edna tried to awaken people to the dangers of the mad dictatorship that was devouring Europe. She dashed off a long series of rhymed stanzas in which the couplet and title, "The tidal wave devours the shore,/There *are* no islands any more," ran like a distraught refrain. In parentheses she added by way of explanation for their imperfection, "Lines written in passion, and in deep concern, for England, France, and my own country." The piece appeared in newspapers and literary journals, and Harper published it in pamphlet form in the spring of 1940.

Huntsman, in spite of its valid poetry, did not do well in sales and Steepletop had to be mortgaged. Despite her wretched condition, Edna made several reading tours in the summer of 1940. She needed a stimulant both before and after performances to get her through—Eugen had a flask of whiskey ready to hand her as she went on and came off stage.

Through all her trials she continued to sound the warning

bell for America to arm against the threat of Nazi aggression. She wrote poems in feverish haste, acutely aware that there was very little of artistic merit in her new volume, *Make Bright the Arrows,* which was to be published in the fall. She took its title from words of the prophet Jeremiah. In one of the two poems that survived and is still quoted, "To the Maid of Orleans," she summons the ghost of Joan of Arc to reinforce her call to arms. "The tidal wave . . ." poetic diatribe that had appeared in pamphlet form was to be included here, and Edna wanted this collection to be issued the same way, but Harpers was not inclined to publish a Millay work that could be thrown away after the message had been absorbed. As usual, Edna consulted Arthur on the matter. He advised, indeed begged her not to publish the book at all.

Privately Ficke felt, as he stated in his notes, that the trouble with the poetry in *Make Bright the Arrows* was not so much "that it was propaganda as that it was *bad* propaganda." It was bad because it was "so largely hysterical and vituperative." Her egocentricity, he felt, "repelled the very people she wished to attract." But he would not voice his harsh views in counselling her not to publish. He did, however, persuade her to omit "at least half a dozen of the most blatant and crude" poems in the original manuscript, saving her from even more pain and embarrassment than she eventually suffered as a result of this book. Almost unanimously, reviewers scolded her for her polemics; one of them labeled the book "nothing but fancy doggerel." Others were "insolent to the point of actionable," she wrote later. Some granted that she had been driven to "a noble fury" in her hasty lines of "passionate loathing," but in the main they all consigned the entire book to oblivion, the worthwhile poems along with the rest.

Millay gained respite from physical pain after consulting a specialist at the New York Neurological Institute who loaded her down with vitamins. At first skeptical, she nevertheless adhered to the prescribed regimen, and in March she had one whole day almost free of pain. By fall she wrote to Hal Bynner that she thought she was cured of her terrible two-year malady. The spring and summer of 1941 also brought a brief period of respite from worry over the ever-increasing fires which led to American entry into World War II. She made a recording of her poems: an album of four sides beginning with "Renascence" and including selections from her other early volumes through to the "Harp-Weaver" ballad, which she read with great feeling, and continuing with poems down through her most recent work. When she read "Maid of Orleans" a note of doom sounded in her voice.

Millay also compiled the selections to be included in her twin volumes, *Collected Sonnets* and *Collected Lyrics,* which Harper had suggested and planned to bring out as soon as the manuscripts were ready. For advice on the former she consulted "the Sage on the Hill," as she called Arthur. He came over at once, taking time off his own work on a new volume of poems in order to assist her with both the selections and a preface she was writing.

One of the sonnets from their early exchanges, beginning, "And you as well must die, belovéd dust," had recently caused a rift between the two poets. At a cocktail party, when Edna was several martinis off her guard, Arthur, murmuring the first line, asked pointedly, "To whom did you write that sonnet, Vince?" She was furious at his indiscretion in asking such a question in the crowded room. She could only counter with his name and let the matter drop. A few days later, however, still upset, she wrote him a letter flatly denying that the sonnet was written to him, though she knew he would be hurt. He did not again bring up the question of that sonnet when they were making the selections, except to be sure it was included. He agreed with her choices and most of her omissions, but persuaded her to leave out all but two from *Make Bright the Arrows.* He also convinced her to shorten and revise the lengthy academic preface she was writing.

Arthur gladly took over the task of correcting the proofs, as well as recommending the final wording of the short preface, which was hardly more than a listing of works she'd omitted. Edna had made many excuses, offering "page after page in defense of the things she left out." He felt that "she knew subconsciously that they were very bad, and could not bear the thought that the reader should agree with her." (From her letters it is evident that she knew *consciously* they were bad; otherwise she would not have agreed to delete them.) After scoring the "self-consciousness" in both her personality and parts of her poetry, Ficke praised the beauty and fearlessness of her convictions regarding sexual love, especially as expressed in the sonnets written during their extraordinary exchange of creativity in the 1918–1922 period of their relationship. Whatever their feelings over the years, judging from Ficke's notes and Millay's letters, the spirit of lovers was always present.

All too soon those summer sessions were over, and the stresses of a strife-torn world supplanted the poetic accents of the *Collected Sonnets* and *Lyrics*. Before the end of the year, America entered World War II, and in spite of the cool reception of her latest poetry, Millay continued to write verses on behalf of her "poor, foolish, bewildered, beloved country." One of these, "Not to be Spattered by His Blood (St. George Goes Forth to Slay the Dragon)," was published in the New York *Times* on December 28, just as word came that a cousin, George Ricker, an Army-Air Force officer, was reported missing. It was almost as if the poem had been written for him, she pointed out to her Aunt Susie, his mother. Two weeks later Ricker was declared dead in a plane accident. Probably partly stirred by his death, after New Year's Edna doubled her efforts, working with colleagues on the Writers War Board and the Red Cross.

The poet's service was without pay. Her reading tours were stopped during the war years. Though the two volumes of collected verse and the record album brought in some royalties, her earnings were not enough to keep her and Eugen going. She wrote to Harper and asked if another loan could be arranged. Harper complied. She drove herself spiritually with the fury of a fanatic powerless to act otherwise, even though repelled by the state of the world she was trying to save, and by her own lack of artistic integrity. On June 10, 1942, word came of the civilian massacre at Lidice, the little Czech village totally destroyed by the Nazis for sheltering underground patriots. The Writers War Board called on Millay to write a memorial poem for a short-wave broadcast. She wrote all summer at fever pitch and managed to turn out a dramatic piece entitled *Murder at Lidice,* which was broadcast over NBC on October 19, 1942, as the featured work on a program with Alexander Woollcott and Clifton Fadiman presiding. Actor Paul Muni read the lines of the rapidly written scenes with deep sincerity and subdued passion. The performance was radioed to England, and Spanish and Portuguese translations were beamed to South America. At the close, the author was escorted to the platform to assist in auctioning the bound manuscript of her play. Edna, frail and skeletal in a long red velvet dress, could scarcely tell what was bid. She was glad when it was over to have made $1,000 for war relief.

Afterward, as she moved slowly back to where Eugen was waiting, she was stopped by wellwishers in the invited studio audience, most of them colleagues in New York literary circles. Among them was Jean Starr Untermeyer, who, stunned by Edna's altered appearance, deplored the fact that Millay had become a "travesty" of her former self; she assumed it was the result of Edna's burning the candle at both ends. This may well have been a factor in Edna's ultimate breakdown—she was drinking heavily in order to keep going—but it was more a matter of overwork than of dissipation. Arthur ascribed her "nervous illness" to the fact that she had lost much of her vast popularity and was no longer "the center of the stage." However, the most destructive force was her own inward awareness that she had written and was continuing to write bad poetry compulsively, an incurable disease.

Still, since Millay had been playing the role of unofficial feminine poet laureate for so many years, it was inevitable that she be called upon to represent the nation's artistic expression in crucial moments, and she continued to receive honors. A few months after the *Lidice* broadcast, the Poetry Society awarded Edna Millay its gold medal "for meritorious work and abiding interest in humanity." Such homage was impossible to ignore—despite her uncertain health, she felt she had to attend the ceremonial dinner on January 31, 1943.

Nineteen forty-three brought a completely unexpected personal tragedy: Edna's sister Kathleen, who had been working in a war plant and was going to join the WACS, suddenly died. Inwardly depressed over the failure of both her career as a writer and her marriage, Kathleen had been taking pills and drinking. When she had not been heard from for a few days, the police broke into her hotel room. It was littered with empty gin bottles, and its occupant lay dead in her bed. The death was a deep blow for Edna.

Around the middle of July another blow came with the news that her long-time editor, Eugene Saxton, had died of a heart attack. The poet wrote to his assistant, Amy Flashner, that she felt "utterly lost" without the reassurance of his calm presence at Harper. Edna had come to rely on him not only as her editor but for arranging financial assistance from her publishers. Now between tears of grief she had to plead with Miss Flashner for understanding of her plight, to ask if Harper could help her. As before, her publishers arranged for her to receive income in advance of future publication.

On June 6, 1944, D-day, the National Broadcasting Company planned a twenty-four hour program of news bulletins, prayers, and special items. Once more the Writers War Board called on Edna Millay, and she put her whole heart into writing a "Poem and Prayer for an Invading Army." The piece was read by Ronald Colman, whose diction and feeling brought out the best elements of the work; but just as before, the glaring fact that the poet had not time for the "masonry of art" stood out in spite of Colman's eloquent delivery. Writing "acres of bad poetry," which she hoped would be ploughed under as soon as its message had taken root in the minds of the people, was a strain on Millay. She was beset by a nagging fear that it would be allowed to stand, smothering the richness of her early poetic flowering. These were besides the sorrows occasioned by the recent deaths, sorrows she tried to drown with drink. It all proved too much for her highly strung system. Shortly after the broadcast, she broke down completely and was taken to Doctors Hospital in New York, where she spent months.

When she came out, she was still weak and trembling, and she suffered from the worst affliction a writer, particularly a poet, can experience: she could not compose a single line. The war had ended, so she should have been able to sing for the joy of peace, but the world was too spent with destruction. She felt drained from the war years and from the losses she and Eugen had sustained. They decided to head for Ragged Island.

The stay on the island might have renewed her poetic powers, but there came alarming news from Gladys Ficke when they returned that Arthur had a malignant cancer and was in constant agony. As the weeks went by he worsened. There was little Edna could do, but she felt she must tell him the truth about the sonnet she had written to him. In the last of several notes she sent him she confessed that she *"did* write that sonnet"* to him—the one he had asked her about at the cocktail party. She admitted that she had denied it at the time because she did not want him to know how terribly in love with him she had been when she composed it. Perhaps, she declared, she was still in love with him when he had asked her about it almost twenty years later. The letter had a terseness that implied the finality of the hour.

Arthur Ficke died on November 30, 1945. At his burial Edna Millay read, in addition to passages from one of his favorite poems, Milton's "Lycidas," this poignant, mutually cherished sonnet of hers written to him, beginning, "And you as well must die, belovéd dust." His death left a void which could not be filled. Now more than ever the poet and her husband confined themselves to their two retreats, Steepletop and Ragged Island. Both were the subjects of new poems when Edna finally began to emerge from the nervous prostration and the frustration of producing propaganda poetry. For a time after Arthur's funeral she remained artistically barren, too heartsick to think of new works. But slowly, with the passing months and improving health, the creative urge returned and she started to bring forth true poetry again.

During this time Eugen watched over his "child" as if she were hovering between life and death. Like some benevolent St. Bernard, he guarded her against unexpected callers, warding off unwelcome intruders. Even close friends like Gladys were discouraged from coming over without an invitation. For some reason, Edna did not want to see Gladys. Perhaps it was because she could not bear the thought of seeing her without Arthur. Or maybe now that Arthur was gone, she felt no need to be friends with Gladys. But the latter was hurt and angry at being turned away. She had often enough resented the peremptory way that Millay expected Arthur to drop his own work to help "Vince" prepare a manuscript or correct proofs— he never seemed to mind. Later, when Edna felt stronger, she did see Gladys, but the ghost of Arthur seemed to produce a continuing edge of rivalry between the two.*

Edna's old friend Bunny Wilson and his wife, Elena, stopped by Steepletop in 1948, on the way back from the Berkshire Festival at Tanglewood. Wilson and Millay were meeting for the first time in nineteen years. He was shocked at the change in her; she seemed on the verge of tears, tremulous and tense at the same time. After a few cocktails, she relaxed a little. But when he asked her to recite "The Poet and His Book," one of his favorites and her own, the air was so charged with

---

* This information comes from an interview with Gladys Ficke in 1968.

emotion—in lines like "read me; do not let me die"—that he could hardly bear it. It was a portentous moment.

In 1949, just as the poems for a new volume were beginning to pile up, Eugen was taken to the hospital for suspected lung disease. The trouble proved a malignancy. An operation was performed, and he appeared to be improving, but then he had a relapse and died on August 30, 1949. Edna, stunned by the swiftness and the bleakness of this final blow managed to stay calm during the funeral for her sixty-nine-year-old husband, but collapsed afterward. She had to spend weeks in Doctors Hospital again. When she came out in late October, she was desolate with grief at the loss of the one man who had cared for her so tenderly. She must have wondered how she was going to cope with the routine of daily living, let alone the fact of her sorrow.

For twenty-five years Eugen had assumed the responsibility of the household as well as serving as business manager for Millay. Now he was gone, but she didn't want anyone else to be at Steepletop. She refused to let Norma and Charles live with her. John Pinnie, the neighboring farmer who had been caretaker and handyman for all the years, could do the chores, and she would manage somehow. She even had the telephone disconnected. She would concentrate on completing her new volume of poetry. And she achieved her goal. As she wrote, her lyric gift returned. Her genius for song resulted in a surge of free-line lyrics of which Robert Hillyer was to say, "Here is Edna Millay at her finest."

In October of 1950, the new volume was almost ready, when she received a request from Rolfe Humphries to read a set of proofs and give him an opinion on his translation of the *Aeneid*. She worked all night of the eighteenth, reading, correcting, now and then sipping a little Alsatian wine. At dawn she started up to bed, first leaving a note for the cleaning woman who came in occasionally to do heavy work and ironing. As she went up the stairs, carrying her glass and bottle of wine, she must have felt dizzy. She sat down on the step above the landing, carefully placing the glass and bottle on the step above. And there on the stair, like a wand in the wind, she swayed forward and died. And there John Pinnie found her when he came in for the second time, at three o'clock in the afternoon.

Edna Millay died in the midst of creating poetry, at only fifty-eight years of age. Perhaps in 1948 when, just prior to her serious intestinal operation, she wrote the sonnet for the feminist leaders, she had had an inscription for herself in mind in the line, "Forget the epitaph; take up the song."

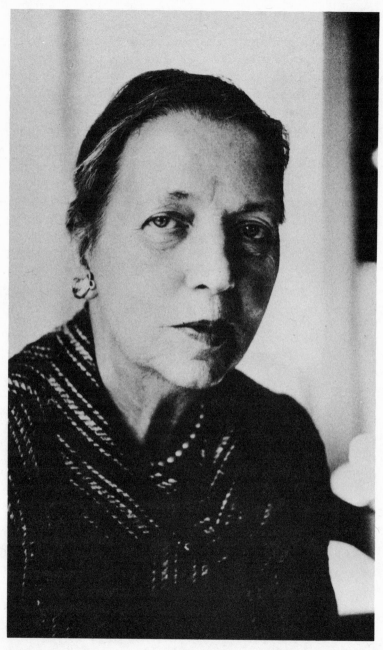

9

LOUISE BOGAN

LIKE Edna Millay, Louise Bogan began life as a waif, moving with her family from one mill town to another. Her early life was marked not only by parental quarreling, but by violence. She, too, was a native New Englander from Maine, born in Livermore Falls on August 11, 1897. She recorded in a journal she began in her late fifties that she must have known violence from birth—a violence "bound up with flight," as she said. In the case of Louise it was her mother who flared up and was constantly fleeing her father's wrath. Both Daniel Joseph and Mary Helen (Shields) Bogan were of Irish descent, and presumably both inherited the Irish temperament, being quick to anger. While Louise was very small these fits of anger passed over her head, except that at one period she went blind for two days. She could recall her vision returning in the sight of the gaslight beside her mother's bureau, but she never knew what caused her to go blind.

Louise's most vivid memory, similar to Millay's view of her father's final leavetaking—but filled with the "utmost terror"

271

rather than sadness—involved the Bogan family trunk. She retained always the sight of its curved lid thrown back and her mother bending over it, tossing things in, crying, the sobs interspersed with sudden screams. Her father, from the shadows of the room groaned each time as if he had been hurt. Then Louise was swept up in her mother's arms and carried out of the room. It was not the first time the scene was enacted, but of the previous instances she remembered only the flight.

The first mill town she recalled with any clarity was Milton, where she and her mother lived in a dingy, down-at-the-heels hotel for a time. She had a brother, Charles, born when her mother was only nineteen. He was ten years older than Louise and away at school during the early unhappy years of her childhood. She had no one close to her to play with except the rough Yankee and French Canadian children who romped in the long rugged pasture back of the hotel.

The hotel building itself housed a dim barroom on the ground floor. The sight of a man's collar stained with blood, lying on the sidewalk outside one Sunday morning, made the impression of sudden violence always threatening. Louise and her mother ate in the hotel dining room, amid, it seemed to the small girl of five, a sea of strange, ugly faces. Her mother became friendly with the waitresses at first, and later had one or two "familiars"; but Louise could only stare with a child's natural curiosity and her intuitive clinical eye at the ugly scars from skin diseases that disfigured the faces of both the men and women who lived in the shoddy hotel. Their bodies, too, were thin as scarecrows or "monstrously bloated." None had a handsome figure like her mother's. Louise was especially repulsed by one of her mother's "familiars," a weaselly little woman who, Louise learned much later, for years had carried on a clandestine love affair with the hotel proprietor, Mr. Bodwell.

After two years in the sordid surroundings of the Milton Hotel, Louise found herself in the first orderly household she had ever known, that of the Gardners in Ballardvale. She and her mother arrived there by train one summer dawn to board until the Bogans, who had decided to give their marriage another try, could find a place of their own. One has only to read the description of Louise's initial glimpse into the bed- room belonging to the Gardners' daughter Ethel, a few years older than Louise, or the detailed outline of this home that held "one of everything," to know that the Gardners and the village of Ballardvale was to Louise Bogan the haven that Camden had seemed at first to Edna Millay. She later sketched as well, in a delicious prose drawing of Mrs. Gardner's kitchen, the mouth-watering picture of her fresh-baked fruit pies and her meals in general.

Following a summer of peace and contentment, the Bogans moved into a house on Oak Street in Ballardvale, where every- thing went "surprisingly well" for a while. In the winter Louise came down with scarlet fever, but the illness had its compensa- tion because she was "bedded down in the parlor," and her brother was home that winter from his school in Portland. As a child he had suffered the same mute agony that she was going through, but now he was a handsome young man of nineteen or twenty, so that he and their mother were on happier terms. They were gayer than they had ever been together, or than Louise could ever be with her mother, because the age gap between the two of them was too great.

However, the main event of that winter, the one besides her brother's presence that made it seem a happy time, was Louise's learning to read. She had been having difficulty mak- ing words out of the mass of letters on a page; her brother and mother had both read to her during her illness. But that was the last time, for suddenly, when she went back to school, she could read. The new-found ability was the beginning of a new life. It spelled escape from the lower-middle-class meanness of her daily home life, the pinched and quarrelsome quality of parental relationships. She would never be trapped in the stormy darkness of that existence again. A way out had been shown her; she was at least partially free of family misery.

The house on Oak Street, after a time the scene of dissonance again, had a narrow space of built-in bookshelves, stacked with her brother's books. There were also some her mother had acquired from door-to-door book salesmen. Louise read them all, shutting out the world around her. But the first book she owned, *Grimm's Fairy Tales*, with the Arthur Rackham illustrations, held the greatest enchantment. She believed all those stories, yet knew they could not be true. The double vision of the born reader, she said, was hers from the beginning.

That summer her mother went away—after her father had gone and come back more than once—and no one knew where she had gone. In August Louise was sent to school at the local convent—Mt. St. Mary's Academy—and boarded at the Gardners' again. It was then she learned to read notes and take pleasure in practicing five-finger exercises in the same delightful little parlor that had been a source of enchantment before she could read. When her mother finally returned, a semireconciliation took place, and the Bogans moved into a big white frame house directly across the street from the Gardners'—the contact with the treasured household continued. In a eulogy entitled "Praise of Mrs. Gardner, Ballardvale, Massachusetts (Circa 1904–1909)," Louise Bogan affectionately and openly spells out her gratitude for all the quiet joys, the things she learned at Mrs. Gardner's. Learning to read notes was one of them—the "din she made on that piano!" she recalled. One revealing item mentioned is the rope swing in the front yard, from which "one had no fear of falling." The emphasis is on absence of fear—no fear at Mrs. Gardner's! Here the future poet learned to "enter into the beauty of a spare but planned life, in which everything was used. No waste. No mess. No quarrels . . ."

No quarrels, a salient detail, for at the Bogans' the quarrels recurred. One cannot help wondering why the disparate couple did not divorce like the Millays, unless it was that they could not accept the idea of excommunication from the Church, which would have been inevitable. Louise continued at the convent until 1909, the year she began writing, first in prose, then in poetry. In 1909 her parents, after a series of violent bickering scenes and a long separation, made a final attempt to live as a couple and a family. They chose to do so in a move to the scrawny outer suburbs of Boston—dreary, dull, and undistinguished by any grace of architecture or landscape. Here in a blocklong, brick apartment building surrounded by vacant lots, Louise lived in a "railroad" flat with her ill-mated parents. In later delineating the effort at decor and the living arrangements, she mentioned matter-of-factly yet pointedly that her father, and sometimes her brother, slept in the smaller, sparsely furnished bedroom off the kitchen, while she slept with her mother in the other, larger bedroom at the front. That had some "respectable" furniture in it.

From this railroad flat the young poet walked, often along a rarely used railroad track, to take the trolley into town. There she attended the Boston Girls' Latin School from 1910 to 1915. They were five most fruitful years, she recorded, for she began writing verse at about the age of fourteen, a soul-saving course to follow in the "purgatory" of her family relationships. She labored as long at her poems as she did at her schoolwork, which was hard and exacting. But it was also her bulwark against the hell around her all during her adolescence—on holidays that hell would burst wide open, with her mother's multiple guilts and grievances literally building up into a high fever.

By the time Louise was eighteen she had a sturdy, steadily growing stack of manuscript stuck away in a drawer of the dining-room sideboard near the square table on which she did her homework. By then, too, she had learned all the essentials, if not the mastery, of her future profession. An early poem entitled "Knowledge," published in Bogan's first book and

quite possibly written during her senior high school year, is
prophetic in the second of its two stanzas:

> I'll lie here and learn
> How, over their ground,
> Trees make a long shadow
> And a light sound.

Her poetry, though it might make a light sound, would cast a
long shadow.

One other source of relief from the family situation was her
weekly music lesson, for which the money was managed somehow. Among the pieces of new furniture her parents bought on
moving to Boston was a cottage piano. Music, as in the Millay
household—indeed universally in those days—had a prominent place in the Bogans' psychosis-afflicted home. Even
Louise's temperamental mother, if she was in a good mood,
would open the piano to play and sing. The sound of music,
mixed with voices, coming over the water at night from a man-
dolin or a guitar during the rare holiday or two spent at a resort
also implanted memories that Louise still recalled with nostalgia in the late 1960s. The only real recreation she had regularly
during her adolescence was the Saturday matinee at the movies,
or occasionally the theater. On Sundays in the suburbs there
was nowhere to go, nothing to do once the midday dinner
dishes were washed. To get away from the bickering in the
dreary flat, she would saunter through the streets with another
teen-age girl or two; they would pass other small groups of the
young, similarly idling away the end of the week.

After a year of education at Boston University, following
her graduation with honors from the Latin School, Louise
Bogan seized the opportunity to free herself physically as well
as mentally from the parental web of insoluble problems. In
1916 she married Curt Alexander, an army officer assigned to a
post in Costa Rica. There the poet spent more than three miser-

able years in the officers' quarters of an army barracks.

Then the tragedy of death struck for the first time in the Bogan family. Louise's brother, who had enlisted in the army when the United States entered the war in Europe, was killed at Haumont Wood in October 1918, a month before the armistice was signed. He had longed as much as she to get out of their parents' emotional miasma and thought the army might be a solution. The blow was devastating to her parents, her mother especially, whose near-psychotic disorders worsened with the loss of the self-love that had kept her going.

Two years later, in 1920, Louise's husband died, leaving her with a small daughter, Maidie,* to care for. If it had not been for her poetry Louise could not have survived. Her work had already appeared in literary magazines—first in the *New Republic,* then in the *Nation.* Like all young poets of the time, she was happy to see her latest poems in Harriet Monroe's *Poetry,* as well as in *Scribner's* and the *Atlantic Monthly.* Poetry was her protective shield against the suffering from past and recent blows. She translated life around her into poetic symbols—she thought lyrically rather than realistically.

Two years after her husband died she spent a year in Vienna, during which she kept a diary. But at the early age of twenty-four she was "so inner, so baffled, so *battered,*" as she recorded in a journal long afterward, that she noticed very little of the life going on around her. She lived with a Frau Weinberger in a prewar luxury apartment that had been converted to a rooming house. The Frau, retaining some sense of elegance, went around the room every day with her duster and lorgnette. Louise saw her but did not then note that incongruity or much of anything else about the Frau or anyone else in the house. Her 1922 diary recorded no description of the neighborhood, the cafes or restaurants, or of the customs, clothes, or manners of

* Now Maidie Alexander Scanell. Occasional mention is made of her in letters to Edmund Wilson.

the Viennese. If any impression of that year remained, it was veiled behind a set of poetic symbols. Coincidentally Edna Millay was in Vienna during the same winter of 1922, suffering emotionally as already described; but the two poets were not aware of each other's existence until 1924.

On her return from Europe, after spending some time with her parents, who kept Maidie while she was away, Louise left her native New England for good and came to New York City, where she lived the greater part of her life. And the city, with its anonymity, excitement, and grandeur—as well as its squalor—was balm to her embittered soul. Coming at "the age of the impossible heart," as she said, she viewed the city and the people who lived in it with warmth and compassion. And she found her feelings returned in the kindred spirits of the literary world, which she soon came to know well. The publishing house of Scribner's had approached her about issuing a book as soon as she had enough poems, and while in Vienna she had been writing new works in addition to selecting, revising, and preparing her manuscript.

Her first volume appeared in 1923 under the telling title, *Body of This Death*. It received uniformly good reviews and placed her at once among the notable American poets of her generation. Edmund Wilson, who reviewed the volume for *Vanity Fair*, was so impressed with her lyrical, yet precise, controlled lines that he sent a copy of the book to Edna Millay, then in England. Millay wrote that she was "thrilled" with the work and commented on the number of "lady poets" coming to the fore. Later, through Wilson, who became a lifelong friend of Louise though never her suitor, the two met. While they did not become intimate friends, there was a warm feeling between them and mutual respect for each other's work. It was Louise who first pointed to Millay's "hampering and sometimes destructive role of poet laureate" that Edna was forced to play because of the enormous publicity she received from the start.

Among the people whom Louise met soon after her first

volume appeared was the young poet Raymond Holden. She was beginning to recover from the dark days of her youth and the more recent emotional blows; the handsomeness of face and figure she must have inherited from her mother was striking. She had thick dark hair and deep-set, brooding eyes, enhanced by smooth ivory skin. Whatever her inner turmoil, there was a serenity about her face that was most attractive to Holden, who was himself a very attractive young man. A good friend and something of a disciple of Robert Frost, he knew everyone in the poetry world. In addition he was a promising poet himself and a lively thinker and conversationalist. It was not long before romance developed between these two very different poets, and in 1925 they were married. For a few years they lived happily together.

Both wrote book reviews and literary criticism as well as poetry; both were making their way as creative artists. They were about the same age—Ray Holden was three years older than Louise—and they were much sought after by the literary world. Ray, who was to become a board member of the Book of the Month Club, a post he held for many years, was often involved with committees. Whether it was because she wanted more solitude for writing or because the marriage to another poet produced conflicts she had not foreseen, in the early summer of 1928, Louise bought a small farm in Copake Ironworks, four miles from Hillsdale, New York. Here she wrote most of her second volume, published in 1929. It was significantly titled *Dark Summer*. Several poems sound the ominous note of impending separation, particularly the title poem:

> Under the thunder-dark, the cicadas resound.
> The storm in the sky mounts, but is not yet heard.
> The shaft and flash wait, but are not yet found.
>
> The apples that hang and swell for the late comer,
> The simple spell, the rite not for our word,
> The kisses not for our mouths—light the dark summer.

This and other poems like "The Mark," which brings in the portentousness of shadows again and the image of apples, this time dropping as if at a signal to yield a ground-harvest that cannot be gathered fast enough to save the fruit from spoilage, won for Louise Bogan the John Reed Memorial Prize for poetry in 1930. The next year she became a reviewer of poetry for the *New Yorker*, a niche that was hers until the end of her life.

Her marital relations did not improve. In 1933 she applied for and received a Guggenheim Fellowship to go abroad to write. She left Raymond behind. He evidently did not expect such drastic action—he sent cables and letters of love professed too late. But Louise felt trapped by marriage, as if she were being used, being made an object. Things were no better when she returned from Europe. Raymond finally agreed to a separation but even then sent Louise importunate messages, in her words "playing [me] like a trout." "Hate letters," she also called them. They were divorced in 1937, and the same year Raymond Holden married Sara Henderson Hay, a poet noted for her light verse.* It is likely that Louise knew of this alliance, as she again applied for and received a Guggenheim grant for travel abroad.

During that year her third volume, *The Sleeping Fury*, appeared, again to uniformly good reviews. William Rose Benét said, "Her poetry is metaphysical and precise. . . . Hers is a lyrical intellectuality." Ford Madox Ford cited her for the same qualities, placing her "in a quiet landscape, with George Herbert, Donne, and Vaughan." This was high praise, and early in 1938 Louise Bogan received the Helen Haire Levinson Prize from *Poetry*.

From this time on, she continued to build her estimable reputation as poet and critic. A collection of her work entitled

---

* It is interesting to note that Holden, in writing his biography for *Twentieth Century Authors*, omitted all mention of Louise or their marriage. Record of that was supplied at the end by the editors. But he made a point of recording the marriage to Sara Henderson Hay, even though the latter was also a failure, ending in divorce more quickly than the former. Sara Hay afterwards married the well-known composer, Nicolai Lopatnikof, and that union lasted until his death in 1975.

simply *Poems and New Poems,* published in 1941, was something of a landmark in her career, in that it brought her unexpected honors. In 1944 she was elected a fellow in American Letters at the Library of Congress, and from 1945 to 1946 she held the Chair of Poetry there. She was invited to be visiting lecturer at the University of Washington and the University of Chicago. In 1948 she won the Harriet Monroe Poetry Award, which had been established soon after Miss Monroe's death in 1937. In 1951 she published a critical-historical work entitled *Achievement in American Poetry, 1900–1950,* and in 1954 she was co-winner with Leonie Adams of the coveted Bollingen Award for contribution to American letters.

Leonie Adams was also one of Louise's subjects in the above book, and a personal friend, whom Louise knew, curiously enough, through her ex-husband. Raymond Holden had launched Leonie Adams' career professionally by taking a collection of her poems to McBrides publishing house, which brought out her first volume, *Those Not Elect,* in 1925, the year he and Louise were married.

Born in Brooklyn in 1899 of southern parentage, Leonie Adams had led a sheltered, literary life—she "composed in metres by seven," she wrote. She came to New York City in 1922, after graduating from Barnard with honors, to try making it on her own. She lived "sketchily" during most of the twenties, holding a wide variety of jobs, from assistant in the bookshop at Best & Company to editorial assistant at the Metropolitan Museum. In 1928, following a year of writing on a Guggenheim grant, she secured a teaching post at New York University's Washington Square campus. There she met William Troy, also a writer on the teaching staff, and in 1933 they were married. Both joined the faculty at Bennington College, where they remained for many years, teaching and writing.*

As early as 1942, the poetry of Louise Bogan and Leonie

---

* Troy died in 1961.

Adams was linked together by their colleague Babette Deutsch, a third poet of keen perception and intellectual power. In her authoritative work, *Poetry in Our Time*, Deutsch saw Leonie Adams' work as "closely allied to that of Louise Bogan," particularly in poems marking "the eternal strangeness of time in its periods and its passage. . . ." She emphasized the "distinction" of Bogan's early lyrics, which gave evidence of the same seventeenth-century roots that formed the basis of Adams' work. Louise herself spoke of an "Elizabethan coloring in her early verse by which Miss Adams' sensitively interpreted nature, thought and feeling have an intensity which often seems to slip over into mystic vision." *Poetry in Our Time* covers the same period (1900–1950) as Bogan's book. Deutsch cited Leonie Adams' concern with the mystery of the diurnal cycle of the sun. In particular she quotes "Evening Sky," in which the poet deplores "all the wild ravage of light. . . . Before the stormy demon fall of night;" and ends with the enormous question, "For how can an eye sustain/To watch the heaven slain and quickening, or do/To stretch in its little orbit and contain/Sky balancing chaos in an inconstant rim?"

One of the poems in Adams' second volume, *High Falcon*, published the same year as Louise's *Dark Summer*, a lyric entitled "The Mount," deals with time as a fiendishly racing charger whose "bin was morning light,/Those straws which gild his bed/Are of the fallen west." She was also concerned with the conflict between body and spirit. Benét deemed her "the finest metaphysical poet writing in this country, and all her work has a rare elegance and eclecticism."

Louise's poetry differed widely in one respect from that of Leonie Adams, who, as Babette Deutsch also pointed out, rarely confronted "things ugly." Louise, on the other hand, never lost sight of stark reality, mingled as it might be with "things lovely," mystical, and light. Her strong, clear, resounding lyrics display a sardonic wit reminiscent of Ben Jonson, enunciated with an economy of words and sense of order that must inevi-

tably have reflected the effect of Mrs. Gardner's exemplary orderly household on the sensitive girl-child whose life otherwise
was filled with chaos. Borrowing a phrase from Yeats, "I Saw
Eternity," as her title, Bogan set down her disillusion with the
concept of eternity in three short stanzas of mocking tone:

> O beautiful Forever!
> O grandiose Everlasting!
> Now, now, now,
> I break you into pieces,
> I feed you to the ground.
>
> O brilliant, O languishing
> Cycle of weeping light!
> The mice and the birds will eat you.
> And you will spoil their stomachs
> As you have spoiled my mind.
>
> Here, mice, rats,
> Porcupines and toads,
> Moles, shrews, squirrels,
> Weasels, turtles, lizards—
> Here's bright Everlasting!
> Here's a crumb of Forever!
> Here's a crumb of Forever!

Yet in spite of such cynicism, Louise Bogan believed and
found comfort in the immortality of art and in its strange power
over people. In "Baroque Comment," an early excursion into
unrhymed free verse, she juxtaposed the chaotic evil of the
inner and outer world—"the empty desert, the tearing beasts,
the kelp-disordered beaches;/Coincident with the lie, anger,
lust, oppression and death in many forms"—with "Ornamental
structures, . . . Fitted marble, swung bells; fruit in garlands as
well as on the branch; the flower at last in bronze, . . . Stone in
various shapes: beyond the pyramid, the contrived arch. . . .
The named constellations . . . palm and laurel chosen as noble
and enduring;/Speech proud in sound; death considered sac-

rifice; . . . the ordered strings;/Fountains; . . ." She ended the piece eloquently with "The turned eyes and the opened mou h of love."

Great artistic fountains held a special fascination for Louise Bogan—she obviously saw them at close range in Rome. She'd gaze in rapture at the ingeniously contrived flow, which she described "with an ultimate exactitude, absolutely as it is," wrote Theodore Roethke. He was commenting on "Roman Fountain," one of her later lyrics. In his opinion, "the opening lines are one of the real felicities of our time":

> Up from the bronze, I saw
> Water without a flaw
> Rush to its rest in air,
> Reach to its rest, and fall.

The second stanza is equally telling:

> Bronze of the blackest shade,
> An element man-made,
> Shaping upright the bare
> Clear gouts of water in air.

In the third stanza, notably the last lines, Roethke says, ". . . we hear the accent of the later work: a tone of resignation, an acceptance of middle age, a comment, often, on the ironies of circumstance. Of these [poems in her latest volume, *Collected Poems, 1923–1953*], I believe 'Henceforth From the Mind' to be a masterpiece, a poem that could be set beside the best work of the Elizabethans. . . ." It may be argued that Roethke was writing from a point of view prejudiced in Bogan's favor, for in the 1930s Louise, who had been one of his literary models—along with Elinor Wylie and Leonie Adams—became his lover briefly and after remained his mentor and friend. Louise and Leonie particularly, in the Elizabethan temper of their lines, had an influence on Roethke's early verse. Indeed it was so marked that Stanley Kunitz, another of his mentors, advised Roethke to read Yeats or some of the up-and-coming American male poets like Richard Eberhart and John Crowe Ransom because his poetry contained more than a touch of the feminine!

Roethke was astonished. He did read Yeats, but he was more influenced by Eliot, and most of all by Joyce, whom he read at Louise's suggestion. However, by the time he wrote *The Lost Son*—even before—his poetry was his own, and Louise Bogan was among those who early recognized the individuality of his genius. She gave him his first laudatory reviews. There was an intimate bond between them, professionally, socially, and sexually, though the last was a flame that flared brightly but briefly at the time of their meeting.

Before she knew it, Louise had enjoyed a full-blown love affair with this big, ebullient, brilliant, erratic, sometimes irascible, but irresistible man. She wrote quite openly to Edmund Wilson about the attraction that Ted Roethke, a younger-than-she, hulking, warm-hearted, warm-blooded fellow rather like an overgrown bear cub, possessed for her. She was amusing in her account, but almost embarrassed as she expressed her feelings about their "enormous love-making" during a three-day drinking binge, and their "bearish, St. Bernard antics" together. Asterisks, followed by, "Such goings on! A woman of my age," denote deleted passages in the selected letters of *What the Woman Lived*, published after her death in 1973 with a title she had used for a lecture she gave shortly before she died. Roethke, born in 1908, was eleven years younger than she. The gap seems to have bothered her, though she was obviously buoyed up by the affair and made no concerted effort to prevent its flowering. She began the above letter to Wilson, dated June 22, 1935, with the remark that she "had been made to bloom like a Persian rosebush."

Once the blossoming had faded, there was no falling off of the friendship between the two poets. When Ted Roethke was married to Beatrice O'Connor in 1948, Louise was matron of honor at their wedding. It was a small but distinguished company that witnessed the ceremony: Stanley Kunitz was best man, and in the wedding party were Leonie Adams, W. H. Auden, and Rolfe Humphries. Louise was the first of his close friends to fill in for him at the University of Washington in Seattle after he had established himself there and felt free to take leaves of absence for reading tours or writing. (All of the above held his post at various times.) Louise was one of his sponsors for a Guggenheim fellowship. And if she ever had any fears for this flamboyant, highly sensitive son of a greenhouse grower, whose wild impulses and escapades made literary history at the artists' colonies—he was hospitalized more than once for his manic-depressive behavior—she never let him see her anxiety for his sanity, or for her own.

Louise Bogan and Leonie Adams were close friends from the time Ray Holden introduced them. Louise often referred to Leonie as "the child" or called her "child." They were closely allied artistically and professionally. They shared not only the Bollingen Award, but other honors, including election to the National Institute of Arts and Letters and the Fellowship Award of the Academy of American Poets. Leonie succeeded Louise at the Library of Congress, probably at Louise's instigation. They were often together, but Louise absorbed none of Leonie Adams's serenity of spirit over their shared success. Instead, Louise, from 1954, seems to have gone into a depression that grew progressively worse.

Although she had help from a psychiatrist, she overcame the "malaise" only in part. Her friends, Leonie in particular, tried to bring her out of it, but could not succeed. The difference in the scope of their subject matter and tone in their poetry grew wider through the years. Nowhere in Adams' ethereal questing does one find the emotional despair of Bogan's tiny two-line couplet whose title is longer than the poem itself. Both speak worlds:

Solitary Observation Brought Back From a Soujourn in Hell

> At midnight tears
> Run into your ears.

Nor would one find in Adams the querying quatrain, "Question in a Field: Pasture, stone wall, and steeple,/What most perturbs the mind:/The heart-rending homely people,/Or the horrible, beautiful kind?" which indicates the perturbed state of her inner life at a time when she was receiving recognition and honors and was firmly established as reviewer and critic. Her affinity for the "heart-rending," desperate souls is evident in her powerful, provocative poem "Several Voices Out of a Cloud":

> Come, drunks and drug-takers; come, perverts unnerved!
> Receive the laurel, given, though late, on merit; to whom
>   and wherever deserved.
>
> Parochial punks, trimmers, nice people, joiners true-blue,
> Get the hell out of the way of the laurel. It is deathless
>   And it isn't for you.

In her journal for January 1954, Louise recorded her unexpected, poignant reactions after rereading the 1933–1937 correspondence between Raymond Holden and herself. She referred to the correspondence in quotation marks as "the packet of letters," when she recorded reliving the memories in a nightmarish period. But she was able to pull herself out of it after a day and a half. The words in quotes form the title of a poem evidently written earlier, which indicates that the separation was a bitter wrench that she'd felt for some time: "In the shut drawer, even now, they rave and grieve—/To be approached at times with the frightened tear," it opens. "There, there, the thugs of the heart did murder./There, still in murderers' guise, two stand embraced, embalmed," is her cold conclusion. The brief trauma from rereading those letters ended when she decided it was all "too *boring* to review any longer"; it was overshadowed by the deeper fear that she was losing her powers of creativity.

The Bollingen Award had come after the appearance of her volume *Collected Poems, 1923–1953,* which Roethke so praised in the critical essay cited above. But for some time she had produced no new poems. She was working on a prose book, *Selected Criticism,* which came out in 1955, but that sort of writing she called "obligatory," rather than the "free setting down of memory and desire" from which her poems derived. Perhaps in an effort to refresh her memory, she revisited the scenes of her adolescence in the suburbs of Boston. Although the memories came flooding back, they deepened her depression. The cloudy impressions of her parents' tirades and troubles were clarified, but the realization of the pathetic nature of their struggle brought on a period of helpless weeping relieved only by medication and psychiatric consultation.

Her neurosis became apparent in her prose writing. She only half-read the books that came to her desk for review, and she could be harsh in her edicts, consigning a work to the wastebasket with a single word. Although she was often enough cutting in her remarks, she was paranoid in regard to comments from others.

Among her last poems is "Psychiatrist's Song," one of a trilogy of which the last is "Masked Woman's Song." There is also a descriptive "Evening in the Sanitarium," first published with the subtitle "Imitated from Auden." The poem indicates a stay in an institution. Louise's "sojourn in hell" was at its worst in the mid-1960s, when she relied on Librium to stop the tears, anxiety, and fears that beset her endlessly. Of the last, she admitted in her journal, to the fear of death—many recent deaths she'd noted were of people her age or younger. Her anxiety was no doubt aggravated by the tragic drowning of Theodore Roethke in 1963. He suffered a heart attack while swimming in a friend's pool and died before he could be rescued. His death at fifty-five at the peak of his career was deeply felt throughout the poetry world.

Louise tried to fathom the reasons for her loss of "psychic energy." She reflected that she had lived optimistically in the past, had surmounted difficulty, "*worked* for life and creativity, and had helped others to work and hold on." Few knew of her own inner suffering. To the end, Louise Bogan maintained an outward calm and control, whatever her inner turmoil. By July of 1966, the final published excerpt from her journal reports "No tears!" And she regained enough energy to write some new poems for a collection covering five decades of her work, which she decided to call *The Blue Estuaries.*

The title of the collection is taken from the second line of a new poem, "Night." Portentous in tone, it speaks in the last stanza of "narrowing dark hours" and bids the reader remember "That more things move/Than blood in the heart." Yet she could still be ironic, almost playful toward death, as in the quatrain, "To an Artist, to Take Heart":

> Slipping in blood, by his own hand, through pride
> Hamlet, Othello, Coriolanus fall.
> Upon his bed, however, Shakespeare died,
> Having endured them all.

There were also songs in this last volume. One, a lovely tranquil lyric with the directive title "To Be Sung on the Water," was without doubt inspired by nostalgic memory of youth and the sound of music coming over the water. There is a delightful, if mournful, "Train Tune" and an intensely dramatic "Song for the Last Act" in three stanzas, the latter a moving piece of masterful craftsmanship. Three "Songs" close the book.

She had written poems about her mother, the earliest, "Portrait," in her first volume. And the title poem of *The Sleeping Fury* obviously depicts her mother's face in death and relates the emotions that aroused in the poet. In the next volume her only sibling appeared overtly in an antiwar poem entitled "To My Brother/Killed: Haumont Wood: October, 1918." Written at the start of World War II, the poem is an affirmation that "all things remain" save "peace alone." The last section of *The Blue*

Estuaries contains a poem called "The Dream," which begins as a nightmare but ends as an idyll of love when the dreamer is rescued by a woman—from certain implications her mother—who transforms attack into love.

An entry in the journal for 1960 warns against bringing back "the bad mother" to justify oneself; the memory should be recalled only to understand oneself. "The Dream" is proof of Bogan's feeling that the artist must resolve the memory of an evil figure into art. In her journal, in an entry written in 1965 after visiting the mean, lower middle-class neighborhood of her youth in Boston, Louise reflected on the courage both of her parents must have had to struggle against the penury, demands, and disparate desires they both felt. And in the end, she undoubtedly forgave them the anguish they caused her, for *The Blue Estuaries* is dedicated "To the memory of my father, mother and brother." She saw it through to press and had the satisfaction of reading praise from the critics. Allen Tate called her "the most accomplished woman poet of our time." Richard Eberhart spoke of a "somber straightforwardness of a strong nature controlling powerful emotions by a highly conscious art. . . ." And Yvor Winters proclaimed that each poem was a "sharply defined segment of experience, raised to something very near major power by the sheer brilliance of the craftsmanship. She is beyond any doubt one of the principal ornaments of contemporary American poetry."

In the spring of 1970, two years after this successful publication, Louise Bogan died during her sleep at the age of seventy-two. In a moving tribute in the report of her death, the *New Yorker* commented on the quiet capability with which she had handled her assignments throughout the years and her reticence in regard to her personal life—she did not care to boast of her reputation or broadcast her name in any way outside the literary world. She herself said, "I am a person who cares a great deal for privacy and anonymity in my life"; the *New Yorker* cited the fact that on her mailbox at her apartment was the sole surname "Holden," a significant detail.

In her poem "Woman," she evidently reflected her own experience in asserting that "Women have no wilderness in them,/They are provident instead,/Content in the tight hot cell of their hearts/To eat dusty bread." This may have been so in part, but Louise Bogan's poetry was the wine of her life. Its clear, distilled light is in contrast to the murky water of much present-day poetry.

10

BABETTE DEUTSCH

BABETTE Deutsch, a native New Yorker born September 22, 1895, merited the praise of her peers from the beginning of her career. Her background could scarcely have been more different from Louise Bogan's. The daughter of Melanie Fisher and Michael Deutsch, Babette was the product of urban intellectuality and early liberalism. She attended the Ethical Culture primary and secondary schools and after graduation went on to Barnard College and Columbia University. She showed a remarkable grasp of words from the time she was a small child. Her earliest known poem, written at the age of five, gives evidence of the scholarly, thoughtful poet she was to become.

> I knew that the sky was blue,
> And I knew that the sun was gold,
> But I never knew that the earth was round
> Until I was told.

During her college years the university faculty boasted such luminaries as Franz Boas, Charles A. Beard, James Shot-

well, and James Harvey Robinson. Babette Deutsch was the sort
of student to respond to such stimulating minds. She also had
contact during those critical years with a prominent liberal
journalist, Randolph Bourne, one of the first regular contributors to the *New Republic,* whose socialist leanings influenced many young minds of the time. Some of Babette
Deutsch's first published poems, like those of Louise Bogan and
Leonie Adams, appeared in the *New Republic.* Some were published as well in the *North American Review.*

Babette received her A.B. degree from Barnard in 1917,
graduating with honors. Since her second interest was political
science, she was briefly connected with the *Political Science
Quarterly.* When she received an invitation from Marion Reedy,
who had published some of Deutsch's poems in *Reedy's Mirror,*
to contribute to his one-man journal of opinion, she submitted
several articles. One of these concerned the noted American
political economist and educator, Thorstein Veblen. Soon after
it appeared, she heard from Veblen, who, evidently pleased
with her grasp of his ideas, asked her if she would act as his
secretary while he was teaching at the New School for Social
Research. She was happy to comply with the request. Veblen
was the author of several books on political economy and at the
height of his career. Babette Deutsch at this time, judging from
an early photograph, was a serious-looking young girl with
great dark eyes that outshone the features of her long thin face.
Her eyes suggested the mingled social consciousness and literary creativity that formed her psyche, and she had a dry wit to
match her intellect.

It was natural that she attracted a man as scholarly as herself, Avrahm Yarmolinsky, chief of the Slavonic division of the
New York Public Library. She met him in the course of her
work. They were married in 1921, two years after publication of
her first volume of poetry, *Banners,* which brought her to the
attention of the literary world.

In 1920 Robert Frost, unbeknownst to her, recommended

Babette Deutsch to his publishers, Henry Holt & Company, for publication in a "young poets" series they were contemplating. Though she did not learn of his recommendation for some time, she was afterwards always grateful to him. However, Holt did not publish her next volume, although Frost said in 1960 that he was always proud of having "discovered" her among the poets he read for Holt's consideration. The firm did later publish her *Poetry in Our Time*.

Babette and her husband, who was of German as well as Russian background, early discovered a mutual interest in translation, and in 1923, *Contemporary German Poetry*, an anthology they compiled and translated together, was published. Shortly after their first child was born, they went abroad for a long journey, visiting Berlin, Riga, Moscow, Leningrad, Warsaw, Florence, Paris, and London. On their return, Babette settled down to writing, teaching—she conducted a private class in poetry and a course at the New School—occasional lecturing, besides looking after her family.

A volume of her verse appeared every two years on the average. *Honey Out of the Rock* (1925) was followed by *In Such a Night* (1927). A poem reprinted in the latter was awarded the *Nation* Poetry Prize in 1926. In 1929, as the Phi Beta Kappa poet at Columbia, she wrote a sonnet series and in 1931 she composed a book-length *Epistle to Prometheus*. That followed *Fire for the Night*, which had appeared in 1930. *One Part Love* appeared in 1939. Both the sonnet series and *Epistle to Prometheus* from the *Collected Poems* volume that was published in 1969 were omitted, although in 1933 she'd stated she hoped to be remembered for *Epistle*. In total, nine volumes of her poetry have been published. They are interspersed with the translations from German and Russian poets that she and Avrahm Yarmolinsky published almost as frequently.

Deutsch also wrote many books of prose, both fiction—three novels on the lives of great figures, including Socrates and François Villon (*Rogue's Legacy*)—and nonfiction in the field of poetry. The first of the latter, *Potable Gold,* was published in 1929 with the subtitle, "Some Notes on Poetry and This Age." It deals in a most accessible way with the making of modern poetry. In it she indicates that for the best definition of cadence one should go to "that most militant of Imagists, the late Amy Lowell."

This Modern Poetry, a volume published in 1935, was expanded in the next decade and a half to a comprehensive work, *Poetry in Our Time, 1900–1950,* published in 1952. Since then an edition updated to 1960 has appeared (1963). The book has become something of a classic in its field and is often used as a text in poetry courses. Yet one cannot help wondering why in the first edition of *Poetry in Our Time,* which went into many printings, Miss Deutsch, of the two hundred and twenty-six poets she discussed, included only eighteen women.* Surely by midcentury there were more women writing poetry worthy of consideration. In a chapter called "A Look at the Worst," she dismissed Edna Millay with a single paragraph, crediting that eminent poet with no more than "a handful of touching songs on the transcience of love and the shortness of life. . . ," overlooking Millay's three great sonnet sequences and the stature of a poem like "Renascence." However, in "A Short Calendar of Events in Poetry," appended to the book, she does note the dates of publication of several of Millay's volumes. No mention is made of Sara Teasdale or of Deutsch's colleague Genevieve Taggard, who founded the magazine *Measure,* for which Babette Deutsch was an editor for a time. And she gave only three lines to Muriel Rukeyser, who by 1950 had produced a body of work warranting more extended discussion.

With the exceptions noted above, Deutsch's perceptions and evaluations are keen and her judgment valid. She says of Louise Bogan, "The texture of her verse is strong and fine, her images, though few, are fit, her cadences well managed."

---

* One of these is British poet Edith Sitwell, since Deutsch dealt with poets writing in English.

Leonie Adams is thoroughly reviewed and quoted in two full-length poems. Elinor Wylie is not overlooked, and Elizabeth Bishop is accorded full credit for her contribution, as are Marianne Moore and the then-young Jean Garrigue.

Babette Deutsch's own poetry is peerless in its fusion of intellect and subtle emotion. Her compassion for the young—for infants and small children, living or dead—and the old is particularly notable. "Heard in Old Age," a three stanza poem dedicated to Robert Frost, written a year or so before Frost's death, asks, in the second stanza, "Is there a song left, then, for aged voices?" adding that they are "half throttled by the thumbs/Of hard self-knowledge. To the old, dawn comes/With ache of loss, with cold absence of choices./What heart, waking to this, drumming assent, rejoices?" The answer comes in the last three lines: "Till the Enigma, in a wandering phrase/Offers a strain never audible before:/Immense music behind a closing door." A few years later, she memorialized Frost in "Lament for the Makers: 1964," a fine, free verse elegy in seven stanzas of seven lines each, mourning the loss of seven American poets—and Yeats and Louis MacNeice abroad—all prominent, gifted "makers" who died around the same time. In America, there was Frost, who, "first famished and then battered/By tragic circumstances, who yet brimmed his verse with a Virgilian calm. . . ." She wrote of William Carlos Williams, who died in the same year (1963), as did Theodore Roethke. The others, who went before Frost, were Wallace Stevens, Kenneth Fearing, Robinson Jeffers, and E. E. Cummings. "How believe that what each left was his last testament?" Deutsch asks. The last stanza begins, "Lament for the makers; it will never be over," and the conclusion is: "There is no end to grief. Nor no end to poetry."

Many poems testify to this poet's affection for infants and small children and the deep pathos she felt for those who die young. "Small Colored Boy in the Subway" asks "What jungle fruit/Droops with such grace as you in the subway corner/In your Saturday suit?" It goes on to describe the little boy's eyes, "dark as plums," and his smooth skin, declaring,

You are a morsel
So fine that you feed the eye as other things . . .
pamper the palate. Now you lean
Lightly against your mother, in the surrender
Of weariness still keeping dignity,
As if, a child, you honorably upheld
What was too heavy for a child to hold. . . .
You sleep. . . .
Yet, even in sleep,
Without defense, darkly your grace proffers
The grave accusation of innocence.

Another poem of rare perception is "To an Amiable Child,"
inspired by the inscription at a small gravesite on upper Riverside Drive, a funerary urn bearing the title words in memory of
a boy who died "in the Fifth Year of his Age, 1797."

Several more poems deal with children, not only those who
have died, but the living: "Afternoon With an Infant," "Feed-
ing the Chickens," and "Urban Pastoral," recreating a scene in
Central Park, where children make "the traffic." All display a
feeling for the dawn and morning of life. Lines inspired by her
own child in "To My Son," written in 1943, when he evidently
was entering the army in World War II, reveal a mother's fears,
anxiety, and tenderness with skillful restraint.

A salient feature of all Deutsch's work is the philosophic
conclusion of each poem, descriptive or discursive. In the midst
of the superbly drawn picture of "String Quartet"—"Fingers
prance on the strings,/Bows dance in air"—she observes, "Time
is undone even where time grows. . . ." Music is another
theme that runs through her poetry as a leitmotif. Besides
"String Quartet," other titles indicating her love of music include "Piano Recital"; "The Prepared Piano," a gentle jibe at
John Cage; "The Belvedere: Mozart's Music"; and "Electronic
Concert," a poem protesting the mélange of noise perpetrated
through electronic music. "Three Nuns Listening to Chopin" is
at once charming and discerning. And in a delicious, sagacious

piece of free verse entitled "At the Green Grocer's," the pears are "shapely as violins." The poetic symbols "song," and "hymn" often appear.

Babette Deutsch has lived most of her long, active life in New York City, the principal locale of her place-name poems, which evoke locations from Riverside Drive to the Battery, and from a subway scene to "Barges on the Hudson." She has immortalized the city.

An independent voter as well as thinker, she has supported liberal causes generally. She was a member of the early Civic Club, predecessor of the American Civil Liberties Union. She participated in the Committee for Cultural Freedom headed by John Dewey. She dissociated herself from the League of American Writers—not to be confused with the Authors League of America—when she realized that it was sectarian. For many years she has been a member of the International P.E.N. Club, which champions freedom of expression for writers everywhere, with emphasis on those interned as political prisoners. Like Louise Bogan and Leonie Adams, she was elected to the National Institute of Arts and Letters, and she remains on the board of chancellors at the Academy of American Poets.

In 1976, her alma mater, Barnard College, announced a scholarship being set up in her name, an honor, she confided with typical self-effacement, that shamed her, "however pleasing" it might be. Other incidents in her career that gave her pleasure, besides Frost's early recommendation of her poetry, provide a further glimpse of her character. W. H. Auden told her that after contracting for a book on prosody he withdrew because she had done the job with her *Poetry Handbook: A Dictionary of Terms* (published by Funk & Wagnalls in 1957, and widely used as a guide to "the craft of verse" behind "the art of poetry") so well that Auden felt it "didn't need re-doing." Another involved her local shoemaker, with whom she "had left a pair of shoes for mending all too long." When she finally called for them, he handed her the brown paper bag containing them, explaining that he didn't know her name. But he had inscribed on the bag in big pencilled letters: "POET." *

For many years Babette Deutsch has taught at Columbia University, where she is a popular figure among the students, who enjoy her wit and lively presentation. Her poem "Moving," reflects her affection for them when she speaks of "papers to destroy," including letters from her students, "golden lads and girls" who have gone away.

Her husband, who started her on translations from the Russian with Blok's "The Twelve," retired from his post at the New York Public Library in 1955. Following that, they collaborated on the tremendous task of compiling a new anthology, *Two Centuries of Russian Verse.* The "Thoroughly Revised and Expanded Edition" was published in 1966.

Few couples among writers were as devoted or worked as harmoniously together as these two, each keeping his/her own individuality. More than one of the poet's books is dedicated to her husband, as the words "and again to Avrahm" on the dedicatory page of *Poetry in Our Time* indicate. Yarmolinsky's death on September 28, 1975, was a deep loss to Deutsch and to the world of literature, as she was well aware. In the credits regarding her own translations she gave full measure to him. Those for her *Collected Poems* of 1969 read: "For the nuances, as well as for the prose sense, the metrics and the rhyme schemes of the Russian poems, I am indebted to my husband, Avrahm Yarmolinsky." Despite his loss and her own illness during the past several years, she has managed to carry on with her "special calm," as Kenneth Rexroth has called it. He characterizes it as a calm "in the face of terror and mystery and miscellaneous excitements of life." He adds, "This evenness of temper is very valuable, as it is an extremely rare quality in modern verse."

Two of her sister poets have summed up Babette Deutsch's

---

* The above incidents were related by Miss Deutsch in a letter to the author, dated October 28, 1976.

work very well. Marianne Moore—for whom Deutsch composed an eighteen-line rhymed lyric, "In Honor of Her
Seventy-Fifth Birthday (November 12, 1962)," italicizing the
first letter of each line so it is visually clear that the poem verti-
cally spells out "Marianne Craig Moore"—wrote: "Compassionate, dextrous, knowledgeable Miss Deutsch . . . one con-
templates her depth, range, straightness, and commanding stature as a poet." And Louise Bogan succinctly arrived at the core
of Deutsch's gifts in two sentences: "Miss Deutsch's lyrics are
dramatically pictorial; she presents moments of everyday reality
that turn out to be mirrors of her informed convictions. She is
an expert translator."

Now in her eighties, Babette Deutsch is a dean among
modern poets, a mentor to many beginners.

SELECTED BIBLIOGRAPHY

1. EMILY DICKINSON

A. Works by—Poetry:

(All except four poems published posthumously)

The Complete Poems of Emily Dickinson. Ed. by Martha Dickinson Bianchi. Boston: Little, Brown & Company, 1925; reprint 1955.

Further Poems of Emily Dickinson (subtitle: Withheld from Publication by Her Sister Lavinia). Boston: Little, Brown & Company, 1929.

Bolts of Melody. Ed. by Mabel Loomis Todd and Millicent Todd Bingham. New York: Harper & Brothers, 1945.

Complete Poems of Emily Dickinson. Ed. by Thomas H. Johnson. Boston: Little, Brown & Company, 1960. Also, *Final Harvest*, Selected Poems, with Introduction by Johnson. Boston: Little, Brown & Company, 1961.

B. Biographical and Critical, Letters:

The Life and Letters of Emily Dickinson. Ed. by Martha Dickinson Bianchi. Boston: Houghton Mifflin Company, 1925, 1957.

Bingham, Millicent Todd. *Ancestors' Brocades.* New York and London: Harper & Brothers, 1945, 1967.

Johnson, Thomas H., Ed., *Letters of Emily Dickinson.* Cambridge: Belknap Press of Harvard University, 1958.

Gould, Jean. *Miss Emily*. Boston: Houghton Mifflin Company, 1946.

Jenkins, MacGregor. *Emily Dickinson, Friend and Neighbor*. Boston: Little, Brown & Company, 1930.

Patterson, Rebecca. *The Riddle of Emily Dickinson*. Boston: Houghton Mifflin Company, 1951, 1975.

Sewall, Richard B. *The Life of Emily Dickinson*, Vols. I & II. New York: Farrar, Straus & Giroux, 1974.

————. *The Lyman Letters*. New York: Farrar, Straus & Giroux, 1971.

Taggard, Genevieve. *The Life and Mind of Emily Dickinson*. New York: Harper & Brothers, 1930, 1967.

Whicher, George F. *This Was a Poet—Emily Dickinson*. New York: Charles Scribner's Sons, 1938.

C. In Drama and Music:

Glaspell, Susan. *Alison's House*. New York: Frederick A. Stokes Company, 1930.

Luce, William. *The Belle of Amherst*. Boston: Little, Brown & Company, 1976. Also recorded by Caedmon with Julie Harris.

D. Musical Settings:

Copland, Aaron. *Twelve Poems of Emily Dickinson*. New York: Boosey & Hawkes, 1948 (?). Many others, including Louise Talma, four poems; Lockrehm Johnson, *Letter to the World*, 1954; Ned Rorem, Poems of Emily Dickinson; and settings by many other composers.

2. AMY LOWELL

A. Works by—Volumes of Poetry:

Of the ten volumes of poetry written by Amy Lowell, those most valuable as source material, read in first edition are: *Sword Blades and Poppy Seed*, New York and London: The Macmillan Company, 1914; *Pictures of the Floating World*, Boston: Houghton Mifflin Company, 1919; and *What's O'Clock*, Boston: Houghton Mifflin Company. Two much later publications, *Complete Poetical Works*, Boston: Houghton Mifflin Company, 1955; and *A Shard of Silence*, Selected Poems of Amy Lowell (ed. by G. R. Ruihley), New York: Twayne Publishers, Inc., 1957, should be cited—the first for its inclusion, in one comprehensive volume, of the entire output of Amy Lowell; the second for shedding light on the poet's emotional and sexual life, her attachment to her friend and companion, Ada Russell.

B. Anthologies:

Three consecutive volumes of *Some Imagist Poets*. Boston: Houghton
    Mifflin Company. Vol. I, 1915; Vol. II, 1916; Vol. III, 1917.
A Miscellany of American Poetry (compiled with Louis Untermeyer).
    New York: Alfred Harcourt, 1917; Vol. II, 1918.

C. Prose Works:

Six French Poets (essays drawn from lectures). New York and London:
    The Macmillan Company, 1915.
Tendencies in Modern American Poetry. New York: The Macmillan Com-
    pany, 1917.
John Keats (biography, 2 vols.). Boston: Houghton Mifflin, 1925.

D. Translations:

Fir Flower Tablets (with Florence Ayscough, translations of ancient
    Chinese poetry). Boston: Houghton Mifflin Company, 1921.

E. Letters:

Published and unpublished, in various library collections.

F. Biographical and Critical, Peripheral Material:

Aiken, Conrad. *Skepticisms: Notes on Contemporary Poetry*. New York:
    Alfred A. Knopf, 1919.
Anderson, Margaret. *My Thirty Years' War*. New York: Horizon Press,
    1969 (reprint of 1930 edition).
Belmont, Eleanor Robson. *The Fabric of Memory*. New York: Farrar,
    Straus & Cudahy, 1957.
Brooks, Van Wyck. *New England: Indian Summer*. New York: E. P. Dut-
    ton, 1940.
Damon, S. Foster. *Amy Lowell, A Chronicle*. Boston: Houghton Mifflin
    Company, 1935.
Fletcher, John Gould. *Life Is My Song*. New York and Toronto: Farrar,
    Straus & Rinehart, 1937.
Gould, Jean. *Amy, The World of Amy Lowell and the Imagist Movement*.
    New York: Dodd, Mead & Company, 1975.
———. *Robert Frost: The Aim Was Song*. New York: Dodd, Mead, 1964.
Hughes, Glenn. *Imagism and the Imagists: A Study in Modern Poetry*.
    Stanford: Stanford University Press, 1931.
Lawrence, D. H. *Selected Letters*. Farrar, Straus & Cudahy, 1958.

————. Unpublished letters to Amy Lowell, c. 1914–1924. Cambridge: Houghton Library, Harvard University.

Putnam, Mrs. William Lowell. "A Glimpse of Amy Lowell's Childhood by her Sister" (unpublished manuscript).

Ruihley, G. R., *The Thorn of a Rose*. Hamden, Conn: Archon Books, 1975.

Sergeant, Elizabeth. *Fire Under the Andes*. Boston: 1927; reprint, Kennikat Press, 1966.

Smith, William Jay. *The Spectra Hoax*. Middletown: Wesleyan University Press, 1961.

Stanford, Ann. *The Women Poets in English* (section on Amy Lowell). New York: McGraw-Hill, 1972.

Untermeyer, Jean Starr. *Private Collection*. New York: Alfred A. Knopf, 1965.

Untermeyer, Louis. "A Memoir," *Introduction to the Complete Poetical Works of Amy Lowell*. Boston: Houghton Mifflin Company, 1955.

Warren, Robert Penn; Brooks, Cleanth; and Lewis, W. R. B. *American Literature Makers*. New York: Appleton-Century-Croft, 1972.

White, Katherine Dana. "Recollections of Amy Lowell in Childhood" (unpublished manuscript).

Wilson, Edmund. *The Shores of Light* (section, "All Star Literary Vaudeville"). New York: Farrar, Straus & Cudahy, 1952.

Numerous reviews and articles, the most valuable among recent studies, "A Musical Apprentice," by William C. Bedford ("Amy Lowell to Carl Engel"), in *The Musical Quarterly*, October 1972.

3. GERTRUDE STEIN

A. Works by—Poetry:

Includes "Operas" and "Plays"—her own verse form.

Tender Buttons. Claire-Marie (pseud. for Donald Evans). Boston: 1914.

Stanzas in Meditation and Other Peoms, 1929–1933. Preface by Donald Sutherland. New Haven: Yale University Press, 1956.

Geography and Plays. New York: Something Else Press, 1966 (reprint of 1922 ed.).

Selected Operas and Plays. Ed. with an Introduction by John Malcolm Brinnin. University of Pittsburgh Press, 1970.

Last Operas and Plays. Selected and with an Introduction by Carl Van Vechten. New York: Vintage Books, 1975.

Four Saints in Three Acts. New York: Mercury Music Corp., 1934.

The Mother of Us All. New York: Mercury Music Corp., 1947.

Gertrude Stein's America. Excerpts from Poems, Plays, Essays, Novels, etc. New York: Liveright, 1974.

B. Prose:

Three Lives (reprint; pub. orig. 1908). New York: Evergreen Press, 1969.
The Making of Americans. Orig. Paris: Robert McAlmon, 1927. Of sub-
  sequent pub. latest is in *Fernhurst and Other Early Writings.* New
  York: Liveright, 1971.
The Autobiography of Alice B. Toklas. New York: Harcourt, Brace and
  Co. (Literary Guild Edition), 1933.

C. Biographical. Letters, Critical Material:

Dear Sammy: Letters from Gertrude Stein & Alice B. Toklas, with a
  Memoir by Samuel Steward. Boston: Houghton Mifflin, 1977.
Anderson, Sherwood. *Sherwood Anderson/Gertrude Stein,* Corre-
  spondence and personal essays. Chapel Hill: University of North
  Carolina Press, 1972.
Brinnin, John Malcolm. *The Third Rose.* New York: Grove Press, 1961.
McAlmon, Robert. Diary–Memoir: *Being Geniuses Together.* Edited by
  Kay Boyle. New York: Harper & Row, 1968.
Scott, Winfield Townley. *Exiles and Fabrications.* New York: Doubleday
  & Company, Inc., 1961.
Thomson, Virgil. *Virgil Thomson.* New York and London: Weidenfeld
  & Nicholson, 1967.
Toklas, Alice B. *What is Remembered.* New York: Holt, Rinehart &
  Winston, 1963.
Wilder, Thornton. *Four in America.* Freeport: Books for Libraries Press,
  1969.

D. Music, Drama, and Recordings:

Gertrude Stein Reads from Her Work. Caedmon, 1956 (orig. 1933).
Gertrude Stein's Gertrude Stein. One-woman show. Recorded in Paris:
  Audiovisuelles. 1969.
Gertrude Stein, Gertrude Stein, Gertrude Stein. One woman show star-
  ring Pat Carroll. New York: 1979.
Carmines, Al. Musical setting of *In Circles.* New York: 1968.
———. Musical setting and dramatization of *The Making of Americans.*
  New York: 1970.
"When This You See, Remember Me." Series of one-act plays set to
  music by Myer Kupferman and other young composers, 1973 (?).
Diamond, David. Setting of "I Am a Rose." Bryn Mawr: 1973.
Rorem, Ned. "Three Sisters Who Are Not Sisters" (one-act opera).
  New York: 1974.
Thomson, Virgil. Setting of "Capital Capitals." New York: 1968.
———. *Four Saints in Three Acts.* New York: 1934.
———. *The Mother of Us All.* New York: 1947.

4. SARA TEASDALE

A. Poetry:

Sonnets to Eleonora Duse. St. Louis: Privately printed, 1908.
Rivers to the Sea. New York: The Macmillan Company, 1923.
Dark of the Moon. New York: Macmillan, 1929.
Strange Victory. New York: Macmillan, 1933 (post.).
Collected Poems. New York: Macmillan, first published in 1937; latest edition, 1966 (23 printings).
Love Songs: Sara Teasdale. Photos by Eric Bauer. (Special edition), New York: Macmillan, 1975.

B. Anthology:

The Answering Voice: Love Lyrics by Women. Compiled by Sara Teasdale. First pub. New York: Macmillan, 1928. New Edition with 50 added poems. Freeport: Books for Libraries Press, 1971.

C. Biographical and Critical:

Carpenter, Margaret H. *Sara Teasdale.* New York: Schulte Publishing Company, 1960.
Drake, William. *Sara Teasdale: Woman and Poet.* New York: Harper & Row, 1979.
Rittenhouse, Jesse B. *My House of Life.* Boston: Houghton Mifflin Company, 1934; also, Untermeyer, Jean Starr, *Private Collection.* New York: Alfred A. Knopf, 1965.
See also *The Letters of Vachel Lindsay,* edited by Marc Chenetier. New York: Burt Franklin & Co., 1979.

5. ELINOR WYLIE

A. Works by—Poetry:

Incidental Numbers. London: William Clowes & Sons, 1912 (pub. anon.).
Nets to Catch the Wind. New York: Alfred A. Knopf, 1921.
Black Armour. New York: Alfred A. Knopf, 1924.
Trivial Breath. New York: Alfred A. Knopf, 1927.
Angels and Earthly Creatures. New York: Alfred A. Knopf, 1929 (post.).
Collected Poems. New York: Alfred A. Knopf, 1932 (post.); reprint, 1960.

B. Fiction:

Jennifer Lorn. New York: Alfred A. Knopf, 1925.
The Venetian Glass Nephew. New York: 1926.
Orphan Angel (based on the life of Shelley). New York: 1928.

C. Biographical:

Letters to William Rose Benét, 1920–1923. University of Virginia Library (recent acquisition, 1979).
Gray, Thomas Alexander. *Elinor Wylie*. New York, 1969.
Hoyt, Nancy (sister). *Portrait of an Unknown Lady–Elinor Wylie*. Indianapolis: Bobbs-Merrill, 1935.
Olson, Stanley. *Elinor Wylie, A Life Apart*. New York: Dial Press, 1979.

6. H.D. (HILDA DOOLITTLE)

A. Works by—Poetry:

Des Imagistes (Chapbook anthology compiled by Ezra Pound). London: privately printed, 1914. Several poems by H.D., her first to appear in print. See also Amy Lowell's anthologies, *Some Imagist Poets* of 1915, 1916, 1917, and *A Miscellany of American Poetry*, mentioned above. Her first volume, *Poems*, appeared 1921, London.
Collected Poems of "H.D." New York: Boni & Liveright, 1932.
Trilogy: *The Walls Do Not Fall; Tribute to the Angels; The Flowering of the Rod*. New York and London: Oxford University Press, 1944, 1945, 1946.
Selected Poems: H.D. New York: Grove Press, 1957.
Bid Me to Live–A Madrigal. New York: Grove Press, 1960.
Helen in Egypt. New York: Grove Press, 1961.
Hermatic Definitions. New York: New Directions Press, 1972.
Sea Garden. London: St. James Press, and New York: St. Martin's Press, 1974.

B. Prose:

Tribute to Freud. Foreword by Norman Holmes Pearsen. Boston: David R. Godine, 1974. First paperback edition, New York: McGraw-Hill, 1975, contains "Writing on the Wall" and "Advent." Most valuable as source material for H.D.'s psychological and emotional makeup, her relationship to Bryher, etc.

C. Biographical and Critical:

Unpublished Letters to Amy Lowell. Houghton Library, Harvard University, Cambridge; 57 letters dating 1914–1922.

Lowell, Amy. *Tendencies in Modern American Poetry*. Chapter on H.D. Boston: Houghton Mifflin Company, 1917; reprint, 1971.

Quinn, Vincent Gerald. *Hilda Doolittle*. New York: 1968.

Swann, Thomas Burnett. *The Classical World of H.D.* New York: Lincoln Press, 1962.

Addenda: *Hilda's Book* (Memoir from the Diaries of Ezra Pound). London: 1979. Also, *The Autobiography of William Carlos Williams*, New York: New Directions, 1951, for material on H.D. and Marianne Moore; and the diary of Robert McAlmon, ed. by Kay Boyle, New York: Harper & Brothers, 1968.

7. MARIANNE MOORE

A. Works by—Poetry:

Poems. London: Printed privately by H.D. and Bryher, 1921 (1st vol.).

Selected Poems, with an Introduction by T. S. Eliot. New York: The Macmillan Company, 1935; London: Faber & Faber, 1935.

Collected Poems. New York: The Macmillan Company, 1951.

Complete Poems. New York: The Macmillan Company, 1967.

A Marianne Moore Reader. New York: Viking Press, 1961.

B. Translations:

The Fables of La Fontaine. New York: Viking Press, 1960.

French Fairy Tales. New York: The Macmillan Company, 1964.

C. Recordings:

Marianne Moore Reading From Her Own Poetry. Caedmon, 1954. Reading her translations, Caedmon, 1965.

D. Prose:

Predilections (essays). New York: Viking Press, 1955.

E. Letters:

Correspondence with executive of the Ford Motor Company, re the naming of a new model. First printed in *The New Yorker*, then in *Marianne Moore Reader*. New York: Viking Press, 1961.

F. Biographical and Critical:

Engel, Bernard F. *Marianne Moore*. New York: Viking Press, 1964.

Hall, Donald. *Marianne Moore*. "Testimony" Collection of Interviews edited by Charles Tomlinson. New York: Prentice-Hall, Inc., 1969.

———. *The Cage and the Animal*. New York: Prentice-Hall, 1970.

8. EDNA ST. VINCENT MILLAY

A. Works by—Poetry:

Renascence and Other Poems. New York: Mitchell Kennerly, 1917. First
published volume. Reissued, as were the second and third volumes,
A Few Figs from Thistles and *Second April,* by Harper & Brothers
directly after 1923, the year that the firm became Millay's permanent
publishers.

The Harp-Weaver and Other Poems. New York and London: Harper &
Brothers, 1923 (winner of Pulitzer Prize for Poetry).

Unless otherwise stated, the following works by Millay were all published by Harper & Brothers, which became Harper & Row in 1962.
Those listed are principal volumes.

The Buck in the Snow. New York and London: 1928.

Fatal Interview. New York and London: 1931 (first sonnet sequence).

Wine From These Grapes (with "Epitaph for the Race of Man," second
sonnet sequence). New York and London: 1934.

Collected Sonnets. New York and London: 1941.

Collected Lyrics. New York and London: 1943.

Mine the Harvest (post.). New York and London: 1954.

Collected Poems (post.). New York and London: 1956.

B. Verse Plays:

Aria da Capo. First published, *Reedy's Mirror,* March 18, 1920, followed
by book publications, most notably, *Twenty-Five Best Plays of Modern American Theatre,* ed. by John Gassner. New York: Crown Publishers, 1949.

The King's Henchman (opera libretto, written separately as verse play).
New York and London: 1927.

Conversation at Midnight. New York and London: 1937.

C. Translations:

Flowers of Evil, from the French of Charles Baudelaire, with George Dillon. New York and London: 1936.

D. Prose:

Distressing Dialogues (pseud. Nancy Boyd). New York: 1924.
Preface to *Flowers of Evil* (on the translation of poetry).

E. Letters, Biographical and Critical Material:

Letters to Charlotte Babcock Sills (roommate), 1917. Vassar College
Library, Special Collections.

Unpublished letters to Arthur Davison Ficke, 1918–1942. Beinecke Library, Yale University.

Letters of Edna St. Vincent Millay. Edited by Allan Ross MacDougall. New York and London: 1952.

Burden, Jean, "With Love from Vincent," *Yankee,* XXII, May 1958. Contains letters to the poet's aunt, Mrs. Frank L. Ricker.

Adams, Franklin P. *The Diary of Our Own Samuel Pepys.* New York: Simon & Schuster, 1935.

Atkins, Elizabeth. *Edna St. Vincent Millay and Her Times.* Chicago: University of Chicago Press, 1936; reissued by Russell & Russell, 1963.

Bogan, Louise. *Achievements in American Poetry.* Henry Regnery Company, 1951.

Dell, Floyd, *Homecoming: An Autobiography.* New York: Farrar & Rinehart, 1933.

———. *Love in Greenwich Village.* New York: George H. Doran Co., 1926.

Eastman, Max. *Great Companions: Critical Memoirs of Some Famous Friends.* New York: Farrar, Straus & Cudahy, 1959.

Ficke, Arthur Davison. *Sonnets of a Portrait Painter,* Revised Edition. New York: Mitchell Kennerly, 1922. "Epitaph for the Poet V (Hymn to Intellectual Beauty), To Edna St. Vincent Millay."

Glaspell, Susan, *The Road to the Temple.* New York: Frederick A. Stokes Company, 1927.

Gould, Jean, *Modern American Playwrights.* New York: Dodd, Mead & Company, 1966.

———. *The Poet and Her Book, A Biography of Edna St. Vincent Millay.* New York: Dodd, Mead & Company, 1969.

MacCracken, Henry Noble. *The Hickory Limb.* New York: Charles Scribner's Sons, 1950.

Munson, Gorham. *Penobscot, Down East Paradise* ("Edna St. Vincent Millay and the Town of Camden"). Philadelphia: J. B. Lippincott Co., 1959.

Powys, Llewellyn. *The Verdict of Bridlegoose.* New York: Harcourt, Brace & Company, 1926.

Sheean, Vincent. *The Indigo Bunting: A Memoir of Edna St. Vincent Millay.* New York: Harper & Brothers, 1951.

Wilson, Edmund. *The Shores of Light: A Literary Chronicle of the Twenties and Thirties.* New York: Farrar, Straus & Young, 1952 (principally, Epilogue, 1952: "Edna St. Vincent Millay," and "Give That Beat Again").

There are privately printed portraits and unpublished papers on Millay in Vassar College Libraries, Yale, and others. The list of articles, reviews, and news stories is far too long to include here. An extensive *Bibliography of the Works of Edna St. Vincent Millay,* compiled by Karl Yost, was published by Harper & Brothers in 1937. A Chronology of Millay press notices in *The New York Times* Index, dating from 1921 to 1964, runs to five pages.

9. LOUISE BOGAN

A. Works by—Poetry:

Body of This Death. New York: 1923 (first volume).
Dark Summer. New York: Charles Scribner's Sons, 1929.
The Sleeping Fury. New York: Charles Scribner's Sons, 1937.
Poems and New Poems. New York: Charles Scribner's Sons, 1941.
The Blue Estuaries. Poems, 1925/1968. New York: Farrar, Straus & Giroux, 1968.

B. Prose:

Achievements in American Poetry. New York: Henry Regnery Co., 1951.
Selected Criticism. New York: Noonday Press, 1955.
A Poet's Alphabet. Literary criticism. Ed. by Robert Phelps and Ruth Limmer. New York: McGraw-Hill, 1970.
What the Woman Lived. Selected Letters, 1920–1970. Ed. by Ruth Limmer. Harcourt Brace Jovanovich, 1973.
"From the Journal of a Poet," excerpts from Bogan's journal, published in *The New Yorker,* January 30, 1978.

C. Biographical, Critical:

Twentieth Century Authors. Ed. by Stanley Kunitz, with staff. New York: H. W. Wilson Co., 1942; also Supplement, 1955.
Articles about the poet, mostly reviews, appeared in the *New Republic* (October 16, 1929); the Wilson *Library Bulletin* (March 1930); *Nation* (April 13, 1940); *Poetry* (April 1942).

D. Anthology:

The Golden Journey, Poems for Young People. Compiled by Louise Bogan and William Jay Smith. Chicago: Reilly & Lee, 1965.

10. BABETTE DEUTSCH

A. Works by—Poetry:

Banners. New York: George H. Doran Co., 1919 (first volume).
Honey Out of the Rock. New York: D. Appleton, 1925.

Fire for the Night. New York: Jonathan Cape and H. Smith, 1930.
Epistle to Prometheus. New York: Jonathan Cape and H. Smith, 1931.
One Part Love. New York: Oxford University Press, 1939.
Collected Poems. New York: Doubleday, 1969.

B. Anthologies—Translations:

Modern Russian Poetry. An anthology chosen and translated by Babette
   Deutsch and her husband, Avrahm Yarmolinsky. New York: Harcourt Brace, 1921.
Contemporary German Poetry (same duo authorship). New York: Harcourt Brace, 1923.
Two Centuries of Russian Verse ("Thoroughly revised and much expanded edition"). Same duo authorship. New York: Random House,
   1966.

C. Prose (on the subject of poetry):

Potable Gold. Some notes on poetry and this age. New York: W. W.
   Norton, 1929.
This Modern Poetry. New York: W. W. Norton, 1935.
Poetry in Our Time (1900–1950). New York: Henry Holt & Company,
   1952.
The Reader's Shakespeare. New York: Julien Messner, 1959.
Poetry in Our Time (updated, 1900–1960). New York: Doubleday, 1963.

D. Biographical, Critical:

Twentieth Century Authors. Edited by Stanley Kunitz and Howard
   Haycraft. New York: H. W. Wilson Co., 1942; also First Supplement
   (Ass't Editor Vineta Colby), 1955.
Articles about: *Poetry:* June, 1931; *Scholastic,* November 24, 1934;
   American Scholar, January 1941; *Poetry,* March 1944.

INDEX